Great Groups

Great Groups
Creating and Leading Effective Groups

David R. Hutchinson
Johnson State University

Illustrations by Hans Bednar

Los Angeles | London | New Delhi
Singapore | Washington DC

Los Angeles | London | New Delhi
Singapore | Washington DC

FOR INFORMATION

SAGE Publications, Inc.
2455 Teller Road
Thousand Oaks, California 91320
E-mail: order@sagepub.com

SAGE Publications Ltd.
1 Oliver's Yard
55 City Road
London, EC1Y 1SP
United Kingdom

SAGE Publications India Pvt. Ltd.
B 1/I 1 Mohan Cooperative Industrial Area
Mathura Road, New Delhi 110 044
India

SAGE Publications Asia-Pacific Pte. Ltd.
3 Church Street
#10–04 Samsung Hub
Singapore 049483

Publisher: Kassie Graves
Associate Editor: Abbie Rickard
Editorial Assistant: Carrie Montoya
Production Editor: David C. Felts
Copy Editor: QuADS Prepress (P) Ltd.
Typesetter: Hurix Systems Pvt. Ltd.
Proofreader: Tricia Currie-Knight
Indexer: Karen Wiley
Cover Designer: Anupama Krishnan
Marketing Manager: Shari Countryman

Printed in the United States of America

Names: Hutchinson, David R., author.

Title: Great groups : creating and leading effective groups / David R. Hutchinson.

Description: Thousand Oaks, California : SAGE, [2017] | Includes bibliographical references and index.

Identifiers: LCCN 2015039146 | ISBN 9781452268347 (pbk. : alk. paper)

Subjects: LCSH: Small groups—Psychological aspects. | Group relations training.

Classification: LCC HM736 .H87 2017 | DDC 302/.14—dc23
LC record available at http://lccn.loc.gov/2015039146

This book is printed on acid-free paper.

16 17 18 19 20 10 9 8 7 6 5 4 3 2 1

Brief Contents

SAGE was founded in 1965 by Sara Miller McCune to support the dissemination of usable knowledge by publishing innovative and high-quality research and teaching content. Today, we publish over 900 journals, including those of more than 400 learned societies, more than 800 new books per year, and a growing range of library products including archives, data, case studies, reports, and video. SAGE remains majority-owned by our founder, and after Sara's lifetime will become owned by a charitable trust that secures our continued independence.

Los Angeles | London | New Delhi | Singapore | Washington DC

Detailed Contents

Preface

This book, *Great Groups: Creating and Leading Effective Groups*, is designed to help students gain a beginning knowledge of how to plan for and develop successful group experiences. It is intended to assist the group work proficiency of graduate students in counseling, social work, and psychology programs, as well as undergraduate students in psychology, social work, or human service programs.

The book should also be useful for experienced group workers. They may find that it has some unique ways of approaching group situations and problems that are helpful. It's designed to be a practical, no-nonsense guide to creating and leading groups that really work.

I have led groups in a variety of human service settings, as well as taught undergraduate and graduate coursework about group work for the past 30 years. In my courses, I always tell students that a course about group work should serve a number of purposes. A course about group work should certainly increase a student's awareness of theory related to group work, and it should give students some "nuts-and-bolts" tools to help them actually run a group. But additionally, it should communicate a belief and passion about the great things that effective groups can do for people. I would hope the same for this book—that it informs about theory; that it shares some practical, useful information about running an actual group; and that it inspires students to run groups and to become proficient group workers.

I see this book as an extension of my teaching about group work, and as such, it is personal and conversational in tone. I want to talk directly with students about this way of working with people and to share some of my ideas about what is effective and how they might avoid some of the mistakes I've made. The book is filled with examples of groups in action, drawn from my own experiences with groups—the names and identifying information of individuals are fictional, of course. I hope that students actually enjoy reading this book and get excited about the groups they might run. This book could also serve as a helpful reference to refer back to once they have groups up and running.

One of the students who used my book about counseling and psychotherapy skills with individuals, *The Essential Counselor*, wrote to me that she considered that book a great "practical skills manual for my professional future." I would hope that this book, *Great Groups*, would do the same for students embarking on careers that will include working with groups.

A NOTE TO INSTRUCTORS

I want this book to be a useful resource for instructors, particularly for instructors who are new to teaching about group work. The 13-chapter format is designed to accommodate a traditional semester-long course, and each chapter affords ample opportunity for students to do some personal reflections—which could easily include written assignments, if an instructor so desires—and opportunities for group work practice. These reflection and group fishbowl lab practice activities could be used as either supplemental or in-class activities. The inclusion of these activities reflects my firm belief that the best learning in "helping" coursework is assisted by a combination of reading, discussion, and hands-on practice of the material. A semester-long course about group work affords the perfect vehicle for discussion of theory and group practice activities.

In particular, the group fishbowl lab practice exercises afford students the opportunity to practice the use of skills in groups. These structured group exercises feature students in the roles of leaders, members, and observers. Students can be encouraged to participate in these exercises in all these roles and to provide one another with supportive, specific, constructive feedback about their activity in the groups. You, the instructor, could also volunteer to participate occasionally, if you want.

The For Further Thought section of each chapter provides instructors with a number of alternative learning activities that could serve to supplement in-class learning. There are clearly more activities provided than could be completed by students during the course of a semester, so instructors can choose those that seem to best fit their students' needs. Some of these activities include using exercises that have been designed by my students in graduate-level courses about group work.

THE ORGANIZATION OF THE BOOK

The book has three distinct sections. The first section, Chapters 1 to 5, deals with foundation information about group work, the theory related to leadership, group dynamics, theories of counseling and psychotherapy as they relate to working with people in groups, and some practical reasons for becoming involved with group work.

The second section of the book, Chapters 6 to 10, helps the student look at all the practical details associated with putting a group together, running it effectively, and then ending it successfully. Each of these chapters discusses some of the features of a group at one particular stage of its life, the tasks and skills necessary to help it move on, and some of the ways problems that might occur can be addressed.

Particular skills are identified in each of these chapters that might be best suited for work with a group at a particular point in its life.

The student should be encouraged to think broadly about the use of skills, using whatever skill might best be suited for a given situation. The assignment of specific skills to some group developmental stage is somewhat arbitrary, so students should be encouraged to think of the use of any skill, discussed in any chapter, that might most appropriately fit a particular situation and need. Again, the aim here is for the student to be armed with some very practical information that can be actually implemented in her or his group work.

The last section of the book, Chapters 11 to 13, deals with some specialized populations that might be typically encountered. Chapter 11 is devoted to looking at groups that might be designed for different age groups, and Chapter 12 discusses groups for some common theme-based issues: addictions, serious and persistent mental health concerns, problems associated with criminality and violence, and grief and bereavement. The final chapter, Chapter 13, discusses group worker self-care and burnout avoidance. It ends with an appeal to those working with groups to extend their work with people beyond the group meeting room—to become effective advocates and activists for social justice on behalf of the people whom they serve. ·

The language of the book reflects an awareness of the fact that group leaders and members might be female, male, or transgender. Anyone leading groups needs to be aware of the fact that groups afford the opportunity for individuals to explore issues of gender and sexuality, and leaders need to be wary of making unwarranted assumptions about either gender or sexuality. "He" and "she" are used alternatively to refer to leaders and members, mostly as a way of avoiding more cumbersome language, like "him or her."

A PERSONAL NOTE TO STUDENTS

This book is about groups, but more basically, it's about relationships. The book will tell you about theory, about applying information from what we know about working with individuals to working with people in groups, and about how to use skills in groups. All this information will only assist you, however, to the extent you are able to actually connect on a human level with the people in your group. The importance of effective *therapeutic alliances*, whether working individually or in groups—or in life—cannot be overstated. Your ability to connect intellectually and emotionally with the people in your groups will be the largest determinant of the success of those groups.

Throughout the book, you will be encouraged to learn more about yourself, particularly in interaction with others. Do what you can to understand the different worldviews of the people who join your groups—travel, expand your intellectual horizons, and live large. You can do some of these on your own, and you can also work with supervisors, professors, and therapists to expand your own understanding of yourself. You can certainly participate in groups to learn more about your interpersonal self. This business of expanding your self-awareness should be thought of as a lifelong, exciting journey.

Acknowledgments

Foremost, I want to thank my editor at SAGE, Kassie Graves. Her knowledgeable guidance, patience, and good humor have made the process of creating this book truly enjoyable. Her professional expertise and personal support have been immensely appreciated, and these have served to make this a better book. It's simply been great working with her.

I also thank her colleagues at SAGE for assisting in the process of getting this book into its final form, for their help in making sure that word gets out about it, and for welcoming me into the SAGE "family." In particular, thanks go to Carrie Montoya for her skillful work in getting the manuscript into production. Other SAGE professionals have provided invaluable assistance. Thanks to David Felts, SAGE production editor; Rajasree Gosh, copy editor; and Anupama Krishnan, cover designer, for their help in bringing the book into production—and for making the process stress free and collegial. And thanks to Shari Countryman, marketing manager, and her staff for their work in helping to get the word out about the book.

It's been great to work with my old friend Hans Bednar on this project. His illustrations serve to bring specific group situations to life. The humanity—and sometimes humor—that they reflect accurately portrays things that actually happen in groups. They lend a visual face to the text. I have very much appreciated his patience and willingness to rework illustrations to achieve the right kind of effect.

I continue to feel grateful to Mary Falcon and Barry Fetterolf for initially encouraging me to write and for their support and friendship through the years.

Much appreciation goes out to my family—Kaki; Katie and her husband, Yves; and Jon and his fiancé, Esther—and my family of friends for their support and patience during the writing of this book. Their good-natured support has been invaluable. Special thanks go to Annemie Curlin, Jon Frew, and Don Schumacher for their ongoing support and encouragement.

While I have recently retired from full-time teaching at Johnson State College in Vermont, I continue to teach part-time and have several colleagues in the psychology and counseling program there: David Fink, Gina Mireault, Eleanor Webber,

Staci Born, Linda Eastman—and in particular Cathy Higley and Vicky Sanborn. I extend thanks to them for their ideas and for their good-natured camaraderie.

There are a number of professionals in the field, professors across the country, who have served as reviewers during the writing of this book. I know that the process of reviewing a book is time-consuming, and I greatly appreciate their input and critical feedback. Their ideas have helped shape this final product. In particular, I'd like to thank Patricia Andersen, Midwestern State University; Devika Dibya Choudhuri, University of Saint Joseph; Susan Eidson Claxton, Georgia Highlands College; Inna R. Edara, Fu Jen Catholic University; John Q. Hodges, University of North Alabama; Tracy A. Marschall, University of Indianapolis; Philip Mongan, Radford University; Benjamin Heim Shepard, City Tech CUNY; and Brian Tilley, National University.

Finally, I want to thank the many students in my undergraduate and graduate group work courses who have helped shape the content of this book. They encouraged me to write this book, and some have even helped by way of contributing the group exercises in the For Further Thought sections of some chapters of the book. Specifically, thanks go to Angel Roy, Lesley Robinson, Brenda Logee, Chris Mitchell, Allison Hayes, Michele Longboardi, and Kathryn Place for use of their exercises. I know that most of my former students have gone on to create and lead some great groups of their own. My continued contact with these students, as well as program graduates, now colleagues in the field, is truly gratifying.

About the Author

David R. Hutchinson prepares both undergraduate and graduate students for careers in psychology and counseling. His areas of special focus are group work, addictions, and grieving. A former Peace Corps volunteer, David's priorities include travel and maintaining an international perspective in his life and work. He has trained counselors in Grenada and established sister school relationships between five schools in Vermont and Grenada. In Vermont, David continues his emphasis on intensive, process-oriented coursework with long weekend retreats at an off-campus lodge near Caspian Lake in the woods of the Northeast Kingdom.

In 2006, David was honored with the Distinguished Faculty of the Year Award. He holds positions on the boards of the New England School of Addiction Studies and Northwest Counseling and Support Services in Franklin County, Vermont. He received his doctoral degree from State University of New York, Buffalo.

Chapter 1

An Invitation to Group Work

Alone we can do so little; together we can do so much.

—Helen Keller

A RATIONALE FOR GROUP WORK

We'd set the stage to start a new group. Jasmine, my coleader, and I had done a lot of planning for this group, and now we were about to have the first meeting. It was a good-sized group, comprising 12 young men and women, though there were a few more women than men.

I'd been watching and listening to some of the informal banter going on before the group started, making some initial mental notes as people talked together before we officially got rolling—seeing who seemed to be initiating conversations, who was holding back, and who was not particularly engaged with anyone. I knew that Jasmine was doing the same. We exchanged some brief eye contact, communicating some nonverbal "coleaderly" solidarity in these moments before we were to launch full throttle into action.

There had been a fair amount of nervous chitchat, and now that we were beginning, everything got quiet. The silence was a signal—this silence signal is true of many beginning groups—that we were about to begin.

Jasmine invited people to briefly introduce themselves, and then she led a discussion about ground rules, the agreements that we share with one another that will help to make this a safe experience—things like confidentiality—and reiterated some of the informed consent issues that people had been briefed on in their pregroup meetings. I then took a little time reviewing our reasons for being together and what people could hope to get out of the experience. This did take some time because it's important, but I was aware that I was talking too much. It was time for others to get involved.

I invited people to talk about their reasons for joining the group and the kinds of things they wanted to get out of this experience. Given that this has been defined broadly as a group for "improving interpersonal relationship skills," I knew that most of the people in the group had some close relationships with partners and friends who were troubled, and that for some the group was suggested by employers or friends as an opportunity to improve their overall social skills. I asked everyone to share something about their expectations from the group.

This was a group with some talkative members, and people began to talk freely. Some talked about current and past work situations and about future work aspirations, and some talked about their families, past and present. Some even began to talk about family difficulties. We didn't do this in any kind of orderly fashion, but everyone did contribute something. Jasmine and I also participated in this by disclosing some personal things about ourselves.

Then Jasmine asked, "And what was it like for you, what were you feeling, as you were waiting to talk about yourself? What kinds of feelings—not thoughts, but feelings—moved around inside you as you thought about what you'd say?"

There was some silence as people contemplated this, but then the conversation began. People talked at first about their thoughts, saying things like "I feel like this is a good beginning" (even though the word *feel* was used, this is really an idea, not a feeling), and we needed to remind them about the differences between thoughts and feelings, and then they started to dig deeper and talked about having been nervous and a little scared. We pushed them to talk a bit about this nervousness, and they then, almost to a person, talked about the fear of being judged and the fear that other people wouldn't like them. Some began to talk about other group experiences they've had and some of them about classes they had taken, where they were actually ridiculed.

As people talked about these experiences, Jasmine and I again exchanged occasional glances with one another. We were sharing an appreciation for how this was going. People in the group were beginning to take little risks in sharing these experiences, and we were acknowledging this with each other. This was the direction in which we hoped our group would go.

In this brief discussion—this small foray into becoming personal and taking some risks—talking about these previous difficult experiences, our new group was being born. We were up and running, good to go. Our new group was under way.

Welcome to the world of group work!

A RATIONALE FOR GROUP WORK

- Practical Reasons for Leading Groups
- Great Groups Can Do Great Things for People
- Challenges of Group Work
- A Brief Historical Perspective on Group Work

Working in groups with people can be remarkably interesting and challenging. This way of working presents the helping professional—counselor, social worker, or psychologist—with some unique benefits and challenges, some of which are similar to working individually with people, some of which are not. Some helping professionals gravitate naturally to this kind of work, while others need encouragement and support to see themselves as ready for group work. Some people are naturally comfortable being group leaders, while others may need to push themselves to assume positions of group leadership.

This chapter will introduce you to some of the reasons why group work is so valuable and so appealing to people who are involved with them. The chapter will also ask you to reflect on some of your own experiences with groups and will afford you the opportunity to talk with others about those.

SOME PRACTICAL REASONS FOR LEADING GROUPS

One of the reasons people frequently cite in making the case for working with groups, as opposed to working with individuals, has to do with the relative *efficiency* of groups. It makes economic sense to be working with a number of people at once (Davies & Gavin, 1994). A couple of hours of a professional's time can be put to much more effective use when dealing with a group of people (Akos & Martin, 2003; Corey, 2008). It also saves a lot of professional energy and time, particularly when doing something like skills training, to say what needs to be said only once, instead of saying it repeatedly in individual sessions. Working with groups of people, in other words, makes great economic sense (Sochting, Wilson, & De Gagne, 2010). Program administrators typically love groups because of this—and even some practitioners in private practice situations love groups because of these economic benefits. Some would maintain that groups could be used even more than they are now in these private settings (Piper, 2008).

However, there is more to making a case for groups than this. Working in groups is a different way of working with people. While there are certainly similarities between group and individual counseling or therapy, it can generally be said that much of the learning that can happen in groups has to do with learning about one's self in relation to others. Individual work, on the other hand, is more generally about learning about one's internal issues and conflicts as well as about one's perceptions of his or her relationship issues. While individual work has to do with learning about one's self, working within a group is more about *interpersonal learning* (Gallagher et al., 2014; Johnson, 2009). While people may talk about relationships in their talk with a professional clinician, groups afford the opportunity for the individual to actually see himself or herself in relationship action.

For you, the professional, there is also the distinct advantage of not having to be the only expert in the room. When you are working with a group, you can rely on others to chime in with their own opinions, ideas, and suggestions for any given situation under discussion (Ferencik, 1992). Thus, while you are still ultimately the leader of the group, this *sharing responsibility* for generating ideas and feedback to group members can be seen as a real asset of group work.

Some of the groups with which you'll work will have a focus on *learning skills*. These skills groups may be almost like classes, where you are the teacher. You may be teaching people with developmental disabilities, for example, skills of daily living, like shopping for healthy food or maintaining an apartment. Or you might be teaching middle school children about nonviolent conflict resolution. In any of these situations, it is easier to teach these skills in groups, where people can assist one another in learning the skills, and where you have an experimental setting, a mini-laboratory, for helping people in trying these new skills out.

For many people in groups, simply learning how to be more socially skilled is the primary issue. *Socialization*, learning how to interact and be with other people in ways that are productive and positive, is a fundamental life skill (Dugatin, 1999). Groups can be a great source of such learning (Kramer, 2009). Moreover, people in groups can learn how to empathically respond to one another. They can learn effective listening skills, learn how to give and receive from one another. *Groups can teach people about how to live in the world with more empathy and compassion.* This is one of the best things that people can learn in groups, and when people learn how to be more compassionate with others, they also inevitably learn how to be more compassionate with themselves.

For me, this is one of the keys to the beauty of group work: *Groups afford people the opportunity to help themselves via helping others.* People in groups learn about themselves, and they also learn more about how to reach out to other people. We all need help, at some point, but we all also need to be able to give help. Groups afford the opportunity to help and be helped.

When people choose to share things about themselves, they inevitably find that others have often had similar experiences, thoughts, and feelings. There is a sense

---

PRACTICAL REASONS FOR LEADING GROUPS

- More efficient and economical than working with individuals
- Best way to help people learn about how they interact with others
- Provides a good way to teach skills, particularly social skills
- Affords people the opportunity to be helped by others—and also to help
- Promotes a sense of connection with others—the universality of the human condition, as well as compassion and empathy for other people
- Provides an opportunity to experiment with new interpersonal behaviors

---

of commonality, a recognition that others share an understanding of one's personal situation. Yalom (1985) uses the term *universality* to describe this understanding. When one feels understood and connected to others in this way, there is also a sense that one belongs to a greater whole.

Any group has the potential for operating as a laboratory for learning about life in interaction with others. People usually interact with one another in much the same way as they do in other social groups. Viewing the group as a laboratory suggests that this is a setting where people can *experiment with new behaviors* and ways of interacting with people. In a controlled and relatively safe environment, people can give and receive information about one another's behavior. This information sharing, also called giving and receiving feedback, is a primary means of important learning in groups.

GREAT GROUPS CAN DO GREAT THINGS FOR PEOPLE

When groups work really well, when people have a high degree of trust and respect for one another, when they experiment with new behaviors and share about themselves, there are wonderful emotional payoffs. Most fundamentally, groups can help people *feel connected to one another*, connected to the human race. Great groups, groups that are productive and cohesive, promote a sense of *belonging* (Kögler, Brandl, Brandstätter, Borasio, & Fegg, 2013; Trotzer, 2006; Woolhouse, Cooper, & Pickard, 2013). It is a fact of life that we are born into the world alone, and that this essential "aloneness" is an existential fact of life as long as we take up space on the planet. Groups afford the opportunity to create some respite from this aloneness. When people share their stories with others and when they share their sufferings, their pains, and their joys, they inevitably find that others share in these. For most people, there is tremendous solace in this shared human experience. Groups promote personal sharing with others that is rare in most other aspects of daily life. People find that behind the facades and everyday demeanors that others present to the world are some of the same fears and concerns that they themselves harbor.

When people share information that is deeply personal, they may get in touch with thoughts and feelings that are powerful, feelings that are rarely expressed. When they feel free enough to contact and express these thoughts and the feelings that accompany them, they may let themselves experience these feelings in the group.

Many people have some serious reservations about revealing themselves emotionally in front of others. Some are afraid of appearing to be "weak" or not in control of ourselves; others may have bad experiences associated with being emotionally vulnerable.

People who do choose to share themselves emotionally in groups invariably find that people usually appreciate and are drawn to this vulnerability. There is something that is cleansing about a good cry, particularly when it is done with others. This is the *cathartic effect* that great groups can provide. My personal belief is that we connect more around our vulnerabilities than our strengths, and when someone in your group chooses to be emotionally vulnerable, it promotes this sense of connectedness, of belonging (Figure 1.1).

In addition to the potential for increased connection and a greater sense of belonging that is promoted by emotional expression, there is the sense that once

Figure 1.1   Great Groups Promote a Sense of Connection With Others

someone experiences strong personal feeling, she or he doesn't typically care so much about what others think. Getting one's emotional feet on the ground is its own reward, and it is accompanied by a sense of being personally powerful.

CHALLENGES OF GROUP WORK

You shouldn't think that this work is necessarily easy.

Great groups can do great things for people, but this is not meant to imply that leading a group is a walk in the park. It can be a *complicated* way of working with people. While we'll discuss a number of specific problem behaviors you might encounter in later chapters in this book, there are some major issues about the complicated nature of group work that can be highlighted here, early on. Primarily, it stands to reason that if the dynamics between two people working together in some kind of helping relationship can be difficult—including their real and imagined ideas about each other and the ways in which one is triggered by the ways the other behaves—then the dynamics of a number of people interacting with one another would be even more complex. As a leader working with groups, you manage an interesting juggling act of paying attention to your own thoughts and feelings, to the thoughts and feelings between you and individual members (and between them, as well), and also to the dynamics of the group as a whole. This means that you will be paying attention to quite a mix of things, some of which are obvious and some of which are hidden.

Some of the material that people bring into groups is out in the open, including the ways they behave and the things they say. Some of the material they bring, however, is less obvious and more hidden. People in groups often hold many of their thoughts and feelings in abeyance. Some of these thoughts and feelings may be eventually shared, but some may remain hidden. Sometimes people even have special, hidden thoughts about the group or individuals in it that are designed to undermine the group. These kinds of *manipulative thoughts or hidden agendas* that people may carry can be difficult things to manage (Barrett, 2012).

People who are coerced or leveraged into groups (e.g., by court mandate, by a work supervisor) can be particularly *resistant and uncooperative* as members of a group. Some of these people may be really tough and challenging and may teach other people in your group exactly the kinds of things you don't want them to learn, like where the safe places to buy drugs are, for example. You are interested in creating groups where people will learn positive things, and you will want to minimize the potential for your group to be a place for *negative learning*.

Sometimes the negative people can do their best to undermine the positive work of a group, as in *intentionally violating confidentiality ground rules*—disclosing information that others have shared—as a way of acting out their resistance.

Additionally, some people you may have in your group are simply not suited for this particular group. *Some may have too many emotional needs* for the group to handle. Others may suffer from serious and persistent mental health issues that prevent them from being able to fully or productively participate in the work of the group. These people may need another kind of group, or perhaps individual attention.

Finally, all kinds of interesting things happen between people in groups that create challenges for your leadership skills. *People can get romantically entangled with one another, or in opposite fashion, develop antagonistic dislikes* for one another. These intense emotional charges between people, whether positive or negative, naturally create interesting opportunities for your intervention.

Some of these challenges may have to do with member selection. If you can screen people before a group starts, you may be able to find out who has some serious mental or emotional health problems, or who may be extremely resistant, and find some alternative ways of helping them. Other situations, naturally, occur once the group is up and running.

I would encourage you to think of any of these group challenges not as insurmountable hurdles but rather as opportunities for you to experiment and think closely about what is needed from you as a group leader. Each challenge is a puzzle, of sorts. Each of these, if skillfully dealt with, can actually provide a positive impetus toward group growth, as well as increase your own confidence and skill as a group leader. I'll help you look at ways you can constructively and creatively deal with any of these challenges in the chapters that follow.

Reflection and Group Fishbowl Lab Practice Exercise

Think about all of the group experiences you've had as a group member or at least the ones that spring quickly into mind. Some of these might have been groups you were in for personal growth experiences, either in school or work settings, or

---

SOME UNIQUE CHALLENGES OF GROUP WORK

- Working with groups can be more complicated than working with individuals.
- Some people in your group might be manipulative or have hidden agendas—they might even violate basic ground rules, like confidentiality, as a way of attacking others.
- Some people might need more personal attention than a group can provide.
- People can learn negative things from other people in the group.
- People may get romantically entangled with one another.
- Some people may become antagonistic—with you or with others in the group.

in some other context. Other group experiences could include coursework (yes, classes are groups, too), sports teams, or even committees. Some of these might have been positive experiences for you, some less so, and some simply aren't particularly memorable.

Think about one or two of your most positive experiences with groups, and then jot down a few notes about what made them so positive. Think about the people involved, the other members, the leader(s), the work involved. Maybe it was simply that the group fit whatever you happened to need at that point in your life. Whatever it was that made this group special, make note of that.

Then think about one or two of your most negative experiences with groups. Jot down a note about what it was that made these so negative—again, whether you think it was other member or leader issues, or something else.

After you have had some time to personally think about these questions, discuss your ideas with others in a group fishbowl exercise.

Here's the way a group fishbowl exercise works with a group of 8 to 15 people. Two people volunteer to be group leaders. If you are one of these, your job is to help lead the group in discussion of these questions. You might want to talk for a few minutes with your coleader to establish how you want to begin the discussion, focusing how you want to proceed and who will take the lead in getting things going.

Five or six people should volunteer to be group members. If you are a group member, your job is to talk with the group about your ideas related to your experiences in groups.

The other people in the group become group observers. If you are one of these, you will sit with the other observers in a circle around the leaders and members (hence the term *fishbowl*). Your job is to closely—and silently—observe the group and its interactions between members and leaders. You might want to take notes while you observe. Pay special attention to how the coleaders stimulate discussion. Do they draw people out, encourage everyone to participate? What kinds of things do they do that seem particularly effective in encouraging discussion?

Make whatever accommodations are necessary to make this work for the number of people you have conducting this exercise. If your numbers are small, perhaps you'll have one leader and only a few group members, for example.

Before the group discussion starts, take a few minutes to assure one another that personal information that is shared, either in the group discussion or in the processing of the discussion that follows, will be held confidentially.

Then take between 20 and 30 minutes for group discussion of the group vignette and the related questions. Take a few more minutes following the discussion for the group observers to share some of their observations. If you are an observer sharing some of what you saw and heard, try to be specific about what you observed, while also being supportive in your comments to the coleaders. They took the risk, after all, in leading this first group fishbowl exercise, and they deserve your support.

GROUP WORK IN CONTEXT: A BRIEF HISTORICAL PERSPECTIVE

The kinds of groups in which we are mostly interested in this book—groups where interpersonal learning is the focus—have become a fact of our cultural life. Groups are everywhere—in schools, in businesses, in mental health and social work agencies, and in all kinds of organizational settings.

The fact that groups are such an integral part of our cultural landscape is the result of a number of events and forces that have shaped our work in human services. It can be helpful to have some understanding of some of the counseling and psychotherapeutic experiments—and of the cultural contexts in which those were held—that have helped shape the group work we do today.

The Birth of the Modern Group

Much of our group work today has its roots in the social work movement of the early 1900s. Chicago's *Hull House* is symbolic of the work that early social workers did in working with groups of people to help find housing, food, and other basics for survival. They found that people could help one another—both for informational reasons and in way of support—in learning some essential survival skills.

Similarly, experiments in working with people in groups were under way at the turn of the century in vocational schools and medical settings. In the vocational groups, people were encouraged to support one another in preparing for and looking for work, and in the medical groups, people were asked to assist one another in dealing with their complicated health problems.

Therapy Groups

In the 1920s and 1930s the psychoanalytic community began to experiment much more intensively with group work formats. Alfred Adler used groups as an extension of his theoretical emphasis on *family guidance* support systems (Papanek, 1970), and Jacob Moreno began to use groups as a way of theatrically highlighting and dramatizing individuals' psychological issues. This special kind of group work, called psychodrama (Moreno, 1949; Nolte, 2014), has evolved into an established—and theatrical—way of working with people.

Much of the way in which analysts worked with these groups used groups as an extension of their individual work. In any given group session, one or more individuals would typically work with the leader, the analyst, on his or her personal issues. Others in the group would observe and comment on this work typically by talking with and through the leader—not generally by direct discussion with other group members. This model of group work, where the leader is seen as the technical expert, stereotypically characterizes some of the differences between counseling and therapy groups today. We'll revisit this distinction again, later.

Self-Help Groups

The 1930s and 1940s also saw the birth and beginnings of *Alcoholics Anonymous*, the preeminent self-help group. Alcoholics Anonymous, as you probably know, does not have a designated group leader; rather, the group meetings are guided by a fixed set of principles and steps, the 12 steps and traditions. This self-help model has become the template on which many other modern-day self-help groups have modeled themselves, and thousands of these groups are now in existence (Gladding, 2008).

Cultural Change and the Role of Groups

It was after the Second World War, however, that the modern group movement really started to take off. Much of the reason for this—in addition to the fact that many of the war's veterans desperately needed treatment, and groups were the best way to provide that (Barron, 1970)—had to do with the cultural context of the times. If you really want to understand how and why groups became so quickly popular in that postwar era, you'll want to become a bit of a sociological history buff. A number of forces came together that helped set the stage for the popular use of groups in all kinds of institutional settings.

The postwar era, that period of time between the Second World War and the Vietnam War, saw tremendous social upheaval. It was a time of relative prosperity, and also a time when many fixed notions about our societal institutions came under fire. The old order, fixed ways of seeing the world, came under attack from all sides: race relations and acts of civil disobedience, the rise of feminism, challenges to the traditional notions of family and divorce, and even questions about the church and the role of religion in our lives.

The popular films of the day included *Rebel Without a Cause* and *The Wild One*, which were tributes to the disaffection of alienated youth. They portrayed the ways young people were beginning to reject cultural traditions and values. When Marlon Brando, the leader of a rebel motorcycle gang, is asked in *The Wild One,* "What are all you young people so angry about?" he answers, "What have you got?" It's a classic line that captures the youthful alienation of the times.

A national news magazine even ran a cover story titled "God Is Dead," which was a poignant comment on the shrinking role of religion in our lives. Divorce rates began to climb, as people began to challenge notions of commitment to marriages that were no longer seen as satisfying. Young women began to demand more equality of rights under the law and more equal opportunity in the workplace.

All these challenges to the authority of the existing order were ultimately designed to afford wider opportunities for people—for civil rights for people of all races, for increased occupational opportunities for both men and women, for lifestyle choices, including whether to marry or stay married. A young woman in the 1950s began to have glimpses of a world where becoming a homemaker, a nurse, or a teacher were no longer her only occupational choices.

With increased opportunity, however, also came increased anxiety. Limited choices, such as occupational opportunities, at least bred a certain amount of security. While most would argue that wider choices and more flexibility in making choices about how to live are a movement in positive directions, there is the unfortunate down side. If I have greater choice in the world, exactly what is it that I'm supposed to do? Increased opportunity yields increased uncertainty, and if I'm challenging the very institutions that used to provide me solace (e.g., the family, the church), to whom do I turn for comfort?

This is the cultural context that laid the foundation for the growth of groups as we know them today. The proliferation of groups in our society was not an accident—it was a logical response to new cultural need.

The Study of Groups

In the midst of all of this cultural upheaval came some new ways of looking at how to use groups. In the late 1940s, Kurt Lewin and some other Massachusetts Institute of Technology psychologists had responded to a small Connecticut city's request for help in dealing with the city's racial tension and difficulties. They set up a series of working groups to help people talk with one another about their perceptions of the situation. What they found intrigued them—that some of the most productive work seemed to be happening around the edges of the actual work that the groups were instructed to undertake. They saw that the *process*, the ways in which people, staff, and participants were working together—not just what they were supposed to be doing—was really important.

Shortly after Lewin's death, his colleagues set up and ran a laboratory in Bethel, Maine (the National Training Laboratory, or NTL), to continue the study of this process work in groups. Their work, coupled with that of other centers around the country (e.g., at Esalen in California), began to focus on the potential for groups to sensitize people to themselves and others—hence the names "sensitivity" or "training" group that were applied to some of these group endeavors.

Groups and the Human Potential Movement

For the growing group phenomenon, the era of the 1960s and 1970s was not just about sex, drugs, and rock and roll—though they were certainly huge influences on these "new" groups—but it was also about new influences in psychology and psychotherapy: *humanism and the human potential movement.* The psychologists Abraham Maslow and Carl Rogers, as well as others, suggested that psychotherapy should no longer be only for those seen as "ill," but it should also be a vehicle for all people to explore the outer limits of personal possibility, to become fully "actualized." They saw groups as having the potential to help with this process of actualization—to help people become more honest with themselves and more authentic with one another.

All kinds of experiments started to happen in the world of groups. Some began to think of groups not only as ways for people to learn more about how they interact with others but also as a way to explore personal limits of consciousness. Hallucinogenic drugs were used in some groups. Some groups encouraged members to take off their clothes. People who ran these groups saw this as a way of helping minimize barriers between people. Some groups met for hours on end, under the assumption that when people got tired enough they'd let down their defenses and become more authentic. These *marathon* groups were designed to help people honestly *encounter* one another. *Bob and Carol and Ted and Alice*, a hugely successful film made in 1969, portrays quite nicely some of the excesses of this era of group experimentation.

Groups Become More Professional

Many professionals in the field became troubled by these encounter groups (Fuller, 2008; Howes, 1981) and, particularly, by the fact that some people seemed to be emerging damaged by their group experiences. They surmised that some people who were leading groups were doing so more for their own gratification and glorification than for the well-being of the people who joined their groups.

The Association for Specialists in Group Work, formed in 1973, established sets of ethical guidelines that stressed professional training and credentialing for group leaders. Irvin Yalom's *The Theory and Practice of Group Psychotherapy* (1970), a seminal text on group work, was published at about the same time as the formation of the Association for Specialists in Group Work, and with its publication came considerable academic support for applying more rigor to group leader training. Counselor, psychology, and social work training programs endorsed standards for training and ethical practice and demanded better training for group leaders.

Groups Today

This increased professionalization of the profession (Scheidlinger, 2000), particularly group leader training, coupled with standards of protection for group members, has resulted in a proliferation of group work in all kinds of social institutions—schools and businesses—as well as agencies that provide community mental health care. Groups are now used in all kinds of agencies, and many of them are quite sophisticated and efficient (Stone, 2001). Savvy private counseling and social work practitioners have integrated groups as an integral part of the services they offer.

Furthermore, the concept of "group" has morphed into all kinds of informal social variations. Book clubs, running groups, and play groups for parents of young children—and now even online groups—provide a forum for people to meet, share, and support one another. Self-help groups—from Overeaters Anonymous to Gamblers Anonymous to support groups for men and for women—have multiplied. In any city newspaper, you can find a support group to fit almost any need.

Groups, in all shapes and sizes, have become an integral part of the way we live.

GREAT GROUPS IN ACTION: A CASE VIGNETTE

Let's take a quick look at an experience I had with a group that did some really good work. This example clearly shows, I think, how a cohesive group can provide concrete assistance and support.

Some years ago, I was working at a large university counseling center and was running a group for students, all of whom were involved in some kind of professional program (mostly social work and counseling). For this group, I didn't have the benefit of working with a coleader.

The people in the group, in addition to being in school, were also working in some kind of human service capacity. Thus, the group was serving a double purpose: (1) it was a vehicle for members' own personal growth, and (2) it was also a training venue for their professional work with groups. I encouraged the people in the group not only to fully engage in the activities of the group but also to occasionally take a "fly-on-the-wall" perspective and to more objectively look at the dynamics of the group. I encouraged them to keep journals of their personal and professional observations.

The group was an interesting mix of people. There was a wide array of backgrounds and work experiences among members. While everyone in the group was currently working locally, most had come from different parts of this country, and a few were from other countries. The varied backgrounds and the cultural mix of members in the group made for some truly rich conversations.

Early on in the group, I was struck by a comment one of the women had made. Her name was Jenna. She was a teacher, looking to retool her resume to serve a different role in a school, perhaps as a school-based clinician or school counselor.

She had said, when asked to clarify her reasons for coming back to school, "I'm not exactly sure what kind of counseling or social work career I want to go for, but I do know that I just want to help people somehow. I need to help. So I'm sampling courses, figuring out where to go next."

What, I wondered, was this "need" to help about?

Later, as the group matured, it came out that Jenna had been raised in a home that was very political. Her parents were both active in local politics, community organizations, and in a variety of honorable causes—fighting poverty, promoting affordable housing, organizing the local food bank. They were highly visible people in the community and were great personalities. Jenna described the two of them together as "a force."

Early on, it had been impressed on Jenna, an only child, that it was her job to continue their work, to fight for social justice, and to help people less fortunate than herself. She had taken this message to heart, and it was easy to see how good she would be at helping others. She had a wonderful way of being with the people in the group—her enthusiasm, good humor, and genuine interest were infectious. All of us liked her.

One day, when the group was coming close to ending, we were using a "big questions" exercise to demonstrate how groups can help people step back and look at the roads their lives are traveling. I suggested that people in the group could consider the appropriateness of using this exercise in their own groups.

The group had broken into smaller groups of three, and each group was contemplating how to use a series of questions like "What would I do if I found out that I had 6 months to live?" "Am I on the right path?" "Do the people I love know it?" with a group. In looking at how to implement such an exercise with their groups, the students in our group couldn't avoid grappling with these questions themselves.

When we got back together, I asked if anyone wanted to briefly share thoughts about the application of the exercise with groups and what had come up personally during these contemplations. Jenna, looking troubled, said, "Well, I think I got involved with this more personally than thinking about it professionally. It got me thinking. I've always had this burning desire to travel. My husband and I always talk about traveling, but we never have time. We get so busy! I'd just love to chuck it all and hit the road." As she said this she was staring at the ground and looking very miserable. Absent were her usual enthusiasm and cheerful demeanor.

"Well, why not just do it?" someone asked. "Between the two of you, you must have some pretty good savings. You don't even have kids yet. Why not travel for as long as your money holds out, and then come back and work?"

"I can't," Jenna replied. "That would be too selfish. It would be all about me. That's just not what I'm supposed to be, or do."

And here we had it. This is what the "need" to help was all about. To paraphrase the motto: "Others before self"—or in her case, others instead of self. The group spent the next few minutes talking with Jenna about this, pointing out that the messages from her parents about being a force for good had been internalized in a way that had become personally oppressive. Maybe her parents wanted her to be a helpful force in the world, someone said, but not in ways that she'd have to sacrifice all of herself.

"How about," the woman sitting next to Jenna said, "combining some helping and some traveling? Is there a way you could do that? I mean, the stuff your parents taught you is all good, but I'm sure that they didn't mean that you should suffer or not pay any attention to what you want."

Then a number of other people voiced support for Jenna doing other things for herself, and some people talked about how much they could relate to the issues Jenna described. Jenna had clearly opened a topic that had some relevance for others.

At this point, as our ending time for the day was rapidly approaching, I short-circuited the conversation by saying, "You know this, like so many other things that have come up here, is a really interesting issue for you, Jenna—and clearly for others, as well. If we had more time today, we could really get into this and work it over. What I can do, however, is suggest you continue looking at this stuff next week. And given that we've only got a couple of meeting times left, maybe you'll also want to look at all this in a more personal, individual way. I can give you the name of a good therapist who you could continue this with, if you want." (This, by the way, is an example of the use of the skill of "cutting off," which we'll discuss again in later chapters.)

A few weeks after that afternoon's session, the group ended, with Jenna only bringing this issue up again briefly, mostly to tell us that she was going to do some personal work with a therapist.

Then, some months later, I got a note from Jenna. Here's an excerpt:

I want to thank you and the group so much for the support and encouragement to continue looking at what is one of my primary issues: "What I want to do versus what I think I'm supposed to do."

My husband and I decided to do some couples counseling, and after a lot of thought and discussion, we've decided to take leaves from our jobs and travel the country. We'll travel for a few weeks, then stop and work in volunteer positions in some place that suits us for a while, and then move on. This way I can manage my guilt about traveling (what our therapist calls my "mantel of codependency").

I couldn't have begun to really look at all this without the push from the group. Please pass this note along to all of them. Maybe I'll be in touch when I return to continue my graduate study. Who knows?

I did pass her note along to the rest of the people who'd been in the group, and for the next few months I got brief update notes from Jenna about her travels with her husband. Finally, I got a letter that said that they had decided to relocate to another state, a place with more sun and warm weather, and that she would continue her studies there.

Reflection and Discussion Exercise

Following are some questions you could contemplate after thinking about this case vignette you've just read:

1. Think about Jenna's current situation and about how that might be influenced by her growing-up years. What reactions do you have to her disclosure in the group, and about the group's responses to her?

2. Is it the role of groups to engage people in such "big questions" exercises? Are there groups where asking these kinds of questions might not be appropriate?

3. Why would Jenna's counselor have used the expression, "mantel of codependency?"

4. How common do you think Jenna's dilemma is among the helping professionals you know?

5. How would you answer some of those "big questions" yourself? Can you think of other such questions that you might pose for a group?

Finally, if you are working on this exercise with other people, take a few minutes to discuss your thoughts with them.

CONCLUDING THOUGHTS

I started becoming interested in and working with groups while a graduate student in Buffalo, New York. We were all expected to be in groups during most of our tenure as students, and I began to see the ways these group experiences positively affected people's lives. I used those groups not only as a way of making good connections with my student colleagues but also as a way of beginning a lifelong journey of self-exploration.

I grew up in a family with emotional difficulties, and I had experienced the death of a brother when I was just finishing high school. I, like so many others who enter the helping professions, wanted to learn how to help people, but I also wanted to resolve some of my own personal questions about the meaning of these difficult life experiences.

Those early groups I was in as a graduate student pushed me to look more carefully at the ways my own life and experience—particularly my own unfinished business—might affect my work with others. They helped me begin to take responsibility for doing my own therapeutic work. I came to see via these groups that awareness and better understanding of my own personal history and myself was prerequisite for working cleanly with others. The importance of group leader self-awareness will run as a theme throughout this book.

I also began to see the ways in which these group experiences improved people's interpersonal skills. I eventually centered my dissertation research on the hypothesis that focused group work can help people increase their sense of empathy for others, even helping them become more effective helping professionals. Then, when I left graduate school, group work became a mainstay of my professional counseling practice. I focused my work on developing groups that encouraged people to become personal and vulnerable, on creating safe spaces for people to learn how to become really personal with one another.

During the nearly 30 years that have transpired since I left graduate school, I have led many groups, and now I teach others about the joys and challenges of group work. Perhaps, as importantly, I have been a member of a number of groups that have served to support me and make my life richer. I look forward to sharing some of those experiences with you in the chapters ahead.

There are, indeed, some unique joys—and challenges—of working with people in groups. While working individually in some kind of helping relationship affords the opportunity for people to learn more about themselves in the confines of an intimate relationship with one other person, group counseling has the benefit of helping people learn more about themselves in relationship with others. The groups we are in help connect us with the rest of the human race—to help all of us see our lives in a context of relationship with others.

Groups, including groups that focus on personal growth, have become an integral part of the social fabric of our lives. They have evolved in ways that fill a critical social need for us. Learning how to negotiate them well, as both a member and a leader, is a great life skill.

FOR FURTHER THOUGHT

1. Look at some of the literature about the history of the development of the use of groups in our society. How do your ideas about this development fit—or not fit—with ideas presented in this chapter?

2. Look at your local newspaper listings for group offerings in your community. What are the other sources of information about groups being held where you live? Check hospital and agency websites, also those of local schools, colleges, and universities for more information about group offerings.

3. Interview one or two people who have had significant experience with groups. They might be counselors, social workers, teachers, or coaches—or anyone else who works regularly with groups. What are their opinions and ideas about their groups? What are their particular joys and challenges associated with group work?

REFERENCES

Akos, P., & Martin, M. (2003). Transition groups for preparing students for middle school. *Journal of Specialists in Group Work, 28,* 139–154.

Barrett, M. (2012). Family dynamics and the educational experience. In H. High (Ed.), *Why can't I help this child to learn? Understanding emotional barriers to learning* (pp. 85–102). London, England: Karnac Books.

Barron, J. (1970). Group psychotherapy: Evolution and process. *Journal of Contemporary Psychotherapy, 3*(1), 27–30.

Corey, G. (2008). *The theory and practice of group counseling* (7th ed.). Pacific Grove, CA: Brooks/Cole.

Davies, P., & Gavin, W. (1994). Comparison of group/consultation treatment methods for pre-school children with developmental delays. *American Journal of Occupational Therapy, 48,* 155–161.

Dugatin, L. (1999). *Cheating monkeys and citizen bees: The nature of cooperation in animals and humans.* New York, NY: Free Press.

Ferencik, B. (1992). The helping process in group therapy: A review and discussion. *Group, 16,* 113–124.

Fuller, R. C. (2008). Review of Esalen: American and the religion of no religion. *Journal of the History of the Behavioral Sciences, 44*(3), 279–280.

Gallagher, M. E., Tasca, G. A., Ritchie, K., Balfour, L., Maxwell, H., & Bissada, H. (2014). Interpersonal learning is associated with improved self-esteem in group psychotherapy for women with binge eating disorder. *Psychotherapy, 51*(1), 66–77.

Gladding, S. (2008). *Groups: A counseling specialty* (5th ed.). Upper Saddle River, NJ: Merrill/Prentice Hall.

Howes, R. (1981). Encounter groups: Comparisons and ethical considerations. *Psychotherapy: Theory, Research, and Practice, 18*(2), 229–239.

Johnson, C. V. (2009). A process-oriented group model for university students: A semi-structured approach. *International Journal of Group Psychotherapy, 59*(4), 511–528.

Kögler, M., Brandl, J., Brandstätter, M., Borasio, G., & Fegg, M. (2013). Determinants of the effect of existential behavioral therapy for bereaved partners: A qualitative study. *Journal of Palliative Medicine, 16*(11), 1410–1416.

Kramer, M. (2009). Review of BAM! Boys advocacy and mentoring! A leader's guide to facilitating strengths-based groups for boys. *Gestalt Review, 13*(3), 302–303.

Moreno, J. (1949). *Psychodrama* (Vol. 1). New York, NY: Beacon House.

Nolte, J. (2014). *The philosophy, theory and methods of J. L. Moreno: The man who tried to become God* [e-book]. New York, NY: Routledge/Taylor & Francis.

Papanek, H. (1970). Adler's psychology and group psychotherapy. *American Journal of Psychiatry, 127*(6), 783–786.

Piper, W. (2008). Underutilization of short term group therapy: Enigmatic or understandable? *Psychotherapy Research, 18*(2), 127–138.

Scheidlinger, S. (2000). The group psychotherapy movement at the millennium: Some historical perspectives. *International Journal of Group Psychotherapy, 50*(3), 315–339.

Sochting, I., Wilson, C., & De Gagne, T. (2010). Cognitive behavioural group therapy (CBGT): Capitalizing on efficiency and humanity. In J. Bennet-Levy, D. A. Richards, P. Farrand, H. Christensen, K. Griffiths, D. Kavanaugh, & C. Williams (Eds.), *Oxford guide to low intensity CBT interventions* (pp. 323–329). New York, NY: Oxford University Press.

Stone, W. (2001). A retrospective of group therapy: A letter. *International Journal of Group Psychotherapy, 51*(2), 169–174.

Trotzer, J. (2006). *The counselor and the group* (4th ed.). Philadelphia, PA: Taylor & Francis.

Woolhouse, S., Cooper, E., & Pickard, A. (2013). "It gives me a sense of belonging": Providing integrated health care and treatment to people with HCV engaged in a psycho-educational support group. *International Journal of Drug Policy, 24*(6), 550–557.

Yalom, I. (1970). *The theory and practice of group psychotherapy.* New York, NY: Basic Books.

Yalom, I. (1985). *The theory and practice of group psychotherapy* (2nd ed.). New York, NY: Basic Books.

Chapter 2

Becoming a Great Group Leader

A leader is best when people barely know he exists, when his work is done, his aim fulfilled, they will say: we did it ourselves.

—Lao Tzu

A short story about one of my former students and her experience with a challenging group might help to initiate a look at what this chapter will highlight as the keys to effective group leadership.

Maya had just graduated from our master's program in counseling, and she was looking for work as a professional addictions counselor. She had had her own difficult journey with alcohol and drugs, had been clean and sober for a number of years, and now she wanted to give back to the treatment community some of what she felt had been given to her. As with many people who enter our field, there was a sense of mission about this work she felt she was meant to do.

Maya had been a star student. She had done well in all of her academic coursework and had completed her field experiences and internships with rave reviews from her clinical supervisors. She had developed a great repertoire of counseling skills, and she showed keen insight into the needs of the clients she served. Moreover, her quick smile and easygoing temperament made working with her a real pleasure. Almost all of her internship experiences were in working individually with people—she'd had very little group experience.

Maya's first job interview was with the superintendent of the local correctional facility. He was overseeing a grant program that was working with soon-to-be released women who had been incarcerated and had been identified as having significant drug problems, which if not treated effectively, would lead inevitably to re-incarceration. The grant was aimed at providing support for counselors to lead intensive 2- to 3-hour psycho-educational groups for these women. The groups were to be a combination of personal sharing among the women—of their histories and concerns—and education about drugs, alcohol, and families.

During the interview the superintendent said,

> You know, Maya, you've got great references, you seem to be really bright, and I've enjoyed talking with you a lot. But I'm concerned that you might be too nice . . . . These women could eat you alive. Are you sure you want to take this on? We'd love to hire you, but I do have concerns.

Maya, despite the warnings of her new boss—and perhaps somewhat in reaction to what she saw as some sexism in his patronizing comments about her "niceness"—took the job. Her primary work was in running three groups of six women each, without the benefit of a coleader, twice a week.

Things did not go smoothly. From the outset, some of the women were openly oppositional, saying that they didn't need this "expletive-deleted" touchy-feely stuff, others were simply silent, and Maya struggled to try to get through some of the basic informational material she was expected to present. The women challenged her on every front: on her youth and inexperience, on her personal appearance, and on just about anything she tried to do.

Maya would call me and her other behind-the-scenes support people in tears, saying that she didn't know how much longer she could take this abuse. Her supervisor at the correctional center provided some support, but he didn't seem to have a good sense of the extent of the difficulty. He didn't know how close to quitting Maya came.

We all encouraged her to just hang in, to use the skills she'd learned during her graduate experience to respond to some of these challenges, and to not allow personal verbal attacks. We also tried to get her to acknowledge these oppositional and defiant behaviors for what they were—defensive, fear-driven responses to invitations to get closer and more honest about their real thoughts and feelings. The women were acting out of their own anxiety, in other words, and this had little to do with Maya. Behind their belligerence and hostility was fear and all of their past bad experiences with trusting other people.

Finally, some of the women started to come around. They started to take little personal sharing risks, and they even started paying more attention to some of the educational and skills training and doing some of the homework assignments. Things were starting to get better. Maya was managing to still be herself, not getting "tough" in response to all the difficult and defensive behavioral posturing, but she was demonstrating an ability to stand up to all the testing and to not be thrown offtrack. She tried to reasonably respond to some of the changes the women requested, but she stood her ground about some of the essential things she felt needed to remain in place. She allowed the women to understand that they had some power and control over how things were going to go, but she maintained her integrity in the process. There was no magic about how she did this; she just didn't quit.

And then a major life event for Maya occurred that, unintentionally, moved the group further along. Maya's sister was in a traffic accident that left her hospitalized with serious, life-threatening injuries. She had been walking across an intersection in a street near her home, and was hit by a drunk driver who'd run a red light. Maya missed 2 weeks of work to help deal with all of this, and then, after she'd seen that her sister was going to pull through—though she was looking at a long and arduous road to recovery—she returned to her groups.

The women in Maya's groups found out about the accident, and they learned about the reasons for Maya's absence. To their outstanding credit, they responded to this awful accident with compassion and understanding. Some of the women sent Maya cards of sympathy, and others brought cards to her personally. Overnight the defiance was gone, and the conversations in the groups became more personal and real. Some of the women talked about having driven drunk themselves, and about the problems and near misses they'd had with drug-related events in their own lives. The accident served as a catalyst for personal sharing.

Through all this Maya shared her appreciation for the comments of support and the increased level of cooperation, while minimally sharing her own struggles with her feelings surrounding her sister's accident. Her supervisory support provided her with the opportunity to deal with her personal reactions to this event and also gave her some guidelines for how much of this to share—or not—with her groups. She was helped to see that these groups were not the primary vehicle for her to deal with her own issues, despite the fact that the women were encouraging her to share more. She correctly saw that what she chose to share—or didn't—could serve as a means for the women to share more about themselves.

EFFECTIVE GROUP LEADERSHIP

Maya's experience with this group is affirmation of some of the ingredients of good group leadership. A combination of some effective personality traits, good skills, and personal kindness, coupled with simple firmness (without getting tough and harsh), resilience, and simply hanging in, will go a long way to helping a group— even a tough one—come together and work well.

Her ability, after some initial problems, to connect with the people in her group set the stage for the group to do some great work. This ability to form an *alliance* with the people in the group is the hallmark of sound group leadership (Crits-Christoph, Johnson, Connolly Gibbons, & Gallop, 2013).

Also, and this probably accounts for at least some of our successes in group work, chance sometimes play a role. Unplanned life events happen, like the accident in this case, and they can be significant factors in helping a group to coalesce and become more cohesive. But I believe that Maya's fierce determination, her grit, coupled with her kind and genuine interest in the women with whom she worked, would have yielded positive group experiences, even without the accident.

There is another observation worth noting about Maya's groups. When given the opportunity, even tough, hardened people can respond with compassion. Certainly as group leaders our job involves caring for and responding as well as we can to the people in our groups, but we can do more than that. If we can provide opportunities for the members of our groups to respond and care for each other, as well, they will have really learned something. We'll talk in later chapters about helping people learn the skills to do this.

We all have times when we need others to care for us, and we all have times when we need to care for others. Great groups can help satisfy these universal needs.

You will bring your own set of unique talents and strengths to the groups you create and lead. You might be naturally outgoing, affable, and comfortable taking control in situations with other people. You might be someone who thrives in challenging interpersonal situations. Or you might be the kind of person who is generally more used to letting others lead. You might avoid groups that have tension and conflict. You might like firmly structured experiences; or you might prefer the looseness and ambiguity of some of the groups you've been in.

Much of this book, particularly the middle portion, will introduce you to many of the *skills* you'll need to be able to do competent group work. The skills, by themselves, are not enough. Who you are as a person is at least, if not more, important than the skills you have at your disposal. In this chapter you will be reading about some of these personal *characteristics* that make for effective leadership. You will also consider how your own interpersonal *style* translates into your perceptions of yourself as a group leader. You have natural inclinations that you can appreciate and respect as you contemplate new group situations, particularly those you will be creating and leading.

Your personal characteristics, your motivations, your knowledge about yourself, and your natural leadership style—coupled with your learned group skills—will be a potent combination in helping to lay the groundwork for a great group.

This chapter will encourage you to look at the characteristics of effective group leadership and the ways in which you can examine your own potential for working well with groups.

EFFECTIVE GROUP LEADERSHIP

- Your Personal Characteristics
- Your Motivation
- Your Personal Style
- Your Self-Awareness
- Your Values
- Your Ethical Awareness
- Your Appreciation for Diversity
- Your Professional Preparation

CHARACTERISTICS OF EFFECTIVE GROUP LEADERS

You'll need to take stock of those personal characteristics of yours that shape your interactions with other people as you approach working with groups. You might believe that you were born with these characteristics. You might think, on the other hand, that your family and other social contacts shaped your personality. Either way, you must assume that these personal characteristics of yours will be important to consider as you approach your work with groups.

Naturally, the ability of a group you lead to do good work rests largely on your shoulders. Leadership skill and leader personality play a large role in the success or failure of a group (Rubel & Kline, 2008). Research suggests that there are a number of personal characteristics that lend themselves to doing good work with groups (Egan, 2006). Most of these traits, like personal *sense of self, integrity, steadiness, and constancy*, are the hallmarks of a person who has a good sense of herself or himself, someone who is grounded in a set of personal values and beliefs, and is not afraid to stand by those (Simons, Tomlinson, & Leroy, 2012). Many of the characteristics of competent group leaders are similar to the characteristics Carl Rogers talked about when he outlined the characteristics of effective helping professionals—*warmth, genuineness, authenticity,* and *being nonjudgmental* (Rogers, 1980).

These characteristics, when combined, create the most critical leadership characteristic: having a *capacity for empathy*. It is this ability to see the world through your group members' eyes that will allow you access to an understanding of who they are, the people behind the challenging behaviors and social roles they most typically display.

It can also be helpful if you have a good sense of *humor*, especially if you have the ability to laugh at yourself and your own mistakes (Wisse & Rietzschel, 2014).

This does not include, obviously, laughing at the mistakes of others (Gladding, 1997).

Many of your best potential leadership traits will simply be an extension of who you are, your essential personality (Tollerud, Holling, & Dustin, 1992). This means that you need to take serious stock of what your strongest personality characteristics are, perhaps even using instruments like the Myers-Briggs to aid your examination (Bates, Johnson, & Blaker, 1982). Your positive personality characteristics, combined with your growing experience as a group leader, will make for a potent leadership combination (Johnson & Johnson, 2012).

Your *self-confidence* will play a huge role in how well you lead groups. You can probably best boost your confidence by repeatedly putting yourself in group situations where you can successfully observe others at work and by remaining open to constructive suggestion and supervision (Bandura, 1997). Undoubtedly, the more success you experience in leading groups, the more self-confident you'll feel about taking on new group experiences.

You are a *model* for the people in your group. Who you are, how you act, what you feel, will be far more important than what you say (Edelwich & Brodsky, 1992). Your group will intuitively know, as they say, if you walk the walk, or just talk the talk. Your own levels of enthusiasm, general happiness, and willingness to show that to your group will have a great influence on how well your group comes together (Chi, Chung, & Tsai, 2011). Ernest Hemingway used to say that people have built-in "crap detectors." Trust that the people in your groups will certainly be listening to theirs. People can sense the truth behind the words being spoken.

Your ability to stay grounded within yourself, to feel confident in who you are, will allow you to let the group do its work without feeling that its relative degree of success is due to who you are. The group, in other words, is not all about you. The best kind of leadership is "*ego-free leadership*." As the quote at the beginning of this chapter suggests, in a group ending it is far better for the members to say, "Look at what a great job we did," as opposed to, "Look at how great a leader she was."

OTHER KEY LEADERSHIP TRAITS: INTEREST, KINDNESS, ENTHUSIASM, AND GRIT

In the early 1950s, when Dwight "Ike" Eisenhower was running in a campaign to become president of the United States, the political slogan that popularized the campaign was "I like Ike." It was a catchy expression that caught on and, certainly, may have helped him win the race.

I think that the "Ike" in this phrase, "I like Ike," can also be used as a corny kind of acronym to characterize some of the best traits of good leadership: interest, kindness, and enthusiasm. These three personal characteristics can go a long way to making your work as a group leader go well. Your genuine, *honest interest* in getting to know the people in your group, and in what they have to say, coupled with your *kindness* toward them, will be great assets in helping the group to coalesce and develop a sense of safety and cohesion. Your *enthusiasm* for working with your group will be infectious. If you believe in the worth of what you're doing, and in what the group is all about, it will be felt by the people around you.

Then there is one characteristic that the literature doesn't discuss much, but that I think is of critical importance. This one is *grit*, or determination, the ability to just hang in and on through difficult situations. This suggests that your ability to be determined and courageous will play a role in your success as a group leader. You could supplement the adage that says, "half of success in life is due to just showing up," by adding, "the other half of success is due to not giving up." Working with groups requires a certain amount of toughness, an ability to ride through difficult times.

THE IMPORTANCE OF YOUR SELF-AWARENESS

Because you are in a modeling role with a group when you are its leader, the degree of self-awareness you bring to the work is of critical importance. Your motivations for working with people, your awareness of your own issues and emotional unfinished business, and your clarity about your beliefs and values are as important as any of the other professional training you have in working with groups (Cavanagh, 1990). Your own life experiences, even the difficult ones, can help you better understand and relate to those of others, but you need to be able to separate your own experiences from those of the people with whom you work.

It should be obvious that a primary reason for increasing your levels of awareness of your own issues (e.g., family history, problematic behaviors, performance anxieties, etc.) is to decrease the likelihood that you will try to work out those issues through the people who participate in your groups (Sommers-Flanagan & Heck, 2013). You want to be able to deal directly with the people in your groups, not simply through the colored lens of your own past experiences.

An example may help clarify this. If, just as example, you grew up in a family where one of your parents or a sibling had an addiction issue and was abusive toward other family members, you may have strong negative feelings about someone in your group who struggles with addiction. These feelings are not solely related to the person himself or herself, but they are in part a throwback to your older family history.

It is this kind of *countertransference* issue (a psychoanalytic term for the ways a helping professional's relationship issues with significant people from his or her past can be triggered by someone who is being helped) that is best brought into your awareness so that you can try to avoid foisting old feelings onto current situations. The more you are aware of and understand the impact life events and people have had on you, the less likely you are to be controlled by those in your current life.

Whenever you find yourself being unusually emotionally reactive (sometimes people call this "getting your buttons pushed") with regard to someone in your group, there may be some of your own old material—not related to this new group situation—that has been kicked into play. This can take a variety of forms. You might be unusually attracted to, angered by, or impatient with one or more people. Whenever it's more about you than the other person, it's something you'll want to take a look at.

This is why you'll do your own personal work—involvement in groups as a member, or your own personal counseling or therapy—as part of your preparation for working with groups. Your coleaders and supervisors will help with this, too. They will help highlight times when they may see that some of your own personal material is influencing how you are responding to things that come up in a group.

Most professional training programs in counseling, social work, and psychology acknowledge the importance of self-awareness in this kind of work and require that their students engage in some kind of personal growth work as an integral part of their educational programming. Typically, while students inevitably do some personal growth activities in their coursework, the bulk of that kind of work is done with professionals—people who are not evaluating student performance—outside of the program.

You can do some of this self-examination work on your own. You can begin to review different aspects of yourself, particularly as they may affect your work with people in groups. I suggest the use of a simple "whole person" model as a starting point for this review (Hutchinson, 2014; Wegscheider, 1986). With this review, you simply consider seven different aspects of who you are and take note of any specific areas that deserve your attention. Looking at yourself this way, you could think about expanding your self-awareness as "selves" awareness.

YOUR "WHOLE PERSON" REVIEW

- Physical Health
- Emotional Health
- Social–Familial Health
- Intellectual Health
- Spiritual Health
- Aesthetic Health
- Working Health

Using this model you can do a quick review your own "whole person," and each of its distinct components. How well is each part of your life faring? Are these different aspects of your life in balance?

For now, simply scan each of these areas of your personal health and ask yourself how "fit" and satisfied you are in that part of your life. If you want to do this more completely, you could look now at the last chapter in this book, where this review is covered more completely.

THE IMPORTANCE OF CULTURAL AWARENESS

A capacity for empathy allows you to appreciate all the unique differences—the diversity—that people bring to groups. There are all kinds of differences that people will bring to your groups and your attempts to understand and your ability to embrace those differences will be key to insuring that those experiences are successful.

People will have all kinds of preconceived notions about what groups can, or can't, do for them. Some basic beliefs about human nature, about what motivates people, and about the nature of human problems are very much culturally determined (Constantine, Miville, Kindaichi, & Owens, 2010). Our research has only begun to look at how cultural background influences how people will do in helping situations, like groups (Jackson, 2003).

There is a remarkable range of differences that you'll encounter: Race and ethnicity, socioeconomic class, gender, sexual orientation, physical capacity, and religion—to name a few of the most outstanding of these. The best that you can do is to become a student of these broad cultural differences. You can certainly begin to read the literature about how some specific kinds of "difference" might shape someone's attitudes about being in a group—and about whether they would even be willing to join in the first place.

In addition to reading, you can try to expand your awareness of these cultural differences in other, more experiential, ways. You can travel to places that are culturally different from where you live. You can spend time in neighborhoods unlike your own. You can go to a place of worship that is different from the one you usually visit—which might be any place of worship, if you don't regularly go yourself. Even eating foods from different places can be viewed as a cultural consciousness expansion. These kinds of personal, lived experiences might, in fact, be the best ways of increasing your personal cultural competency (Okech & DeVoe, 2010). Push yourself out of your cultural comfort zone.

In a sense, every helping encounter—either in a group or individually—is an experience in cultural difference. Beyond those broad categories of difference mentioned earlier, each of us lives in our own cultural world. Each of us has a unique world perspective. While this should not be an excuse for trying to broaden an understanding of cultural differences, via reading or lived experience, it does mean that in each encounter we have with someone we can let him or her be our teacher. Take a serious interest in how the world looks through his or her eyes, and let the people in your groups explore some of these differences with each other.

Finally, don't get so caught up in looking for difference that you lose sight of the commonalities we all share. These include our experience of joy, of suffering, of frustration, and of connection with others. At the same time, you are encouraging people to learn about differences from one another, you can be helping them to engage around the universal truths of the human condition.

Gaining experience with groups can expand your ability to respond empathically to all the different kinds of people in your groups (Granello & Underfer-Babalis, 2004). You can also search out other experiences, like service learning (Brown, 2011), or other strategies that can help you expand this ability to respond (Turner, 2013). When your group senses that you are fully in the experience with them, the stage is set for more interpersonal risk taking to occur (Chapman, Baker, Porter, Thayer, & Burlingame, 2010).

THE IMPORTANCE OF PROFESSIONAL—INCLUDING ETHICAL—PREPARATION

Your professional, academic preparation is a critical aspect of your group leadership "personality." You need to understand some of the theory about the forces that have influenced your group members' lives, about how they have developed, about different approaches for working with groups, and about basic assessment strategies. You need to know about ethical issues and potential problem situations that might occur in your groups. Professional training programs in social work, counseling, or psychology will supply you with the coursework and tools that are prerequisites for doing group work.

Any of these professional programs will also provide you with knowledge of the ethics involved in working with people in groups. That knowledge of your profession's approach to ethical issues, coupled with guidelines specific to group work, will help you insure that you are adequately protecting the people in your group, the profession, and yourself from unfair practices. Toward this end, in addition to the ethical guidelines specified by your professional organization, make sure that you familiarize yourself with those established by the American Specialists in Group Work (Thomas & Pender, 2008).

Life experience has helped shape your life. The more diverse and divergent your life experience and exposure to people, the better prepared you are to empathize with and relate to the people who will present themselves in your groups. Similarly,

TRAITS OF EFFECTIVE GROUP LEADERS

- Solid Sense of Self   Integrity   Steadiness   Constancy
- Warmth   Genuineness   Nonjudgmental   Authenticity
- Self-Awareness and the Capacity for Empathy
- Ability to Use Yourself as a Model
- Appropriate Humor
- Self-Confidence
- Ability to Provide "Ego-Free" Leadership
- Appreciation of Diversity
- IKE: Interest, Kindness, and Enthusiasm
- Grit, Determination

Figure 2.1   Grit and Determination Can Help You Get Through the Tough Times

your academic training, your field experiences, and the coursework you take will provide you with tools to better understand these people and the group situations you encounter. Your best professional preparation, then, is a marriage of your ongoing experience of life and your more formal academic training.

These characteristics of effective leadership described here are not abstract concepts. They relate to you directly. These traits, as they are reflected in how you work with people, will have a lot to do with how successful your group experiences will be. I would encourage you to look at your areas for needed growth as a group leader.

When you've finished reading this chapter, you can take the brief, simple questionnaire in the "For Further Thought" section at the end of this chapter. Then you can discuss your reflections with your colleagues (Figure 2.1). Later, you can use other sophisticated instruments (e.g., the Myers–Briggs) to help you gauge your skills and competency as a group leader (Woo & Hsu, 2012).

EFFECTIVE GROUP LEADERSHIP: LEADERSHIP STYLE

You will bring yourself, your own personality, to your groups—and you will also bring your own style, your way of working, to these groups. Some of your style is simply an extension of who you are, your natural way of being with people. Other aspects of this style, however, can be adjusted to meet the needs of your group. You can thoughtfully shift how you are being with a group depending on the characteristics of its members and the particular issues that are emerging in it.

The literature about leadership in groups has historically talked about three basic styles of leadership: autocratic, democratic, and laissez-faire (De Cremer, 2006; Rast, Hogg, & Giessner, 2013; Schneider, 1965; Van Vugt, Chang, & Hart, 2005). The first of these styles, *autocratic*, refers to a leader who is solidly in control. This leader plans the action, is clearly visible as the person in charge, and is generally in control of the group decision making. This leader may be kind and benevolent, yet is definitely in command. The second leadership style, *democratic*, suggests a leader who is comfortable sharing in the planning and group direction functions and with the group arriving at its own decisions. He or she may play an active role in making suggestions and providing direction but is generally willing to let go of a directive role in favor of group consensus or majority rule.

SHIFTING LEADERSHIP STYLE WITH A DEVELOPING GROUP

- Birth of the Group → The Working Group → End of the Group
  With a Leadership Style That Is One of the Following:
- Autocratic → Democratic → Laissez-Faire
- Directive → Nondirective
- Active → Less Active

Finally, the *laissez-faire* leader takes a passive approach to leadership. This leader lets the group act on its own, providing little direction. In a group with a laissez-faire leader, it is oftentimes difficult to tell who the leader is. This kind of leader blends in with the group and may appear to be just another member.

Another way of looking at the issue of leadership style is to think about the degree of direction you want to provide and how active you want to be in your group. There is no right or wrong style of leading a group, but generally, groups will need a lot of firm direction and for you to be quite active at the front end (making your leadership style roughly "autocratic"). Then, as your group matures and begins to take more responsibility for itself, you can provide less direction and lie back a bit more (a more "democratic" approach). The group that is capable of making its own decisions will rankle, in fact, under the leadership of someone who refuses to give up the reins of control (Van Vugt, Jepson, Hart, & De Cremer, 2004). Eventually, at least with groups that have the capacity to become largely self-directing, you can become very nondirective and minimally active (analogous to the "laissez-faire" leader).

You should strive to comfortably shift into whatever leadership style is needed by your group. We'll talk more of these different group "needs" and how this will influence your leadership style in later chapters. In reality, however, you are probably most comfortable with one of these styles and will need to push yourself to use the others. The following reflection and discussion exercise asks you to consider your own preferred style.

Reflection and Group Fishbowl Lab Practice Exercise: Leadership

Think about your own personality characteristics and style of leadership. You could use the terms *autocratic*, *democratic*, and *laissez-faire* to consider this style, or you may be more comfortable with *directive* and *nondirective* and *active* or *less active* to describe this style.

Think about some of the groups you've been in—formal groups, committees, classes, or teams. Focus in on one particular group experience you've had. Did this group get its work done well? Did people get along and work cooperatively? Did you look forward to going to this group, and did you enjoy the experience? What role did leadership style play in all of that?

Now consider the group experience described at the beginning of this chapter. Go back and reread the example of Maya's group experience. What personal reactions do you have to this group experience? How would you have managed this group, if you had been in Maya's shoes? What suggestions would you have offered Maya, as her supervisor, when the going was really tough?

When you have had ample time to reflect about these leadership questions, create a group fishbowl exercise to discuss your reflections with others.

EFFECTIVE GROUP LEADERSHIP

- Personal Traits + Personal Style + Skills

Again, this exercise will work best with a group of 8 to 15 (or more) people. Two people volunteer to be group leaders. If you are one of these, your job is to help lead a group in a discussion about leadership. You'll try to encourage people in the group to talk about their own personal reactions and reflections and about their own perceived strengths and styles for leading groups. Encourage people to talk personally about leadership, not just about leadership as an intellectual concept. Have them talk about their own leadership abilities and style.

Before you begin, the coleaders might want to consult for a few minutes to establish how they want to initiate the discussion, focusing on how they want to proceed and who will take the lead in getting things going.

Five or six people should volunteer to be group members. If you are a group member, your job is to talk with the group about your ideas related to your perceptions of your own group leadership personality and style.

The other people in the group become group observers. If you are one of these, you will sit with other observers in the fishbowl circle around the leaders and members. Your job is to closely—and silently—observe the group and its interactions between members and leaders. You might want to take notes while you observe. Pay special attention to how the coleaders stimulate discussion. Do they draw people out and encourage everyone to participate? What kinds of things do they do that seem particularly effective in encouraging discussion?

Make whatever accommodations are necessary to make this work for the numbers of people you have conducting this exercise. If your numbers are small, perhaps you'll have one leader and only a few group members, for example.

Take between 20 and 30 minutes for this group discussion. Then take a few minutes for the group observers to share some of their observations. If you are an observer sharing some of what you saw and heard, try to be specific about what you observed, while also being supportive in your comments to the coleaders.

CONCLUDING THOUGHTS

The best way to learn about groups is to get personally involved with groups, initially as a member. Try out a few different groups. Being a member will allow you to participate and observe without feeling the responsibility of leadership. If you get involved with a group that has a leader, it will afford you the opportunity to observe leadership in action. If you get involved with a leaderless support or self-help group, it will allow you to watch how groups grow and develop—or don't—without the benefit of leadership.

If you're in an academic program, you could consider forming a support group with some of your student colleagues. You could even hire a leader, someone experienced in group leadership, from the local social service community. You don't need to wait for an instructor to assign it as part of a course requirement. Doing this would serve a double purpose: providing you with group experience, as well as providing opportunities for increasing your own self-awareness. The more group experience you have—before you're expected to be on the point with leading a group—the better.

If you're not in an academic program, you can either start a group or look for groups in the newspaper. Hospitals and local human services networks often advertise groups they are sponsoring, and you could join one of those. Again, and this is worth repeating, the more experience you have with groups as a member, the more confident you'll feel when you're in the position of actually leading one.

FOR FURTHER THOUGHT

1. Locate two people in your community who lead groups in different kinds of settings. One of these might be a school counselor, for example, and another might work in a community mental health agency. Interview them about their joys and frustrations of doing group work and about their own evolution as group leaders. What natural personal traits do they see themselves as having that help in this work, and what have they most needed to work on to become more proficient?

2. Begin to survey the literature about cultural diversity in therapeutic relationships. Consider the implications that your investigation has for the groups you might lead.

3. Following is a simple, brief, 15-item inventory that asks you questions about your own personal traits and characteristics and your potential for working with groups of people. Each question has a ranking of answers, from 1 (rarely) to 5 (almost always). Naturally, this will be helpful to you to the degree that you can be honest with yourself as you answer each of these.

GROUP LEADERSHIP INVENTORY

1. I am genuinely interested in hearing what other people have to say.

    Rarely   1   2   3   4   5   Almost Always

    Comments:

2. I have a good command of the skills needed to draw people out (e.g., warmth, active listening skills, etc.).

    Rarely   1   2   3   4   5   Almost Always

    Comments:

3. I have a strong and positive sense of who I am, and I am confident in my abilities.

    Rarely   1   2   3   4   5   Almost Always

    Comments:

4. I have a good sense of humor, and I know how to use it appropriately—meaning, never at someone else's expense.

    Rarely   1   2   3   4   5   Almost Always

    Comments:

5. I plan well and I take pride in my organizational abilities.

    Rarely   1   2   3   4   5   Almost Always

    Comments:

6. I can be trusted to hold information confidentially.

    Rarely   1   2   3   4   5   Almost Always

    Comments:

7. I maintain a high level of integrity in my dealings with others.

    Rarely   1   2   3   4   5   Almost Always

    Comments:

8. I am comfortable in managing interpersonal situations that are complex.

    Rarely   1   2   3   4   5   Almost Always

    Comments:

9. Being around people who are expressing strong emotions—anger, sadness, joy—doesn't make me unduly uncomfortable.

    Rarely   1   2   3   4   5   Almost Always

    Comments:

(Continued)

(Continued)

10. I approach my work with people with enthusiasm and considerable positive energy.

    Rarely　　　　1　　2　　3　　4　　5　　Almost Always

    Comments:

11. I think of myself as a kind person.

    Rarely　　　　1　　2　　3　　4　　5　　Almost Always

    Comments:

12. I am assertive in my relations with others.

    Rarely　　　　1　　2　　3　　4　　5　　Almost Always

    Comments:

13. I am adept at managing conflict.

    Rarely　　　　1　　2　　3　　4　　5　　Almost Always

    Comments:

14. I think that people enjoy being around me, and I enjoy being with people.

    Rarely　　　　1　　2　　3　　4　　5　　Almost Always

    Comments:

15. I am able to work well with diverse (e.g., racial, ethnic, religious) groups of people.

    Rarely　　　　1　　2　　3　　4　　5　　Almost Always

    Comments:

Review your responses to this inventory. Take a little time with this, as you think about your personal strengths and areas for attention and growth that will affect your work as a group leader. Take stock of those items that strike you as most revealing. What implications does this review have for the kinds of groups you might be most naturally suited for leading?

As you look at this inventory and your responses, which questions seem to you to reflect attributes that you can work on to improve, and which seem to simply reflect characteristics of who you are as a person, things that will remain essentially the same?

Discuss your reflections with two to three of your colleagues, and hear about theirs, as well. Does any of this discussion affect any of the ways you perceive your own strengths and areas for needed growth? Then widen the discussion to include the larger group.

Examine the literature and research about effective leadership in groups. Then also look at the literature and research about leadership in organizations and the business world. What kinds of similarities and differences do you see in this review of the literature?

REFERENCES

Bandura, A. (1997). *Self efficacy: The exercise of control.* New York, NY: W. H. Freeman.

Bates, M., Johnson, C., & Blaker, K. (1982). *Group leadership: A manual for group counseling leaders* (2nd ed.). Denver, CO: Love.

Brown, M. A. (2011). Learning from service: The effect of helping on helpers' social dominance orientation. *Journal of Applied Social Psychology, 41*(4), 850–871.

Cavanagh, M. (1990). *The counseling experience.* Prospect Heights, IL: Waveland Press.

Chapman, C. L., Baker, E. L., Porter, G., Thayer, S. D., & Burlingame, G. M. (2010). Rating group therapist interventions: The validation of the Group Psychotherapy Intervention Rating Scale. *Group Dynamics: Theory, Research, and Practice, 14*(1), 15–31.

Chi, N., Chung, Y., & Tsai, W. (2011). How do happy leaders enhance team success? The mediating roles of transformational leadership, group affective tone, and team processes. *Journal of Applied Social Psychology, 41*(6), 1421–1454.

Constantine, M. G., Miville, M. L., Kindaichi, M. M., & Owens, D. (2010). Case conceptualizations of mental health counselors: Implications for the delivery of culturally competent care. In M. M. Leach & J. D. Aten (Eds.), *Culture and the therapeutic process: A guide for mental health professionals* (pp. 99–115). New York, NY: Routledge/Taylor & Francis.

Crits-Christoph, P., Johnson, J. E., Connolly Gibbons, M. B., & Gallop, R. (2013). Process predictors of the outcome of group drug counseling. *Journal of Consulting and Clinical Psychology, 81*(1), 23–34.

De Cremer, D. (February 2006). Affective and motivational consequences of leader self-sacrifice: The moderating effect of autocratic leadership. *Leadership Quarterly* [serial online], *17*(1), 79–93.

Edelwich, J., & Brodsky, A. (1992). *Group counseling for the resistant client.* New York, NY: Lexington Books.

Egan, G. (2006). *The skilled helper* (8th ed.). Pacific Grove, CA: Brooks/Cole.

Gladding, S. (1997). The creative arts in groups. In H. Forrester-Miller & J. Kottler (Eds.), *Issues and challenges for group practitioners*. Denver, CO: Love.

Granello, D., & Underfer-Babalis, J. (2004). Supervision of group work: A model to increase supervisee cognitive complexity. *Journal for Specialists in Group Work, 29*(2), 159–173.

Hutchinson, D. (2014). *The essential counsellor: Process, skills, and techniques* (3rd ed.). Thousand Oaks, CA: Sage.

Jackson, Y. (2003). Research in ethnic minority communities: Cultural diversity issues in clinical psychology (with vignette by Anne K. Jacobs). In M. Roberts & S. Ilardi (Eds.), *Handbook of research methods in clinical psychology* (pp. 376–395). Malden, MA: Blackwell.

Johnson, D., & Johnson, F. (2012). *Joining together: Group theory and group skills* (11th ed.). New York, NY: Pearson.

Okech, J. A., & DeVoe, S. (2010). A multidimensional exploration of the impact of international experiences on counselors' cross-cultural awareness. *International Journal for the Advancement of Counselling, 32*(2), 117–128.

Rast, D. I., Hogg, M. A., & Giessner, S. R. (2013). Self-uncertainty and support for autocratic leadership. *Self and Identity, 12*(6), 635–649.

Rogers, C. (1980). *A way of being.* Boston, MA: Houghton Mifflin.

Rubel, D., & Kline, W. (2008). An exploratory study of expert group leadership. *Journal for Specialists in Group Work, 33,* 138–160.

Schneider, E. (1965). Theoretical problem of leadership and group atmosphere. *Psychological Reports* [serial online], *16*(2), 416.

Simons, T., Tomlinson, E. C., & Leroy, H. (2012). Integrity. In K. Cameron & G. Spreitzer (Eds.), *The Oxford handbook of positive organizational scholarship* (pp. 325–339). New York, NY: Oxford University Press.

Sommers-Flanagan, J., & Heck, N. C. (2013). The initial interview with diverse populations: An introduction to the special issue. *Journal of Contemporary Psychotherapy, 43*(1), 1–2.

Thomas, R. V., & Pender, D. A. (2008). Association for specialists in group work: Best practice guidelines 2007 revisions. *Journal for Specialists in Group Work, 33*(2), 111–117.

Tollerud, T., Holling, D., & Dustin, D. (1992). A model for teaching in group leadership: The pre-group interview application. *Journal for Specialists in Group Work, 17,* 96–104.

Turner, L. M. (2013). Encouraging professional growth among social work students through literature assignments: Narrative literature's capacity to inspire professional growth and empathy. *British Journal of Social Work, 43*(5), 853–871.

Van Vugt, M., Chang, K., & Hart, C. (December 2005). The impact of leadership style on group stability. *Chinese Journal of Psychology* [serial online], *47*(4), 380–394.

Van Vugt, M., Jepson, S., Hart, C., & De Cremer, D. (2004). Autocratic leadership in social dilemmas: A threat to group stability. *Journal of Experimental Social Psychology, 40,* 1–13.

Wegscheider, S. (1986). *Another chance.* Palo Alto, CA: Science & Behavior Books.

Wisse, B., & Rietzschel, E. (2014). Humor in leader–follower relationships: Humor styles, similarity and relationship quality. *Humor: International Journal of Humor Research, 27*(2), 249–269.

Woo, S., & Hsu, Y. (April 2012). Development of the Group Leadership Competence Scale. *Chinese Journal of Guidance and Counseling* [serial online], *32,* 1–31.

Chapter 3

The Varieties of Groups

It's as simple as this. When people don't unload their opinions and feel like they've been listened to, they won't really get on board.

—Patrick Lencioni

While I was a doctoral student in Buffalo, New York, I did my clinical counseling internship at the university's counseling center. This was a good-sized counseling center, and we served a large population of undergraduate and graduate students. The counseling center staff comprised a number of skilled clinicians from a variety of disciplines, as well as a handful of graduate student interns like me. We generally met with our clients once a week, and we also met weekly for scheduled clinical case consultations, as well as for individual and group supervision.

Our supervision sessions operated under the assumption that supervision and counseling are parallel processes and that the dynamics between the supervisor and the counselor and the counselor and the client are similar. During our group supervision, considerable, sometimes excruciatingly long, periods of time were spent in examining the relationship issues between supervisors and supervisees and in looking at the dynamics of the relationships among all of us clinicians in the group. The idea was that a counselor's learning about his or her issues and responses to a supervisor would translate into more effective work with clients.

This was my immersion into the world of *process-oriented groups*. In this group, we were not interested in accomplishing tasks (though I sometimes found myself fervently wishing we were talking more about the clients we served, as opposed to ourselves) but rather interested in how we were approaching the work. The more we could learn about ourselves in relationship with others, so the thinking went, the better would be our work with our clients. Our group supervision sessions, by analyzing the process by which we interacted with one another, would translate into good clinical work.

This term *process*, when applied to group work, suggests that the focus of the work is on how things are getting done, the ways people are interacting with one another, and how their needs are being satisfied, or not, as this unfolds. The term *processing* refers to the discussion that the group has about these interactions and the dynamics of the group. These supervision groups personified this kind of process orientation. The coleaders assumed a fairly laissez-faire style of leadership and allowed the group interminable amounts of time to "process" the dynamics in the group.

Coincidentally, at the same time when I was doing this internship, I was working as a volunteer on a presidential primary campaign. I would typically leave my counseling internship site and go directly to campaign headquarters to find out what my duties for the day would be. Two people with a tremendous amount of political and organizational expertise headed our group of volunteers. Their "people skills" were minimal, however. Oftentimes in our planning sessions, individuals would be soundly criticized for tasks left undone. Rarely was anyone praised for work done well. Some of these meetings erupted into heated arguments that left people feeling hurt and abused. These group sessions were generally really unpleasant. There was only one purpose, or goal, for the existence of this group: getting the candidate elected.

The contrast between these two group experiences, the counseling internship group supervision sessions—with their interminable process-oriented discussions—and the political campaign volunteer group meetings—with its single-minded focus on content, where we were told what to do, where to go, and how to do it—was stunning. The political campaign group cared little about relationships, about feelings people had for and about one another, and how each of us were doing personally. It was all about winning the primary. It was about accomplishing the *task*. Getting the work done meant that the task of the group, or its *content*, was of primary importance. Nobody seemed to care anything about how anyone else felt.

I kept a personal journal all through my years as a graduate student, and many of my entries during this internship/political volunteer period reflected on the differences between these groups, and in particular the stark contrast between a group that works nearly exclusively in the process realm and a group that has its eyes set only on content and task. I thought then—and still do—that if my supervision groups could have more frequently actually gotten some work (content) accomplished and if my political action group could have paid some attention to how things were being done, to how people were thinking and feeling, to the process, both would have been better off. (Our primary candidate, by the way, lost handily.)

DIFFERENT GROUPS FOR DIFFERENT PURPOSES

Your leadership approach to the group you're leading will depend on the kind of group it is. If your group–work life is anything like mine, you will probably find yourself running groups with very different goals and ways of operating. It will be important for you to know about some of the features and characteristics of these different kinds of groups, so that you can think about adjusting your leadership approaches to these accordingly.

This chapter will help you look at the varieties of groups you might lead. It will help you to distinguish these different kinds of groups by the relative amount of weight each group will typically devote to "process" or "content" material.

VARIETIES OF GROUPS

- Task/Work Groups
- Psycho-Educational Groups
- Counseling Groups
- Psychotherapy Groups
- Self-Help Groups
- Online Groups
- Other Support Groups

PROCESS AND CONTENT IN GROUPS

Most broadly, as you saw in the example that started the chapter, groups can be characterized as being primarily process or content oriented. Content-oriented groups have a task orientation. They have defined goals, and there is work to be done, specific things that they are charged to do. Work committees, planning groups, even classrooms typify these kinds of groups. They are concerned with what needs to be done, who needs to do it, and how these goals will be accomplished.

Process-oriented groups, on the other hand, are more interested in how the group works together. They are interested in the dynamics that unfold in the group, the relationships between people in the group, and the ways people learn from one another about how they behave interpersonally (Roman, 2003). Much of the talking that goes on in these kinds of groups is focused on how people can learn from one another about how they are perceived and received. This information that gets shared, this potential for interpersonal learning, is seen as a major benefit of process-oriented groups.

Most groups, of course, are not entirely either process or content oriented (Holmes-Garrett, 1989). As a group leader, you will want to pay attention to both process and content in your groups and be able to respond to either, depending on what seems most relevant and important at the time (Hulse-Killacky, Kraus, & Schumacher, 1999).

Process and Content in Groups: An Example

Consider a situation in which a group of young adult college students has been meeting for a number of weeks. The general purpose of the group is to provide support for students who are about to graduate and who are dealing with some anxiety about dealing with life after college—finding a job, finding a place to live, and general economic uncertainty.

The students in the group have been talking about their searches for graduate schools, searches for work, parental expectations, and romantic relationships with other students. On this particular day, one of the students, Julie, has been talking at length about her strained relationship with her mother. Her mother wants her to move back home while she sorts out the next steps of her life. Julie is unclear about what to do, but seems reluctant to move back home. The group has been asking lots of questions about the specifics of the relationship with the mom (and dad), the history of the relationship, what the new living arrangement would look like, and Julie's thoughts about the situation.

If you were one of the leaders of this group, you have some choice points as to how you might add your own intervention.

You might respond to the *content* of the discussion with some kind of question or reflection about the specifics of Julie's situation: "Julie—how much of your decision will be affected by the history you've got with your mom?" Or "Tell us more about what exactly moving back into your family's house would mean for you." Or maybe you would be asking her about her job search, her relationships with peers, or any of other aspects of her situation that seem unclear.

Alternatively, you could respond with some kind of a *process* intervention. For example, "It's really interesting that there are so many ideas about how Julie should proceed. Her dilemma seems to have struck a chord." Or "This has been a really engaging discussion . . . lots of suggestions about what Julie should do."

There are no right ways or wrong ways of responding. Your choices will be based on what you think fits best for where the group is at any given time—about what might help drive it further and deeper into thinking about whatever is at hand.

Much of your decision making about whether to respond to process or content in a group discussion will also be affected by the kind of group you're running. If it's a group that is primarily task or work oriented, for example, you'll primarily be responding to content. If, on the other hand, it's some kind of counseling group, you might want the bulk of your responses to be focused on process.

Let's take a look at some of these different kinds of groups you might find yourself leading.

Task/Work Groups

These are groups where people are working together to make decisions, to solve problems, and to get something done (Conyne, Wilson, & Ward, 1997). Some specific task or work is the focus of these groups, and they are heavily content oriented. Committees, sports teams, and classrooms can be thought of as task/work groups, given that content, whether it's winning games, finishing a group work assignment, or learning material, is the primary goal of the group (Figure 3.1).

Figure 3.1 Winning Coaches Know How to Turn a Group of Individuals Into a Successful Team

TASK/WORK GROUPS

- Examples: Committees, Teams, Classes, Boards
- Primarily Content Oriented
- Some Attention to Process
- Oriented to Getting Work Done

These groups need to get work done. To work efficiently and smoothly, they need to pay primary attention to content, but they can't ignore process. People have needs for affection, inclusion, and control in groups (we'll look at these more closely in the next chapter), and to be effective, these groups need to pay attention to these needs. In other words, paying attention to process—how people are interacting with one another—in these groups is necessary, to the extent that it serves the purpose of getting the work done more effectively. Thus, process is secondary to content but is still really important in these groups.

Running task groups efficiently and effectively takes real skill. When you work with this kind of a group, and do it well, you keep your eye on the primary goal—getting the work done. Everyone needs to have an opportunity to share what he thinks, and everyone's opinion needs to be valued.

I once participated in a values clarification exercise where I was one of a group of people told to think of ourselves as a hospital board. We were given a make-believe task of picking one hypothetically sick person from a slate of candidates to receive critical, life-saving care. Each of the candidates had some personal characteristics that were to be factored into our decision making. We were given a fixed amount of time to pick our candidate and were told that no one would receive the necessary care if we couldn't arrive at a consensual decision by the end of the allotted time.

It took us some time to arrive at a decision, but with a couple of minutes left in the exercise, we felt confident that we had arrived at a good choice. Then, out of the blue, one man who hadn't said anything previously, said he disagreed with the choice the group had made. We spent the next couple of minutes scrambling to accommodate his concerns and then to make a choice, but we couldn't arrive at a consensus. We had to end without picking anyone.

Even though this had been only an exercise, all of us in the group were crushed, thinking that we hadn't been able to save even a single hypothetical candidate. Though this had been a simulation experience, the potential consequences felt very real. We had learned a significant lesson: Make sure everyone is heard from, early on, to insure that last-minute monkey wrenches aren't thrown into the decision-making works.

In addition to the need to pay attention to process in task groups, there are also the mechanics to attend to in insuring that a group can get its work done well.

I'm sure you've been part of at least one frustrating, unproductive work group—I've certainly lived through a few. If you're like me, you've endured meetings that go on and on, well beyond the allotted time, from groups that suffer from people who always come late, or from groups that stray from the business they're expected to discuss.

You don't want a group you are running to be one of these. Some of the following tips may help you to keep your committee on task and running efficiently.

TIPS FOR RUNNING EFFECTIVE TASK/WORK GROUP MEETINGS

- Have clearly defined group goals and expectations.
- Make sure everyone is aware of and buys into the work to be done.
- Take time to do introductions—help to connect people personally.
- Distribute an agenda, with time allotted for each item, well in advance of each meeting.
- Stick to the agenda, with time for each item.
- Start on time and end on time (or earlier).
- Include everyone—make sure all opinions are valued.
- Don't approve of late-coming behavior: Avoid recapping when members come late.
- Make assignments for the next meeting: The three W's—*w*ho (is responsible), *w*hat (should be done), by *w*hen (completion date).
- Praise publicly, for work done well (in front of the group).
- Criticize privately, for work not done, or for problem behavior (not in the group).

Psycho-Educational Groups

This kind of group is primarily geared toward teaching people specific things or skills. These groups are a combination of process and content, where oftentimes equal amounts of time are spent on helping people look at how they're interacting with others and in teaching skills.

Psycho-educational groups have been shown to be helpful in assisting people in dealing with a variety of emotional and behavioral issues (Bains, Scott, Kellett, & Saxon, 2014; Canfield, 2014). They have also proven effective in helping people to become more interpersonally skilled and in becoming more compassionate and understanding of others' difficulties (Yildiz & Duy, 2013).

The group itself serves as a learning laboratory where people can experiment with new skills. Oftentimes the skills being taught are those having to do with making relationships with others better. Examples of these groups include groups teaching people how to be more assertive or manage anger more productively. Psycho-educational groups can combine these interpersonal skills training with other kinds of skills, like skills of simple daily living—shopping for groceries and maintaining a household. Sometimes these groups may combine education and more traditional psychotherapy (Canete & Ezquerro, 2012).

I know counselors who work with people with significant developmental disabilities who use psycho-educational groups as a way to help people negotiate the skills of daily living. They sit and talk with their group members about how to put together shopping lists, then actually put together the lists, and finally go shopping

> **PSYCHO-EDUCATIONAL GROUPS**
>
> - Teach Some Sort of Skill: For Example, Assertion, Anger Management, Stress Management
> - Aim to Improve Interpersonal Skills
> - A Mix of Content and Process
> - Oftentimes Follow a Curricular Agenda

as a group. Money management, dealing with the public, the logistics of getting to the store, all of these become part of the "curriculum" of this group. The people in the group also need to learn how to get along with one another in the groups and on these excursions. Time will be spent examining these relationship issues. Thus, these groups are a combination of both content and process activity.

Some of the counseling courses I teach could also most likely be called psycho-educational groups. While the classes are clearly designed to teach things about working with people, they are also designed to model the material that they instruct. So, for example, a class that is teaching about working with groups—in that it is itself a group—would be modeling leadership skills as the class unfolds. The teacher in this situation is the group leader. The course is not, of course, a counseling group, so the emphasis needs to remain on the content, but it still affords the opportunity for some immediate learning about group process and leadership.

Reflection and Group Fishbowl Lab Practice Exercise: A Psycho-Educational Activity—An Introduction to Assertiveness Training

Assertiveness training is the kind of activity that might be included as part of a psycho-educational group curriculum. I have found that some variety of assertiveness training can be helpful for many of the people in groups that I've run. Many people have trouble with being assertive. They are either too passive in their relations with others (i.e., not standing up for themselves) or can be overly aggressive. Learning how to ask for what is wanted, clearly and politely, and learning how to say "no" are skills that most of us can stand to have refreshed occasionally.

This exercise might serve as an introduction to a longer assertiveness training experience, perhaps a series of group sessions that would allow members to fully explore some of their own difficulties around being assertive, as well as practicing some of the skills necessary to become more personally effective in this.

For this exercise, begin with a period of personal reflection about one experience where you were left feeling less than satisfied about how you had handled yourself. This might have been with someone who is close to you, or perhaps with someone who was providing a service for you (e.g., fixing your car or repairing your computer). Think about the specifics of one or two situations that caused you difficulty: who the person was, what happened, where it happened, and how it left you feeling. When you have assembled your thoughts about at least one difficult episode, get together with others for a group fishbowl discussion.

As with the fishbowl exercises you've done previously, two people volunteer to be group leaders. If you are one of these, your job is to help lead a group discussion about the difficult situations you've all just reflected on. You'll try to encourage people in the group to talk about their own personal reactions and reflections. You might want to talk for a few minutes with your coleader to establish how you want to begin the discussion, focusing on how you want to proceed and who will take the lead in getting things going.

Five or six people should volunteer to be group members. If you are a group member, your job is to talk with the group about your ideas related to your own "assertively challenged" situation.

The other people in the group become group observers. If you are one of these, you will sit with other observers in the fishbowl circle around the leaders and members. Your job is to closely—and silently—observe the group and its interactions between members and leaders. You might want to take notes while you observe. Pay special attention to how the coleaders stimulate discussion. Do they draw people out and encourage everyone to participate? What kinds of things do they do that seem particularly effective in encouraging discussion?

Make whatever accommodations are necessary to make this work for the numbers of people you have conducting this exercise. If your numbers are small, perhaps you'll have one leader and only a few group Members, for example.

Take between 20 and 30 minutes for this group discussion. Then take a few minutes for the group observers to share some of their observations. If you are an observer sharing some of what you saw and heard, try to be specific about what you observed, while also being supportive in your comments to the coleaders.

Counseling Groups

Counseling groups lean heavily toward a process orientation. They are designed to help people look at and improve their interactions with others and are oftentimes theme based. Sometimes the groups are simply labeled as "personal growth" experiences.

This means that there is generally a topic or some specific concern, or perhaps a characteristic, that the members share. Thus, there are issue-oriented groups—for addiction issues, for relationship problems, or for grief resolution (MacKinnon et al., 2014), for example—and there are groups for specific age groups:

men, women, teens (Choate & Manton, 2014), and children (Lopez & Burt, 2013). Generally, these groups are designed to help people resolve some problems in living by providing an opportunity to share concerns and struggles about those problems with others. For many people, and for some specific issues, groups are preferred to individual counseling as a way of working with people (Csiernik & Arundel, 2013).

The leaders of these counseling groups—typically social workers or counselors—are people who see themselves as fellow travelers on life's road, though perhaps a bit farther down that road and more experienced than the rest of the people in the group.

Psychotherapy Groups

These groups, too, rely on a process orientation. They are similar to counseling groups, but—and this can be an overgeneralization—tend to see the members as people with more significant, serious issues, typically mental health problems (Liu et al., 2015; Thimm & Antonsen, 2014).

The people in these groups are seen as being in greater need of some kind of repair work, and the leader is generally seen as more of the "expert" in the group.

The leaders of these groups could be from any of the helping professions, with psychologists and psychiatrists more likely leading psychotherapy, as opposed to counseling, groups.

More of the communication in the group tends to go through the leader, as opposed to the counseling group, where communication patterns have a tendency to be more equally shared among members and leaders. The table below characterizes some of the stereotypical differences between counseling and psychotherapy groups, though it should be remembered that sometimes the differences between these groups are blurred. In day-to-day practice, these groups may look quite similar.

Some counseling and psychotherapy groups have either some or all of its membership comprising people who are *mandated* to attend. They may have perpetrated

COUNSELING GROUP	PSYCHOTHERAPY GROUP
• Leader is memberlike	• Leader is technical expert
• Members work on problems or to improve communicaiton	• Members have significant emotional/ mental health issues
• Communication shared among members and leader(s)	• Communication tends to move more through leader(s)

offenses against others (e.g., domestic assaults, sex offenses) or have been con-victed of some kind of drug-related offense where the court has offered treatment as an alternative to jail. Part of the work you'll have, should you have some or all of your members mandated to be there, is to work through some of the resistance associated with being leveraged into the group.

If you are dealing with mandated people in a group, you can always begin to put some of the resistance aside by making it clear that even though someone else (typi-cally the court system, but sometimes another third party, like a school administration) is "mandating" attendance, that people always have a choice about being there. The alternatives might not be attractive, but there is always choice. Even if you are running groups in a correctional center, someone can always opt out—though that may mean going back to a cell. Thus, in fact, there should never be anyone in your group who is not truly a voluntary participant.

Self-Help Groups

There are other kinds of groups, as well, that attract people who are looking to connect with others. Oftentimes there is some kind of personal concern—a health issue, for example—which motivates someone to seek out support and advice from others who share that concern. These are generally not groups you will be leading, but at some point you might join one of them as a member.

Self-help groups are designed to help people help themselves—usually to grapple more productively with recovery from some kind of problem, like addic-tion, or overeating, or the loss of a child. Alcoholics Anonymous (AA), Overeaters Anonymous, and Compassionate Friends are all examples of these.

There has been a remarkable proliferation of self-help groups in the past 20 years, groups that provide support for people dealing with all kinds of problems and concerns. Groups for women with disabilities (Mejias, Gill, & Shpigelman, 2014), for people with serious and persistent mental illness (Schlögelhofer et al., 2014), and for people dealing with problems related to Internet addiction (Woods, 2013) are but three examples of the many kinds of self-help groups.

These groups are typically leaderless, though there may be someone who orga-nizes space and sets things up. Instead of being led by a leader, most self-help groups are led by a set of principles and a program of activity (called "steps," e.g., in AA). These groups are a combination of a process (mutual support) orientation and content and learning skills (like reducing or stopping drug use).

Most self-help groups are modeled after the first and most well-known of these, AA. While some of these groups, like AA, have a program of principles and "steps" that guide the participants in their work in the groups, other recovery groups don't work with similar principles or steps.

SELF-HELP GROUPS

- Leaderless
- Peer-to-Peer Support and Guidance
- Guided by a Program of Principles
- Reduction of Stigma in Seeking Help

There are also self-help groups that are meant for support, but not necessarily for recovery from any kind of problem. Bible study groups and support groups for people with similar physical afflictions are but two examples of these.

A major advantage of these peer-to-peer groups is that they can minimize the stigma associated with seeking help for specific problems. People who join these groups might also think that peers would understand their problems more compassionately. Someone seeking help for an addiction problem, for example, might feel more comfortable seeking out others who are similarly struggling, as opposed to a professional who might—they fear—not truly, personally, understand how difficult coming to grips with an addiction is.

Many self-help groups embrace questions of spirituality in ways that professionals oftentimes don't. This can be an advantage that self-help groups have over more professionally oriented ways of dealing with the problems for which people seek help. These groups may use terms like *higher power* to suggest that there are larger forces, outside of ourselves, at play in the world and in our lives. While these groups allow for a great range of interpretation about how a term like *higher power* is viewed, these self-help groups don't shy away from alluding to this hunger for meaning that people have. Their incorporation of spirituality into their essential credo is greatly appealing to many people who become involved in these groups.

Not all self-help groups embrace spirituality as a part of their credo. Rational recovery, for example, eschews spirituality as part of its step program. Other self-help groups, as well, do not invoke "higher powers."

It's important that those of us who professionally lead groups stay in touch with what is happening in the self-help community so that we can make informed referrals for people who might benefit from them (Riordan & Beggs, 1988). We need to see these groups as allies and partners in the lives of those we serve.

Online Groups

The surging world of technology and the Internet have spawned a wealth of new online groups. There are websites where people can find existing groups that deal

with specific issues, like some kind of medical problem, for example, http://www
.dailystrength.org/support-groups.

There are also websites that advertise the ability to create your own, new group.
Some of these cost money, and some advertise themselves as free, like http://www
.groupbox.com. This kind of group, which is most likely a combination of process
and content, is great for people who want to connect with people with similar conditions, issues, or concerns and who may be living in distant places.

Many people who work with groups have a preference for face-to-face group
work (Lubas & De Leo, 2014). Some suggest that developing relationships between
people is a particular challenge facing online groups (Kozlowski & Holmes, 2014;
Mishna, Tufford, Cook, & Bogo, 2013). This kind of group does seem to be well
suited for people who may be reluctant or simply not ready to join a face-to-face
group, for any variety of reasons (Haberstroh & Moyer, 2012), and there is demonstrated evidence that this kind of group can be helpful for people dealing with
some distinct kinds of problems (Dölemeyer, Tietjen, Kersting, & Wagner, 2013).
It has also been demonstrated that an online group supplement (to individual and
group counseling) can be helpful in addictions treatment (Campbell et al., 2014).

Other Support Groups

And then there are other, less formal, groups that can provide support and information for people. Play groups, women's groups, men's groups, parenting groups,
book groups, support groups for specific illnesses and health concerns—all are
examples of these. There is a vast array of these.

Many of these groups simply spring up out of a desire of a collection of people
to associate for some reason, like providing mutual support or learning some skill
(Kees, 1999). Other groups can be sought out for support around specific concerns.
Most support groups are leaderless, but some are led by professionals.

Someone who is interested in finding a support group can usually look in a
variety of places to find a group that seems personally appropriate: in local newspapers, online, in state agency websites, and at local hospitals or health centers.

BENEFITS OF A SUPPORT GROUP

- Reduce Anxiety
- Connect With Others Who Have Similar Concerns
- Learn Some New Coping Skills
- Obtain Information About Helpful Resources
- Gain a Sense of Control

Reflection and Group Fishbowl Lab Practice Exercise: Varieties of Group Experience

You have just read about a wide variety of group experiences: groups that are primarily work and task oriented, counseling and therapy groups that are geared toward personal growth, and support groups that are either face-to-face or online.

Take a few minutes to think about and review the array of group experiences in which you have personally been a member, and think about which of those have influenced you the most. Which of these varieties of groups did you enjoy the most, and which did you find the most rewarding? What implications does this review have for the kinds of groups you'll search out, either as a member or a leader, in the future? After you've taken some time to think about these group experiences, and perhaps made a few notes about your reflections, get together with a few others for a group fishbowl discussion of this.

Again, this experience will work best with a group of 8 to 15 (or more) people. Two people volunteer to be group leaders. If you are one of these, your job is to help lead a group in discussion about the groups you've all just reflected on. You'll try to encourage people in the group to talk about their own personal reactions and reflections. You might want to talk for a few minutes with your coleader to establish how you want to begin the discussion, focusing how you want to proceed and who will take the lead in getting things going.

Five or six people should volunteer to be group members. If you are a group member, your job is to talk with the group about your ideas related to your perceptions of the groups you've been in.

The other people in the group become group observers. If you are one of these, you will sit with other observers in the fishbowl circle around the leaders and members. Your job is to closely—and silently—observe the group and its interactions between members and leaders. You might want to take notes while you observe. Pay special attention to how the coleaders stimulate discussion. Do they draw people out and encourage everyone to participate? What kinds of things do they do that seem particularly effective in encouraging discussion?

Make whatever accommodations are necessary to make this work for the numbers of people you have conducting this exercise. If your numbers are small, perhaps you'll have one leader and only a few group members, for example.

Take between 20 and 30 minutes for this group discussion. Then take a few minutes for the group observers to share some of their observations. If you are an observer sharing some of what you saw and heard, try to be specific about what you observed, while also being supportive in your comments to the coleaders.

CONCLUDING THOUGHTS

Evidence, cited earlier, suggests that involvement in groups can assist helping professionals in becoming more sensitive to the needs of others. They become more empathic. People who use groups for their own support and growth, in other words, can become more effective in their work with people. Active participation in groups is a great way to increase awareness of one's self in interaction with others. This, again, is part of the reason why professional training programs encourage involvement in groups for their students.

There is more to involvement with groups, however, than the professional benefits that can be derived. They're also interesting, engaging, and even fun. I can attest to the fact.

Over the span of my professional career as a counselor and counselor-educator, groups have been important parts of my own personal and professional life. I have certainly led lots of counseling groups, encouraged participation in self-help groups, and taught lots of psycho-educational course groups. All of these have been rewarding, and most of them have been fun.

Support groups have also played a large role in my professional and personal lives. When I was in graduate school, I belonged to a graduate student support group. This was not a program-required group, rather something we chose to do because we thought it would be a great way to get to know one another better. We talked about school, about our professors, about our relationships, and about our professional plans. We went on hikes, cooked meals together, and sowed the seeds of enduring friendships. Some of these relationships continue to this day.

After I started working as a counselor in the field, another of kind of support group experience spanned more than a 10-year period. A group of us who were aspiring to create things—music, art, or writing—got together every couple of weeks to share our artistic efforts with one another. We cooked meals together (food is a necessary staple in most of my groups), we talked about our work, and. we talked about our families and our lives. It was wonderful, and it served to make each of us not only more productive in our artistic endeavors but also more connected with one another and more personally anchored and satisfied.

All these groups have served to make my life significantly richer. I hope that both the groups that you lead, as well as the ones you participate in, can be as rewarding for you.

FOR FURTHER THOUGHT

1. Explore the self-help group options in the area where you live. You can look online, in your local newspapers, and at notices posted on your community

bulletin boards. Should you choose to go to a meeting of Alcoholics Anonymous, I suggest going to an Open Speaker meeting. Consider joining one of these groups, if you think it might be personally helpful.

2. Alternatively, if you know anyone who goes to any of these groups, consider asking him if you could come along to a meeting.

3. Examine other support group options in your community. Consider attending one of these.

4. Talk with a coach of a sports team. Beyond the talent of individual players, what helps to create a successful team? What does a cohesive team look like: What are its characteristics, and how does he or she know when it's all coming together?

5. Examine the literature about the rise of online groups and of their effectiveness. Look at the ways they might be most effectively used. What does the literature say about the effectiveness of online groups as compared with face-to-face groups? What's your opinion about the use of online group experiences?

REFERENCES

Bains, M. K., Scott, S., Kellett, S., & Saxon, D. (2014). Group psychoeducativecognitive-behaviour therapy for mixed anxiety and depression with older adults. *Aging & Mental Health, 18*(8), 1057–1065.

Campbell, A. C., Nunes, E. V., Matthews, A. G., Stitzer, M., Miele, G. M., Polsky, D., . . . Ghitza, U. E. (2014). Internet-delivered treatment for substance abuse: A multisite randomized controlled trial [Correction]. *American Journal of Psychiatry, 171*(12), 1339–1340.

Canete, M., & Ezquerro, A. (2012). Bipolar affective disorders and group analysis. *Group Analysis, 45,* 203–217.

Canfield, J. (2014). Traumatic stress and affect management in military families. *Social Work in Mental Health, 12*(5–6), 544–559.

Choate, L. H., & Manton, J. (2014). Teen court counseling groups: Facilitating positive change for adolescents who are first-time juvenile offenders. *Journal for Specialists in Group Work, 39*(4), 345–365.

Conyne, R., Wilson, F., & Ward, D. (1997). *Comprehensive group work: What it means and how to teach it.* Alexandria, VA: American Counseling Association.

Csiernik, R., & Arundel, M. (2013). Does counseling format play a role in client retention? *Journal of Groups in Addiction & Recovery* [serial online], *8*(4), 262–269.

Dölemeyer, R., Tietjen, A., Kersting, A., & Wagner, B. (2013). Internet-based interventions for eating disorders in adults: A systematic review. *BMC Psychiatry, 13,* 207.

Haberstroh, S., & Moyer, M. (2012). Exploring an online self-injury support group: Perspectives from group members. *Journal for Specialists in Group Work, 37,* 113–132.

Holmes-Garrett, C. (1989). The crisis of the forgotten family: A single session group in the ICU waiting room. *Social Work With Groups: A Journal of Community and Clinical Practice, 12*(4), 141–157.

Hulse-Killacky, D., Kraus, K., & Schumacher, B. (1999). Visual conceptualization of meetings: A group work design. *Journal for Specialists in Group Work, 24,* 113–124.

Kees, N. (1999). Women together again: A phenomenological study of leaderless women's groups. *Journal for Specialists in Group Work, 24,* 288–305.

Kozlowski, K. A., & Holmes, C. M. (2014). Experiences in online process groups: A qualitative study. *Journal for Specialists in Group Work, 39*(4), 276–300.

Liu, Q. X., Fang, X. Y., Yan, N., Zhou, Z., Yuan, X., Lan, J., & Liu, C. (2015). Multi-family group therapy for adolescent Internet addiction: Exploring the underlying mechanisms. *Addictive Behaviors, 42,* 1–8.

Lopez, A., & Burt, I. (2013). Counseling groups: A creative strategy increasing children of incarcerated parents' sociorelational interactions. *Journal of Creativity in Mental Health, 8*(4), 395–415.

Lubas, M., & De Leo, G. (2014). Online grief support groups: Facilitators' attitudes. *Death Studies, 38*(8), 517–521.

MacKinnon, C. J., Smith, N. G., Henry, M., Berish, M., Milman, E., Körner, A., . . . Cohen, S. R. (2014). Meaning-based group counseling for bereavement: Bridging theory with emerging trends in intervention research. *Death Studies, 38*(3), 1–5.

Mejias, N. J., Gill, C. J., & Shpigelman, C. (2014). Influence of a support group for young women with disabilities on sense of belonging. *Journal of Counseling Psychology, 61*(2), 208–220.

Mishna, F., Tufford, L., Cook, C., & Bogo, M. (2013). Research note: A pilot cyber counseling course in a graduate social work program. *Journal of Social Work Education, 49*(3), 515–524.

Riordan, R., & Beggs, M. (1988). Some critical differences between self-help and therapy groups. *Journal of Specialists in Group Work, 3*(1), 24–29.

Roman, C. P. (2003). It is not always easy to sit on your mouth. In R. Kurland & A. Malekoff (Eds.), *Stories celebrating group work: It's not always easy to sit on your mouth* (pp. 61–64). Binghamton, NY: Haworth Social Work Practice Press.

Schlögelhofer, M., Willinger, U., Wiesegger, G., Eder, H., Priesch, M., Itzlinger, U., . . . Aschauer, H. (2014). Clinical study results from a randomized controlled trial of cognitive behavioural guided self-help in patients with partially remitted depressive disorder. *Psychology and Psychotherapy: Theory, Research and Practice, 87*(2), 178–190.

Thimm, J. C., & Antonsen, L. (2014). Effectiveness of cognitive behavioral group therapy for depression in routine practice. *BMC Psychiatry, 14,* 292.

Woods, J. (2013). Group analytic therapy for compulsive users of Internet pornography. *Psychoanalytic Psychotherapy, 27*(4), 306–318.

Yildiz, M., & Duy, B. (2013). Improving empathy and communication skills of visually impaired early adolescents through a psychoeducation program. *Kuram Ve Uygulamada Eğitim Bilimleri* [serial online], *13*(3), 1470–1476.

Chapter 4

Putting Group Theory
Into Practice

He who loves practice without theory is like the sailor who boards ship without a rudder and compass and never knows where he may cast.

—Leonardo da Vinci

Some of the best groups I've led are the ones that have gotten off to the rockiest starts. One of these immediately springs to mind. This was a group I led with one of my colleagues, Samantha (she preferred to be called Sam). We were working in a residential treatment facility for young adults with drug problems, and we had nine participants in our group—five men and four women—all in their late teens.

The group had been set up to help these young people hone their job-seeking skills. We wanted to help them increase their ability not only to get but also to hang onto good jobs, and we'd designed a number of specific skills training modules designed to assist them. Helping them see the relevance of sound interpersonal skills in the job search—and spending time working on those—was also a primary goal of this group.

Getting satisfying work was important to people in the group, so most of the members were eager to learn some of the skills we'd highlighted. Early on in the group, however, Sam and I were particularly frustrated with two people in the group who, for very different reasons, seemed to be reluctant to "get with the program." Justin was one of these, a very bright and articulate young man. He thought he knew more about most things than anyone else—Sam and I included—and maybe he did, but his intellectual arrogance was doing little to endear him to any of us.

Wendy was the other reluctant member. Her resistance, almost the opposite of Justin's, was tied to her incredible shyness. She would come to each group session, sit in the corner, literally curl up in a ball, and remain silent unless pointedly asked something.

Things finally began to turn around on the day when, after one of Justin's lectures to the rest of us about the unfairness of the state minimum wage (a point that, while it had some merit, was only tangentially related to our skills training that day), Sam suggested that it might be helpful to do a group check-in. Her intent was not only to short-circuit Justin's lecturing but also to draw others out.

Sam asked each of us to make a short statement about what we were thinking and feeling, right now, to the extent that it felt safe and OK to share. A couple of people talked about being bored, a couple of others talked about things going on in their lives, and I said that I was looking forward to getting on with the training business of the day. Then, when it came to be Wendy's time to talk, there was a long silence. To her credit, Sam didn't ask questions. She waited her out.

Just when the silence was starting to become painfully long, Wendy finally spoke. "Justin reminds me of all the kids in my school who used to think they were so much smarter than me. They used to talk down to me, too, just like Justin. They didn't have a clue about who I was or what I knew. They just assumed I was stupid because I was quiet. And here it is, happening again. I'm not stupid!"

I remember thinking, "Good for her! What courage!" And clearly the group felt similarly. They asked her more about what this meant and about her school experiences.

Wendy didn't say much, but she did at least answer their direct questions.

Sam wanted to make the whole experience more immediate, so she asked Wendy to talk about how what Justin had done reminded her of those past experiences ... and, importantly, she asked if Wendy could say those things directly to him. Again, another long silence, but finally Wendy did (sort of) look at Justin and told him how he was being intimidating and discounting of her.

Wendy's disclosures marked a turning point in the group. Others talked about their dissatisfactions with Justin's lecturing, and Sam and I tried to help Justin listen to, without being overtly defensive, the things people were saying. We also tried to protect him from getting hammered too badly by the resentments that others were now articulating, mostly by forcing people to be specific and nonjudgmental with their feedback to him.

This group went on to do some very nice work. Wendy and Justin never became good friends, but I think that they did come to learn more about each other, and even to have some respect for each other. Other people in the group talked about learning a lot about having a respect for different interaction styles after watching and listening to the ways Wendy and Justin learned to negotiate each other. I'd also like to think that along the way they all learned something about getting good jobs from the skills training we did.

Mostly, for me, this came to symbolize what I now take for granted—that once a group has started and gotten off the ground, it will inevitably go through some relatively predictable growing pains on its way to becoming a more cohesive working unit.

This chapter is about those predictable growing pains: the beginnings, the bumps in the road, and the eventual coming together of a group that works well. Knowing something about these predictable changes in a group, about its developmental changes, can help to insure that your group will become a great group.

THE IMPORTANCE OF THEORY TO YOUR GROUP WORK

Theory gives you a foundation from which to work and a feeling of solidity as a group leader that would be impossible if you were simply winging it on your own. Your knowledge of theory connects you to the knowledge that legions of people who've worked with groups before you have learned.

This is a little like learning how to fix a car. You could approach your car's faulty fuel injection system, for example, with a wrench and a positive attitude about the car and your mechanical ability—but wouldn't it also be helpful to know something about how fuel injection works? Wouldn't it be helpful to read the manual before popping the hood?

Why should it be any different in learning how to work with groups of people? Learning about how other people have worked and approach their group work and exploring what has been culled from years of practice as being optimally effective can help you avoid making some significant mistakes.

There are actually two primary strands of theory that concern and inform your work with groups. The first of these is the theory about groups and how they work. This is the world of group dynamic theory. How groups are born, how they live, and how they disband all come under the purview of group dynamic theory (Brabender & Fallon, 2009). So, too, do ideas about group member needs and behaviors in groups. This is the kind of theory we'll explore in this chapter.

The other major body of theory that concerns you—at least if you will be leading a process-oriented, personal growth kind of experience—is that theory related to counseling and psychotherapy. Theory that informs your work about the individual counseling that you do, regardless of your professional orientation, has been adapted for group work. You can bring the same theoretical perspectives from your individual counseling work to your work with groups. These perspectives include basic assumptions about the nature of people, about how they behave, and about

GROUP DEVELOPMENT AND DYNAMICS: A PRACTICAL APPROACH TO THINKING ABOUT GROUP DEVELOPMENT

- How Groups Develop
- What People Need in Groups
- What People Learn in Groups
- What People Can Get in Groups That Become Cohesive

optimal ways of providing therapeutic assistance. The next chapter will explore the application of counseling and psychotherapy theory to group work.

Meanwhile, this chapter on group development will help you learn more about some specific aspects of group dynamic theory as it applies to the group work you will do.

GROUP DEVELOPMENT AND DYNAMICS

A group begins, the group meets over a period of weeks or months, and then the group ends. That's probably about as simple a way as you can talk about the developmental life span of a group. It's born, it lives, and it dies. While technically accurate, this simple description of the life of the group doesn't capture the richness and complexity of the group experience. Just as in thinking about the development of a human life we want to consider all the dimensions of its experience, so too with groups do we want to describe, with some predictive accuracy, some of their natural transitions.

Knowledge of group development theory is particularly helpful for you in learning how not to take everything that happens in a group too personally. It can be really liberating to know that when conflict is happening between members, or between you and members, for example, that might be exactly what the group should be doing at this point in time. It might not be because of some mistake you've made. Knowledge of how groups typically develop allows you to anticipate certain behaviors and changes in group temperament that are natural—and not necessarily the result of some either negative or positive thing that you've done.

There are many theoretical models that talk about how groups develop. Most— though not all (Yalom & Leszcz, 2005)—of these are linear, meaning that these theories suggest that things happen in a regular sequence during the life span of a group. These are probably the least complex of the theories about group development. Other theories take other approaches to looking at group development—like talking about how individuals change in groups, about how decision making changes as groups grow, or about the interaction of groups with their environments. As you become more involved with group work, you will want to explore these in more depth.

Mostly, you are interested in knowing about these group life span issues because they affect how you will plan what to do for your group at different points along that timeline. You can also interpret and respond to different things that happen in your group depending on where it's at in its life cycle. While, for example, you might have a lot of activity planned for the beginning of a group, you might have less for when the group has coalesced and is working well. Or, as another example, you will respond differently to conflict that happens between members depending on where the group is developmentally. We'll talk more of this later.

For our purposes here, we can consider one of the most familiar ways that group growth and development has been described: forming–storming–norming–performing–adjourning (Tuckman, 1965; Tuckman & Jensen, 1977). Because this description is quite descriptive and easy to remember, it is one of the most utilized and repeated theories in use today, though many have modified it for their own purposes (Maples, 1988). This approach suggests that a group comes together (forms); then experiences some conflict after the initial newness of the group wears off (storms); eventually settles into some typical, predictable behavior patterns (norms); then proceeds to become cohesive and do some good work (performs); and finally disperses (adjourns).

This "Forming–Storming–Norming–Performing–Adjourning" model works pretty well. It describes the process of the birth, life, and death of a group in understandable, descriptive fashion. For the most part, this is how I've come to think about groups, but with some modifications. I've taken this theory and tailored it to more accurately outline my own experience of how groups develop, as well as to reflect the work that needs to be done at each stage of a group's working life. I include some additional features I think are important, and I've tweaked a couple of the stages to more accurately look like what I've seen groups negotiate from my own experience. I've changed *storming*, for example, to *engaging*. I'll explain the reason for this shortly.

Following is a list and description of how I think about the different stages of group development. Each developmental stage is only briefly described here. The second section of this book is devoted to an in-depth look at each one of these developmental components and the tasks and challenges that await you in your work with a group.

Planning

A great deal of thought and organizational work goes into getting a good group up and running, regardless of the setting in which you work (Hill, Marshall, &

Harris, 2011; Letendre, 2009). Much of this happens long before people even enter the room. This is the work that you do alone, or with a coleader, that plans for the ways you can make this experience successful. You formulate the goals and ideas for outcomes that you'd like to see this group embody. You think about who this group will ideally serve, and then plan for all the logistical details—like where the group will be held, how you will recruit people, and how long the group will run— that will help to guarantee that this experience works smoothly and efficiently.

Forming

The first few times a new group meets can typically be filled with some anxiety. New members are trying to figure out about how this is going to work, about how they will be received, and whether this will be a safe and interesting place to meet and engage with new people (Vernelle, 1994). Much of your work as a leader will be to create some structure, or activity, within these initial meeting times so that this anxiety can be contained and people will begin to feel safe with one another.

Engaging

I prefer the term *engaging* to *storming* in that many groups with which I've worked do not seem to go through a process of negotiating a lot of conflict and difficulty. Certainly, conflict can happen (Cornish, Wade, Tucker, & Post, 2014; Glyn, 2010; Kraus, 1997), but more typically, I've seen groups simply leave the initial stages of coming together, with all the politeness and cautionary behavior that entails, to a point where members become more honest and direct with one another, and with the leader. People get clearer about what they want and about what dissatisfies them with what's happening. This is where conflict, some storming, can occur if all is not handled well (Unger, 1990). We'll talk in Chapter 8 about how you strategically plan for avoiding storming and what to do if it does, in fact, erupt in your group.

Norming

Your group will eventually settle into some usual, predictable ways of behaving. Some people will talk more than others. One of your members might become the group clown, regularly joking and generally trying to lighten the group mood when things get heavy. Some people may help make things work well, others may be more resistant to productive work. People may even start to sit in the same places every time you meet.

These behavioral patterns, called *norms*, are usually taken on unconsciously and simply reflect the fact that your group is settling in for some longer-term work (Huebner, 2004; Nosko, 2003).

People will behave in your groups in ways that demonstrate their needs for affection, inclusion, and control. Their behavior, in other words, is their attempt at needs fulfillment. While they may behave differently in different groups, because they'll have varying needs for affection, inclusion, and control in different group situations, you can assume that they behave in roughly similar fashion in most group settings. Your group is a mini-laboratory setting in which you and your group's members can observe how other people in the group typically relate in social situations, and this provides opportunities for learning when people give one another information about how this behavior affects them.

People will have different styles of behavior, and some of these styles will be more helpful than others in moving the group in positive directions. Some people will be more understanding of others and more obviously interested in forming relationships with others in the group. Others may be hostile or aggressive, and still others may simply withdraw (Schein, 1969).

How individual group members choose what behaviors are most comfortable probably has a lot to do with utilizing behaviors that have worked for them in past group situations, starting with their first, most important group, their family. How we all behave in groups harkens back, to varying degrees, to how we were shaped behaviorally by our own families.

When you think about growing up in your own family, particularly if you had brothers and sisters, you can think about the behaviors each family member exhibited, about the *roles* that they played. People unconsciously settle into patterns of behavior in their families that gain them some kind of rewards and, particularly in troubled families, help them get through chaotic times. A number of people who research and write about families, particularly families where there are emotional difficulties, have looked a lot at these roles and the impact they have on people in later life (Wegscheider, 1986). Names like *hero*, *mascot*, *lost child*, and *scapegoat* have been used to identify some of these roles. You may want to read more in the family counseling literature about these roles, but for our purposes, it should be fairly easy for you to consider some of the behaviors that would be associated with those names. The hero is often the oldest child, the mascot the youngest.

To varying degrees, these same roles, and others, may be at play in your groups. Broadly speaking, you will have some people who will want to be helpful in moving things in a positive direction (*facilitators*) and some who are bent on making things more difficult. These could be called *obstructers* (Capuzzi & Gross, 2013).

Within these broad categories, you will see lots of variation. If you think back to the groups you've been in, even the classrooms, you will be able to come up with any number of names that characterize these roles that people play: the clown, the monopolizer, the intimidator, the lover, the compromiser, the competitor, the placater, and so on. These are some of the more positive names I've given to some of the roles I've seen, but there are also the slackers and the whiners. I'm sure you can imagine what behaviors those names imply.

Reflection and Discussion Exercise: Group Dynamics and Behavior

Think about the ways you've seen people behave in the groups you've been in. How have these behaviors configured themselves into regular roles that people have played in these groups? Create your own list of positive and negative group role names. Have fun with this.

Then consider some of the typical ways you behave in groups. Are you generally talkative and outgoing, or more reserved, waiting for others to initiate? Do you usually take an active role in moving things in a positive direction, or are you more comfortable in letting other people lead the direction in which the group goes?

Also consider the role(s) you may have played in your own family. Did you play the role of "hero," or "mascot," or one of the other family roles described earlier? How did your behavior—your role—in your family affect how you are in other groups you've been in?

If you're part of a group that is reading this, get together with other people to talk about your reflections on roles in groups, including your thoughts about some of your own typical group behaviors. How congruent are your thoughts about your behavior with how others in the group see you?

Working (or Performing)

If the group achieves a moderate level of trust and cohesion, where people feel safe in taking some risks, the group will start to do good work. Group cohesion is of critical importance, and groups will perform well in direct proportion to how well people have come together (Ellis, Peterson, Bufford, & Benson, 2014). Members begin to do more self-disclosing about things that are important to them, and people start to interact with one another more honestly.

In this view, "performing" does not mean acting in any sense. Rather this refers to the time when the group will be doing its most serious work (DeLucia-Waack, 2006).

Great groups provide their members with opportunities for significant interpersonal learning—and this is the stage in your group's life where much of that occurs.

Ending

Everything in life ends. At some point, your group, too, will end. The ending of the group may come after some fixed number of sessions, or the group may be in charge of deciding itself when to end. Regardless of how well the group has fared, no matter how much people have come to rely on one another in the group, at some point, it will end.

A PRACTICAL MODEL OF GROUP DEVELOPMENT

Planning → Forming → Engaging → Norming and Working → Ending → Following Up

Immature Group → Mature Group

Very Active Leader → Less Active Leader

This is one of the most important stages of your group's life. In a sense, it is a replication of all the endings you and your group members have had, and this group ending needs to be orchestrated thoughtfully. It is an opportunity to look carefully at and talk about, with awareness, all the thoughts and feelings that endings can ignite.

Following Up

Even after your group meets for the last time, there may be some things you need to do to complete it. There may be some loose ends of unfinished business that need to be managed. Primary among these has to do with the needs of some of your members who may be left feeling adrift and needy in the wake of the group's ending. You will want to insure that no one in your group is simply left high and dry when the group ends and that there are sufficient supports in place to take care of what they need. This may include providing any variety of case management services, like connecting them with appropriate community supports.

There may be other follow-up concerns, as well. Some of your group members may want to plan a reunion, for example. All these concerns need to be addressed before you can comfortably say that your group is over.

Finally, you'll want to make some provisions for evaluating the group experience to get a sense of how well it's gone. Have people's behaviors or attitudes changed as a result of the experience? Have they enjoyed it and thought it beneficial? Are there things that need to be changed if you do this kind of group again?

WHAT PEOPLE NEED IN GROUPS

If you ever took a course in introductory psychology, you were undoubtedly exposed to the ideas Abraham Maslow had about what people need. His description of the hierarchy of individual needs has become a widely accepted model of what each of us seeks out in our own lives. In this model, Maslow suggested that we have to satisfy basic needs first, before we can really think about anything else. He said that once we have established some basic safety (meeting biological needs for shelter, food, security, etc.), we can attend to establishing connections with others and establishing our own place in the world through our work and other achievements. Only then we could pursue other needs for knowledge, beauty, and self-awareness.

Later in his life—and this is oftentimes left out in discussions of his needs model—Maslow also talked about the ways evolved people—people who have satisfied their own needs for safety and belonging and have pursued their own self-actualization—also pursue a need to share what they know with others (Maslow, 1970). They are then able to connect with others in ways that help others develop themselves, as well. Self-awareness, for these people, is not enough—a drive to share what is known becomes a compelling need.

This, I think, has serious implications for us as helping professionals and as group leaders: Our work with people is, in a real sense, satisfying an upper-level need of our own.

At about the same time Maslow was originally devising his hierarchy of needs model, another psychologist, William Schutz, began to write specifically about people's needs in groups. He said that people have three compelling needs in their relations with other people in groups. Schutz assumed that people in groups have satisfied basic needs for physiological safety, so he focused more on balancing midlevel needs for connection with others and personal autonomy.

He said that one of these needs people have in groups is the need for *affection*. This is simple. People want to be liked. Second, Schutz said that people need to feel *included* in the plans and activities of others. They want to feel that others will want to involve them. And finally, he said that people have a need to *control* how things will go. They want to be able to exert some influence on decision making. Schutz designed ways to test how people exhibit these needs in group situations, specifically by utilizing instruments he designed to look at communication and individual needs in groups (Schutz, 1958).

You can assume that these needs for affection, inclusion, and control will be very much alive and active among the members of your groups. Every person is different, however. Each person will have his or her own variable desire for each of these needs. Some people will have more need for affection, some for control. Furthermore, though each person's need for each of these will be relatively constant in different groups, there will be some variability. Thus, someone might have strong needs for affection with one group of people, with little need to control or influence things, but might want more control and less affection in another group experience.

Naturally, you have your own needs for affection, inclusion, and control. Your needs, as well as those of every other member of your group, will be at play as your group moves along the developmental continuum. Thus, not only will you be watching for the subtle signs that your group is making developmentally, you will be paying attention to individuals and how their needs are making themselves known.

> **WHAT PEOPLE NEED IN GROUPS**
>
> (After Basic Safety Needs Are Met)
>
> - Affection
> - To Be Included
> - To Have Some Control or Influence

WHAT PEOPLE LEARN IN GROUPS

In the first chapter, we reviewed all the good things that groups can do for people. Groups can help people learn skills, and they can also help people learn more about themselves in relation to others. People learn about themselves, as well as about their relationships with others, in these group experiences.

There is a helpful model about interpersonal learning in groups that was developed years ago, just as the group movement was coming into its own, by Joseph Luft and Harry Ingham. The model, called the Johari Window (named after Joe and Harry—no kidding), describes the four broad areas of what is known and what can be learned in any group (Luft, 1984). If you've taken an introductory course about group dynamics, you've most likely already run across this model, but it's worth reviewing here. It's still relevant, and it does have implications for how you'll work with your own groups.

In this model's first area, or quadrant, is all that information that someone knows about himself, and that everyone else in the group knows, as well. Let's consider Justin and Wendy as examples here. Remember them, the know-it-all young man and the shy young woman in the vignette that opened the chapter? If you recall, Justin was very talkative and he liked to share his ideas about virtually any topic that came up. The fact that he has views on lots of issues is known to both him and the group. Also, the fact that Wendy is shy and reserved is known to all, including her.

In the second quadrant is all that information that the group knows about Justin and Wendy, but that they are not aware of. In that group, Justin may have had no clue about how arrogant he was sounding until Wendy let him know about her personal reactions to him. Similarly, the group may share some ideas about Wendy that it hasn't told her about before.

The third area contains all that is known by the person himself or herself, but not known to the group. Justin has probably had some reactions to what Wendy has told him, but the group won't know about those unless he chooses to share them with the group. In choosing to share personal information, Wendy has expanded the group's knowledge of her.

And finally, the fourth quadrant holds all the information that is not known to either the individual or the group. Things may have happened early in Justin's childhood, for example, that he doesn't remember and that may have contributed to his need to appear to be so confident, self-assured, and knowledgeable. Similarly, Wendy may have had some early childhood experiences, which are now out of her awareness and which have helped shape her shyness. There is no way anyone else in the group could know anything about these things either.

You can see how, when these four areas are laid out, they resemble a window.

The Johari Window: Information in Groups

QUADRANT I	QUADRANT II
Known to Self	Not Known to Self
Known to Others	Known to Others
QUADRANT III	QUADRANT IV
Known to Self	Not Known to Self
Not Known to Others	Not Known to Others

Two of these areas present the greatest opportunity for learning in groups—Quadrants II and III. Quadrant II, which represents the material that the group knows about someone in the group, holds great potential for this is where people can tell someone about how he or she is being perceived and how his or her behavior is affecting others. This is what *feedback* is all about. When the group gives someone information like this, then the person can make a choice about what to do with it—ignore it, take it in but do nothing, or take it in and in some way change behavior (Crits-Christoph et al., 2011). Naturally, feedback about someone's impact on others can be either positive or negative.

The other area that poses the greatest potential for learning is Quadrant III, where people know things about themselves that they can choose to share, or not, with others in the group. The ability that you have to connect with people in the group, to form the all-important therapeutic alliance—also so critical in working individually with people—helps make it possible for people to share information about themselves with others. This sharing, this *self-disclosure*, is where people choose to let others into their internal world in ways that they typically don't do in most social situations. To choose to reveal these more hidden aspects of one's self, if appropriate and handled well, can be one of the best things someone can do in a group (McDonnell, Gillam, & Bergin, 2004; Shechtman & Rybko, 2004). We'll spend more time exploring this in later chapters.

The analogy of "people as onions" is sometimes used to describe the ways people can let others know about what they are thinking below the surface of what is usually presented to the world (Mehrgardt & Curen, 2005; Zytowski, 1994). In this line of thinking, a typical way of responding to the question, "How are you doing?" is "Fine, fine, everything's fine." Someone might choose to take a bit of a risk, and peel back a few layers of the onion (doing some self-disclosing), responding with, "Well, I'm generally OK, but I've been feeling kind of blue lately." If this peeling back is continued, the person becomes more and more vulnerable, sharing things toward the core that are rarely shared with others. At the core of the onion, meaning of the person, may be deeply held convictions—both positive and negative—about oneself.

Quadrant I contains that information that is known to everyone—the outer layers of the onion—and if a group spends a lot of its time dealing with only this kind of information, it will quickly become boring. People learn best when there is a little anxiety, where pushing the limits of what is known, and taking reasonable risks become the norm. The onion's layers start to get peeled away. People shut down, however, when there is too much anxiety, and thus trying to promote a balance of safety in a group—maintaining just an edge of anxiety—is one of the challenges of group leadership. This, too, we'll talk about later.

Finally, Quadrant IV contains that information that neither the individual nor the group knows about. In the case of our example, things may have happened to Justin and Wendy as children that they have forgotten, and there is no way that either the group or they would know about those things. This area is better suited for individual counseling and reflection. They could be assisted in remembering some of those things that had happened. For people who have forgotten, or hold out of awareness painful or difficult things, this can be important learning and remembering. These are the inner layers, the core, of the onion. This is the area of learning where individual counseling is the preferred mode of working with someone.

PRIMARY SOURCES OF INTERPERSONAL LEARNING IN GROUPS

- Learning Skills
- Giving and Receiving Feedback
- Self-Disclosure

WHAT PEOPLE CAN GET IN GROUPS THAT BECOME COHESIVE

Yalom and Leszcz (2005) identify a number of good things that being involved with "growth" groups can do for people. Here is a paraphrased and shortened list of what they see as the best that groups can do for people:

- Give members a new sense of hope
- Help people see that their problems are not unique and that they are not alone
- Learn new skills, including socialization skills, and ways of looking at the world
- Release feelings: the cathartic effect
- Help people recognize and take responsibility for themselves
- Promote a feeling of cohesion and connection with others

These are all positive reasons for leading and being involved with groups. If only one or two of these things happen for someone in your group, it's a worthwhile experience—even better when more of these factors are in play for that person.

Most of these positive things will happen only when a group comes together cohesively, when there is a sense of shared purpose and commonality. This sense of cohesion occurs when individuals in the group make the shift from "I" to "we" in their thinking about the group.

All this suggests that you'll want to do everything you can to promote this sense of shared purpose, this cohesiveness, in the groups you lead. In later chapters, we'll look at how—at each stage in the life of your group—you can help set the stage for this to happen.

Group Vignette: Feedback and Self-Disclosure

A few years ago, I ran a group for people who had been married and divorced. Some of the people in the group had been married multiple times. Each person in the group wanted to meet someone new and build an intimate relationship, but none of them wanted to repeat the same mistakes that had led to their divorces.

There were 10 people in the group, seven of whom were women. One of the three men, Dan, was a big—and I mean, really large—man. He was about 6 feet 4 inches, or 6 feet 5 inches, and he probably weighed at least 220 pounds (1 pound = 0.45 kilogram). He looked very fit, like he worked out a lot, and most of his size appeared to be solid muscle. Thus, he probably looked even bigger than he actually was.

Moreover, his voice was also loud. Even in the small room where we met, he usually spoke with a big, booming voice. His physical size, coupled with the way he carried himself and the way he spoke, meant that he took up a lot of space in the group. It didn't take too many of my keen observational skills to notice that most of the other people, particularly the women, were intimidated by Dan. No one sat very close to him, and when he spoke, people almost visibly leaned away.

For a couple of weeks, we had been talking about the difficult act of juggling jobs and kids, and how difficult all that made to meet people. Some of the people in the group were still engaged in legal custody battles related to their children, and others had worked out relatively amicable child-rearing plans with their former spouses.

On this particular day, when it came to be Dan's turn to talk, he railed at length about how unfair and "rotten" his ex-wife was being. He told us about all the ways she'd made his and their two children's lives miserable—not showing up on time to pick up the kids, hassling him about money, always making more demands, and so on. As he talked, his voice, which was always full volume, even went up a decibel notch, or two. His face got red, and he seemed to get even larger in his chair. His anger seemed to inflate his size.

Finally, Dan's rant lost steam, and he slumped back in his chair. The room got quiet. Then, one of the women, Marie, said, "Dan, can you tell us about your kids?"

And Dan did. He told us about his son and daughter, both preteens, about how proud he was of them, and about how much he wanted to help them avoid being hurt too badly by the divorce or by the anger between him and their mother. He told us about their sports, about their music, and about his hopes for their future. His affection and concern for them was clear, and what was truly interesting was how his whole demeanor, including the volume of his voice, changed as he told us about them. He had gotten visibly softer.

When he had finished talking, I said, "Dan, it was wonderful to hear you talk about your kids. And about the stuff going on with your former wife, as well, what was interesting to me—and I don't know if anyone else here noticed this—was that there almost seemed to be two different 'Dans.' One Dan talked about the trouble with the former wife, and the other talked about the kids. And they were really different."

Very quickly, Marie said, "Oh yeah. I saw that, too. One Dan was all big—and kind of scary—and the other Dan was gentle and compassionate."

Other people nodded their agreement, and then some offered their own "take" on this. "The first Dan," one woman said, "makes me cringe. I get nervous. But the other Dan, the one who talked about his kids, seems like someone I'd like to get to know better." Another woman said, "Dan, I liked it a lot better when you weren't acting so tough and angry. I think that if all I ever saw was the tough stuff, I'd be too nervous around you to have much of a relationship with you. I sure wouldn't want to sit too close to you."

This was a key moment in the group for Dan. To his credit, he didn't get defensive and self-protective. Instead of denying people's reactions to him, he seemed really interested in what they had to say. I asked him if he'd like more information, from other people, and what he would like to know. He said he did. What, he wondered, did they see as the specific differences in how he'd talked about his former wife and his children? Had the women been afraid of him before today's talking? What about the men; were they intimidated, too?

When the group had finished giving Dan lots of comments about their reactions about the ways he'd presented himself, a couple of people told him how much they'd appreciated his willingness to hear what they had to say, how much they respected his openness.

All this talking, with Dan telling us about his family, and then the conversation about how he had affected others, had taken quite a bit of time. Seeing that we were going to need to end soon, I tried to summarize some of what I'd seen.

> This has been something. Dan you've gotten lots of information about how people have reacted to what you've done here today, and you can choose how you want to use that, how you want to go forward. And what's also been really interesting to me is how much, particularly in the ways people have responded to you, they have indirectly said about themselves. Maybe some will want to talk more about that, about how what's happened here today is personally relevant, particularly in terms of their relationships.

With that, and after a couple of people had weighed in with saying that they did, in fact, want to talk more about this, we ended for the day.

One of the best things that happened in subsequent weeks was that two of the women in the group were able to talk about their having been in relationships with men who had been physically abusive. They talked movingly of the terrible incidents that they'd endured, about the trouble their children had witnessed, and about how difficult it had been to escape those relationships. They talked about how automatically, when around large, imposing men—like Dan—they shut down and don't even try to get to know more about those men. They talked about their appreciation for Dan's willingness to try to act in ways that were more accessible, less threatening, and Dan talked about his desire to be known, not to be perceived as someone who is inaccessible.

Group Vignette Discussion

This case vignette nicely demonstrates the best ways groups can promote people's understanding of themselves in relationship with others. In this scenario, Dan has gotten a lot of information from others in the group about how he's perceived. This feedback about how intimidating he can be—and also how approachable he can be—is information he can use, or not. He'll be able to consider whether he'll want to try to bring out that "approachable" side more with the people in the group.

More important, this information about how he's perceived is information he can carry into his life outside the group. The group can be thought of as a small microcosm of his social world. How he behaves and is perceived in this group, in other words, is representative of how he behaves and is perceived in the wider world. If people in the group are intimidated by some of how he behaves, it is likely that others in his life are, as well. Similarly, if there are ways that he behaves that people in the group find attractive, that, too, will most likely be mirrored in his world outside the group. The information he has received from different people in the group—the feedback he's been given—can then help him decide how he wants to behave differently, or the same, in the group going forward, as well as in his greater life outside of the group.

The other major kind of learning that is taking place, though it may be less apparent in this case vignette, is that associated with the personal talking that people are doing about their lives—Dan's talking about his ex-wife and kids, the women in the group who talk about their past history of abusive relationships. These kinds of self-disclosures, when done in a safe and supportive environment, can promote a sense of connection with others in the group. Also, simply the telling and the sharing of personal and vulnerable information can serve a cathartic effect. This will be particularly meaningful if the telling is accompanied by the expression of feeling. The support one feels from others, coupled with the cleansing effect that is felt in the telling, is a powerful combination.

Naturally, all this has implications for the ways you lead your groups. If you want people to be able to give and receive feedback, you'll want to make sure that they know how to do this well, so that it can be given cleanly and heard by others. Similarly, you'll want to create guidelines for how people self-disclose and how information is held by group members. When your group feels safe and when people know the rules and the basics of what's expected, good things can happen.

Reflection and Group Fishbowl Lab Practice Exercise: Self-Disclosure

Sit quietly for a few minutes and think about something about yourself that you don't typically share with groups. This might be some skill you have, or something that makes you nervous. Maybe it's some experience you've had, or something you've always wanted to do. This "thing" about you is something that (assuming you are reading this book with others) you'll be sharing with others, so make sure it's not overly personal, too heavy, or potentially too embarrassing.

Here are some examples of things that I've shared with some of the groups I've been in: my dislike of public speaking, my love for sea kayaking, my secret desire to become a lounge singer in my spare time (thankfully, that one is no longer current), the fact that I see myself as an introvert who's learned how to make it in an extrovert world, some of the places I'd like to see before I die—I'm sure you get the drift. I've chosen not to share anything that is too deeply personal, and certainly not anything that represents something that I haven't come to grips with in my own life. This should hold true for what you think about sharing about yourself, as well. Certainly, don't share anything about which you'd feel embarrassed later or that could come back to haunt you if someone in your group shares it with someone outside the group.

Once you've had a chance to contemplate what you'd like to share, get together with the rest of your group. Create a group fishbowl exercise, as you've done previously, with leaders, members, and observers. Allot yourselves an adequate amount of time for everyone to share and for there to be some discussion. Each person should take a turn sharing, but—and this is important—there shouldn't be any discussion about what's been shared. That includes asking questions about the shared material. This is meant to be an experiment in sharing, not analysis of what's shared.

There should also be mutual agreement regarding confidentiality. Everyone in the group should agree to not share with anyone outside of the group any personal information that other people share. This is important, and your group should take the time to make sure that everyone buys into a confidentiality pact for this exercise.

After everyone has shared something, there could be a period of reflection about the general themes of sharing (but, again, without referencing specific material that any one person shared). People in the group could also share their feelings about having shared and having listened to others share—their feelings, not thoughts or ideas. Finally, people in the group could discuss whether doing this seemed to have any meaning, either for the group or for themselves personally.

When the group has finished with the entire process of sharing and reflection, the observers can provide supportive feedback to the leaders about what seemed to be most effective in moving the discussion along.

CONCLUDING THOUGHTS

You'll want to keep in mind that the development of your group will not necessarily progress in a simple straightforward line, like the "planning–forming–engaging–working–ending–following-up" model suggests. The model is simply a way of thinking about how groups can ideally progress. In reality, sometimes a group will move back and forth, for example, between working and engaging—there can be some regression, as events occur, in other words. Sometimes personality conflicts will emerge, even in a group that seemed really cohesive, and things don't go quite so smoothly. Nevertheless, the model does provide a way of looking at group development that you should find useful, and many times, it will work with your groups exactly as outlined.

I'd suggest maintaining notes after each group session, even if your workplace doesn't require it. That way you can track how the group is moving forward, as well as noting issues that need to be addressed. Additionally, this is simply one more good reason to have a coleader, someone with whom to consult and compare notes with between meetings.

FOR FURTHER THOUGHT

1. Think about one of the best classes you've ever taken. Try to remember how it got started, what happened during the life of that class that made it so good, and then about how it ended. Was part of the reason that the class was so successful because of the ways people in it came together, that it became cohesive? What helped make that happen?

   Then look at the class from a group development perspective. Compare the ingredients of group development described in this chapter with the development of that class experience.

2. Have you ever been part of a sports (or other kind of) team? Was it successful, either in terms of wins and losses, or in terms of how you and others simply felt about it? Did people on the team come together, cohesively?

   If you were to apply what you've learned about group development to that experience, how would you handle the team differently—or the same—if you were leading it at some point in the future?

3. Examine the literature about theories of group development. Look at both linear and other kinds of interactive group development models that those theories describe. Compare and contrast those with the linear one highlighted in this chapter.

4. Talk with someone who leads groups (and you can include teachers and coaches in your list of group leaders), and ask him or her about their perspectives on what makes for good group experiences. Ask specifically about what is done at different stages in the life of the group to make it successful.

5. Think about any popular films you may have seen that portray groups in action. Again, think widely about groups that may have been portrayed—counseling groups, sports teams, other kinds of groups. How did the groups

shown in the films develop in ways that can be compared/contrasted with what you've read about group development here?

REFERENCES

Brabender, V., & Fallon, A. (2009). Group development: Integrating theory, research, and practice. In *Group development in practice: Guidance for clinicians and researchers on stages and dynamics of change* (pp. 249–267). Washington, DC: American Psychological Association.

Capuzzi, D., & Gross, D. R. (2013). Group counseling. In D. Capuzzi & D. R. Gross (Eds.), *Introduction to the counselling profession* (6th ed., pp. 228–255). New York, NY: Routledge/Taylor & Francis.

Cornish, M. A., Wade, N. G., Tucker, J. R., & Post, B. C. (2014). When religion enters the counseling group: Multiculturalism, group processes, and social justice. *The Counseling Psychologist, 42*(5), 578–600.

Crits-Christoph, P., Johnson, J., Gallop, R., Gibbons, M. B. C., Hamilton, J., & Tu, X. (2011). A generalizability theory analysis of group process ratings in the treatment of cocaine dependence. *Psychotherapy Research* [serial online], *21*(3), 252–266.

DeLucia-Waack, J. L. (2006). *Leading psychoeducational groups: For children and adolescents*. Thousand Oaks, CA: Sage.

Ellis, C. C., Peterson, M., Bufford, R., & Benson, J. (2014). The importance of group cohesion in inpatient treatment of combat-related PTSD. *International Journal of Group Psychotherapy, 64*(2), 180–206.

Glyn, D. (2010). What and who belong in the group? Managing early crises. In S. Fehr (Ed.), *101 interventions in group therapy* (Rev. ed., pp. 287–291). New York, NY: Routledge/Taylor & Francis.

Hill, R., Marshall, L., & Harris, J. (2011). From idea to implementation: Planning and training strategies for establishing groups in addictions. In R. Hill & J. Harris (Eds.), *Principles and practice of group work in addictions* (pp. 91–101). New York, NY: Taylor & Francis.

Huebner, R. A. (2004). Group procedures. In F. Chan, N. L. Berven, & K. R. Thomas (Eds.), *Counseling theories and techniques for rehabilitation health professionals* (pp. 244–263). New York, NY: Springer.

Kraus, G. (1997). The psychodynamics of creative aggression in small groups. *Small Group Research, 28,* 112–145.

Letendre, J. (2009). Working with groups in schools: Planning for and working with group process. In R. T. Constable, C. Massat, S. McDonald, & J. Flynn

(Eds.), *School social work: Practice, policy, and research* (7th ed., pp. 595–609). Chicago, IL: Lyceum Books.

Luft, J. (1984). *Group processes: An introduction to group dynamics* (3rd ed.). Palo Alto, CA: Mayfield.

Maples, M. (1988) Group development: Extending Tuckman's theory. *Journal for Specialists in Group Work* [serial online], *13*(1), 17–23.

Maslow, A. (1970). *Motivation and personality.* New York, NY: Harper & Row.

McDonnell, K., Gillam, S., & Bergin, J. (2004). Member self-disclosure: "But this is how I feel!" In L. E. Tyson, R. Pérusse, & J. Whitledge (Eds.), *Critical incidents in group counseling* [e-book] (pp. 149–157). Alexandria, VA: American Counseling Association.

Mehrgardt, M., & Curen, V. (2005). Dialectic constructivism: An epistemological critique of gestalt therapy. *International Gestalt Journal, 28*(2), 31–65.

Nosko, A. (2003). Adventures in co-leadership in social group work practice. In R. Kurland & A. Malekoff (Eds.), *Stories celebrating group work: It's not always easy to sit on your mouth* (pp. 175–183). Binghamton, NY: Haworth Social Work Practice Press.

Schein, E. (1969). *Process consultation: Its role in organization development.* Reading, MA: Addison-Wesley.

Schutz, W. (1958). *FIRO: A three dimensional theory of interpersonal behavior.* New York, NY: Holt, Rinehart, & Winston.

Shechtman, Z., & Rybko, J. (2004). Attachment style and observed initial self-disclosure as explanatory variables of group functioning. *Group Dynamics: Theory, Research, and Practice, 8*(3), 207–220.

Tuckman, B. (1965). Developmental sequence in small groups. *Psychological Bulletin, 63,* 384–399.

Tuckman, B., & Jensen, M. (1977). Stages of small group development revisited. *Group and Organizational Studies, 2,* 419–427.

Unger, R. (1990). Conflict management in group psychotherapy. *Small Group Research, 21*(3), 349–359.

Vernelle, B. (1994). *Understanding and using groups.* London, England: Whiting Birch.

Wegscheider, S. (1986). *Another chance.* Palo Alto, CA: Science & Behavior Books.

Yalom, I., & Leszcz, M. (2005). *The theory and practice of group psychotherapy.* New York, NY: Basic Books.

Zytowski, D. G. (1994). A super contribution to vocational theory: Work values. *Career Development Quarterly, 43*(1), 25–31.

Chapter 5

Laying the Foundation

Developing Theoretical and Ethical Competency

> *Everyone desires relationship and community. Most people want to belong to a cohesive, like-minded group. It staves off loneliness. It promotes identity. These are natural and very human instincts.*
>
> —Joshua Ferris

COUNSELING THEORY AND GROUP WORK

In addition to the group-related theory and research that can help inform your work, there is also the theory about psychotherapy that may influence how you work with psychotherapy and counseling groups. Theories about psychotherapy and counseling with individuals have been applied to work with groups. You will want to familiarize yourself with this range of theoretical approaches.

I would encourage you to eventually establish your own theoretical base. After you've carefully examined the range of counseling and psychotherapy theories (from reading, coursework, discussion, and observation of theories in practical application), decide which theoretical approach best suits you and your beliefs about how people behave and how we can best respond therapeutically to their needs. Include in this examination a review of the research related to how these theories work with different populations of people. You want to be able to articulate which theory or theories most suit your beliefs and the way you want to work, and ground your group work to that theoretical approach.

THEORIES OF PSYCHOTHERAPY AND COUNSELING

- Insight-Oriented Approaches
- Action-Oriented Approaches
- Humanistically Oriented Approaches
- Postmodern Approaches
- A Developmental Approach to Using Theory in Group Work

Once you have thought through these different approaches and found one that suits you best, think more broadly about the ways other theoretical approaches might best suit the specific needs of people in a variety of situations.

You want, in other words, to be able to draw on a variety of tools and skills from different theoretical orientations, as different group situations arise. These different ideas and skills, or tools, from different theoretical stances can be used with different kinds of groups and group situations. Much of this decision making about what theoretical stance to use can be determined by the developmental level of the people in the group. I'll describe more completely what I mean by this developmental approach in applying theory to practice after looking briefly at some of the more common theoretical approaches to group work.

Insight: Psychoanalytic Approaches

These approaches are all variants of Freudian ideas about human behavior and about how to work therapeutically with people. Freud believed that human behavior is shaped by early childhood influences, particularly by parents, and that therapy with adolescents and adults involves exploring all of these childhood influences in a way that these influences can be better understood. With understanding, or *insight*, regarding these early influences, comes a greater ability to control the present, so the theory goes. Working with others in a group is a way of helping individuals gain insight about their hidden motivations and forgotten memories (Livingston, 1999).

Key psychoanalytic ideas and concepts that are relevant to group work include the following:

- The *unconscious*—This assumes that many things that have happened to us have been "forgotten," or *repressed*, perhaps because they were painful. Part of the goal of group work, then, would be to help individuals recover some of these memories, to make the unconscious conscious.

- *Transference* and *countertransference*—The idea here is that we continue to work out our unconsciously held memories of significant people from our past—especially our parents—through relationships with people in the present. Most analysts see looking at these phenomena as centrally important in therapeutic work (Strupp, 1992). We "transfer" our thoughts and feelings to these people in the present. Thus, we may respond to those in authority, like teachers or bosses, as we might have to our parents. Or we might even look for characteristics in lovers that remind us, again unconsciously, of a parent.

When it is our group members who are doing the transferring, particularly when it involves us as the group leader (e.g., seeing in us some characteristics that are parent reminders), it is transference. When it happens to us, as group leaders, it is called countertransference (e.g., being particularly annoyed by or attracted to a group member that is some reminder from our past).

- Defense mechanisms—Freudians believe that we unconsciously protect ourselves with a variety of little mind tricks that we play. With *projection,* we see in others those characteristics that are most difficult to accept in ourselves. With *denial* (e.g., "What do you mean I've got a drinking problem?") and *rationalization* (e.g., those grapes looked sour anyway), we gloss over the harshness of the reality of our situation by minimizing it.
- Dreams—There is great meaning to be derived from dreams, analysts would say. Our dreams are seen as vehicles for working out the unfinished business of the day, for fulfilling all those wishes that we can't tolerate considering in our waking lives.

Thus, in a psychoanalytic group, a significant amount of time would be spent with members looking at the past and how relationships with others are affected in the present (Woods, 2013). Dreams might be analyzed, thoughts and behaviors would be *interpreted* (significant life events and thoughts would be linked together via the leader's suggestion), and people's past would be examined. People wanting to work with groups from this kind of perspective would be advised to search out specific training related to conducting analytic group work (Horwitz, 2014).

Some contemporary versions of the psychoanalytic group focus on the ways people's current relationships are affected by relationships with significant others from the past. This *object relations* approach assumes that current relationships are configured in an attempt to work through issues in those older relationships with significant others, so much of the group's work is focused on looking at how past relationships (which have been psychically internalized) affect current relationships with others (St. Clair, 1996).

INSIGHT-ORIENTED GROUPS: KEY CONCEPTS

- The Unconscious
- Transference and Countertransference
- Defense Mechanisms
- Interpretation
- Dream Work
- Object Relations

Action: Cognitive and Behavioral Approaches

These theoretical approaches have a very different perspective as to what shapes our lives and how we feel about ourselves. People who lead cognitive/behavioral groups would say that it is less important to look for hidden motivations or underlying causes of behavior than it is to simply change the behavior. Adherents of these kinds of groups have generally done a good job of demonstrating that this approach can be effective in helping people with a variety of problems (Khoo, Dent, & Oei, 2011; McEvoy, Burgess, & Nathan, 2013; McGillivray & Evert, 2014).

By aiming to change behaviors, particularly behaviors that are causing individual members problems, the idea here is that people will automatically feel better about themselves as the behaviors change.

Rational emotive behavior therapy (REBT) assumes that feelings and behaviors follow thoughts. When we feel badly about ourselves, these theorists would say, it's usually because we have some unrealistic thought or belief that is to be blamed. Albert Ellis, who championed REBT, said that three particularly unrealistic and damaging belief systems cause people problems. In short, these are, essentially, that people get into trouble when they believe that they should perform perfectly in all situations, that everyone else should like them, and/or that life should be fair (Ellis, 2003). REBT groups force people to confront their own personal versions of these false belief systems. These groups help members look at the ways these beliefs create shame and self-distrust and try to help people replace these beliefs with more realistic, positive beliefs about themselves.

Other kinds of *behavior therapy* groups may try to teach members to change maladaptive behaviors (e.g., problems with being assertive) with more self-supporting ones. They might use role playing, homework assignments, or discussion of strategies to help someone change behaviors. Again, the emphasis here is not in finding out why someone might not be doing well with a certain kind of behavior, like assertiveness; rather it's focused on directly teaching skills to help someone become more effective.

ACTION-ORIENTED GROUPS: KEY CONCEPTS

- Correcting Self-Destructive Thought Patterns
- Examining Action–Consequence Patterns
- Skill Building
- Homework
- Role Playing
- Self-Regulation

One particular kind of behavior group therapy, called *dialectical behavior therapy*, was designed specifically to deal with people with serious emotional problems, particularly borderline personality disorder. It is now used more widely with a variety of different populations of people (Blackford & Love, 2011; Feldman, Harley, Kerrigan, Jacobo, & Fava, 2009; Linehan & Dimeff, 2001).

Dialectical behavior therapy is founded on the interesting assumption that people need to both change behaviors that are self-destructive and also become more self-accepting. These seemingly opposed assumptions (the dialectic) use some basic concepts of behavior therapy coupled with some ideas taken from writings about mindfulness and meditation to help people learn to be more comfortable with themselves and others. Individual and group work are combined in a highly structured fashion that is designed to help people become more emotionally self-regulating, more skillful interpersonally, and more self-accepting. Visit behavior-altech.org for more information.

Humanism: Person-Centered, Gestalt, and Existential Approaches

In contrast to both the analytic and cognitive–behavioral approaches to group work, the humanists talk less about resolution of past personal issues or changing specific behaviors than they do about people realizing their potential, for becoming more self-actualized, and for becoming more authentic. The purpose of a group, they would maintain, would be to provide an environment where people can obtain support from others in becoming more in tune with their own basic wishes and desires, while also becoming more connected with others. Phrases like "becoming more authentic" and "exploring your human potential" might characterize much of what they believe are good goals for people in their groups.

Person-centered theory, which was developed and championed by Carl Rogers, suggests that people experiencing difficulty in life have learned to live with so-called conditions of self-worth, to not trust their own basic instincts and inherent goodness. Instead of being met with unconditional love, they have been met with attitudes like, "You'll love me as long as I behave in ways that meet your approval (like getting good grades, hanging around with the right people, etc.). The function of group work here is to provide a therapeutic climate of empathic understanding, genuineness, warmth, and caring, so that people can drop their normal defensive posturing and experiment with new ways of relating with others (Rogers, 1970).

Gestalt therapy theory, designed by Fritz and Laura Perls, Paul Goodman, and Ralph Hefferline, is similarly designed to help people become more authentic and "whole" by working with them to look at their "unfinished business" and integrating aspects of themselves that they may find unacceptable. While some of the early Gestalt therapy groups (which were not actually groups, rather individuals working with a therapist individually in front of a group, in the so-called hot seat), particularly those led by Fritz Perls, were highly confrontational and theatrical, Gestalt therapy has evolved into a system of therapy that is generally much more relationally based (Polster, 1995). Gestalt group leaders encourage honest, open "contact" among group members and try to let their own subjective experience of members and the group as a whole inform their interventions in the group (Fairfield, 2004).

For many Gestalt therapists, groups are the preferred way of working with people (Frew, 1988). Gestalt groups are sometimes characterized by little experiments designed to help people examine aspects of themselves that they have difficulty acknowledging and accepting, as well as an encouragement to fully experience the emotion that may accompany material that is brought into awareness (Schoenberg, Feder, Frew, & Gadol, 2005; Zinker, 1978).

Existential therapy, which is an applied extension of existential philosophy, looks at the big questions of life–death, meaning, aloneness, and personal freedom (Bugental, 2008; Yalom, 1980). Groups that are existentially oriented encourage the development of self-awareness and promote the notion that we are all essentially alone, no matter how much or closely we try to connect with others—that our ability to act truly freely relies on our ability to grasp the fact of that "aloneness." Basic tenets associated with the usefulness of group work—the concepts of cohesion and universality—are solidly based in existential thinking (Sayın, Candansayar, & Welkin, 2013).

These groups might use dreams, creative writing, painting, or other means of personal creative expression as a way of helping people access these themes of meaning in their lives (Provost, 1999). That being said, existentialism is highly supportive of intimate relationships between people, but only in ways where people in those relationships act as true individuals—not looking to another for validation.

We are, the existentialists would say, the architects of our own lives. Given that life is inherently meaningless, they would also say, our job is to find a game worth playing and to play it as if our life depends on it—because it does.

HUMANISTICALLY ORIENTED GROUPS: KEY CONCEPTS

- Relationships Between Members and Leaders
- Cohesion
- Authenticity
- Self-Actualization
- Issues of Personal Meaning

Postmodern Approaches

The past 40 years have seen the proliferation of newer approaches to working psychotherapeutically with people. Most of these approaches have been developed in reaction to older theoretical perspectives (the ones that we've just reviewed), which tend to focus on people's problems. The older established theories also historically ignored issues of cultural differences, including gender.

The newer approaches, called postmodern—literally because they come after the modern era of psychotherapy (behavioral, humanistic, etc.)—turn the approach to psychotherapy on its head. They suggest that instead of dealing with people's problems, we should be dealing with their strengths. Instead of ignoring gender differences, they say, we should look carefully at those and begin to challenge prevailing cultural stereotypes and assumptions about gender. Instead of assuming that everyone looks at the world through the same cultural lens, we should begin to appreciate and respond to all the different way people perceive the world given their unique cultural heritage and outlook.

Notions about how personality develops, in contrast to those older theories, suggest that we all have shifts in personality that are largely dependent on circumstance and the situations in which we find ourselves. Postmodernists would assume that the best way to work with these "shifts" would be to let the client be the teacher and to talk about the specific situations and the ways in which she or he is affected by those. The therapist's role would be to help reframe those perspectives and instruct about the larger political realities that affect and have shaped those perspectives.

Each of these different postmodern approaches has a specific means for working with people. Following are brief descriptions of five of these approaches.

Multicultural psychotherapeutic approaches would look carefully at the ways an individual's perspective on the world has been shaped by his or her background—racial, ethnic, religious, and so on—and current living situation. These theorists would look at similarities and differences between the therapist's and the client's cultural world view and try to understand and reconcile those (Sue, Ivey, & Pederson, 1996).

Feminist theory asserts that people, women in particular, have been burdened with a cultural paradigm regarding gender assumptions that is oppressive. A therapist working from this perspective would help a client become more politically aware of that cultural oppression and would strive to assist her—or him—in becoming more personally assertive and also more able to negotiate gender role assumptions in a way that is more personally satisfying (Enns, 2004).

Strengths-based approaches help people, as the title suggests, focus more on their strengths than on their problems as they move forward with their lives. It utilizes concepts from the field of positive psychology to work with people in this less problem-oriented way. Through a close examination of personal strengths, as well as in practicing the use of those, a client would be assisted in maximizing his or her strengths for use in future situations (Jones-Smith, 2014).

In *solution-focused* therapy, the client would be assisted in finding the keys toward resolving his or her problems via a close examination of the strategies he or she has utilized effectively in the past to work toward achieving goals set in the present (Berg, 1994; de Shazer, 1985).

A *narrative* therapist would look at the stories someone has manufactured about his life. He would help the client to look at how some of those stories have been shaped by other people, and the client would be assisted in creating an alternative, personally meaningful, narrative (White & Epston, 1990).

Four Different Approaches to the Same Group

It might be helpful to take a look at how these very different theoretical approaches might play out when applied to an actual group.

Let's consider for a moment a group of high school students, all of whom have families that are experiencing significant difficulties. Following is a brief overview of how these three theoretical orientations—insight, action, and humanistic—might deal with such a group.

Insight-oriented group leaders would encourage these group members to talk about their families, their histories with their parents, and their current lives. Exercises might be used to encourage this discussion, and interpretations would be made linking past histories with current life situations. Students would be encouraged to look at how they were acting, or not, with the leaders and other members as they might with their parents—transference issues, in other words. The group would be seen as a replication of the family, with the leaders symbolically as parents and the members as the kids in the family. If any of the student members have behavioral problems, defusing those through an investigation of hidden motivations would be a primary goal.

Action-oriented leaders would approach this group very differently. There would be little discussion of the symbolism of relationships between leaders and members, and little attention would be paid to underlying motivations. The emphasis here, instead, would be in providing reinforcement (support) for thoughts and behaviors that are constructive and self-supporting, gentle confrontation of thoughts and behaviors that are undermining and counterproductive. There would undoubtedly be training sessions where specific skills to deal with problem behaviors (anxiety, troubling feelings, or drug use) like relaxation, anger management, or refusal skills are taught. Role playing and homework assignments might be used to supplement the work done in the group.

Leaders with a *humanistic* orientation would have their own approach to this group. These leaders would do all they could to create a warm and supportive environment where people would feel safe in letting down personal defenses. It would be assumed that a warm, supportive atmosphere could be a good counterbalance to the tumult and turmoil that these kids might be experiencing in their homes. These kids would be encouraged to drop their usual role-bound behavior so that they could honestly encounter, in more authentic fashion, one another. The leaders would strive to point out commonalities among the students, despite their outward, more superficial, differences. Building relationships between leaders and members, and among members, would be a key goal, in addition to helping members examine some big life questions and their personal wishes and dreams.

Finally, leaders utilizing one of the *postmodern* approaches would use the group as a way to instruct about cultural differences in the group and about larger political realities and the ways those shape individuals' experience of the world. They would use the group to help people learn from one another about these differences and would help individuals recognize and support one another's strengths. People in the group would be encouraged to view their lives through political, as well as psychological, lenses. Typically, the emphasis would be on building strengths, as opposed to focusing on problems. Films, guest speakers, and readings might be used to supplement in-group conversation and activities.

Using Theory in Group From a Developmental Perspective

Again, I would encourage you to explore the varieties of theories of psychotherapy and counseling and to eventually identify one of these as your personal theoretical home base. This "base" may shift over time as you gain experience as a group leader or a therapist, and you'll be able to track some of your own professional development via these shifts.

In working with groups, however, I would encourage you to pragmatically use tools from a variety of theoretical positions to fit the developmental level and needs of the people in your group. Thus, while you might naturally gravitate to using interventions and skills based on your primary theoretical orientation, you would also have at your disposal a variety of tools from other orientations to meet the immediate needs of your group. This is similar to the approach to thinking about the use of theory I've advocated in working with individuals (Hutchinson, 2014).

Very broadly speaking, you will have two very different kinds of folks in your groups. The first category will comprise people who need significant direction. These may be children. They may be people with significant, persistent mental illness, or they may be people whose lives are out of control with substance use disorders. For these groups, you will probably want to use skills from the action-oriented or postmodern categories of theories. These will most likely be psycho-educational groups that combine some content (teaching) with some discussion of process (interpersonal relations). These approaches help people learn new skills for dealing with life's difficulties in new ways.

The other broad category of people is comprised of those who have lives that are functionally sound. These will be people who are emotionally, physically, and economically self-supporting. They may need to learn some skills, so occasionally some action-oriented approaches are appropriate, but more likely they will be look-ing for a group that is more heavily process oriented. They will be less interested in learning new skills than they are in simply talking with others about their lives. In this case, the humanistic, insight, or postmodern theoretical approaches would be more appropriate.

This means that how you screen and select people for your groups will be of real importance. You'll want people in your group who are operating at roughly the same level of development. Then you can create strategies and plans for the group, applying theoretical interventions that are appropriate for that developmental level.

Reflection and Group Fishbowl Lab Practice Exercise: Use of Theory in Groups

Now that you've had a chance to read about the use of counseling and psycho-therapy theories in groups and have also had a chance to see how they might be used in group situations, think about how this might apply to your own work with groups. While you may or may not have had much exposure to these theories, other than what's been presented here, do you have any immediate reactions regarding which might have more appeal for you and the work you want to do?

Given what you know about people, human behavior, and development, what theory or theories of counseling and psychotherapy appeal most to you? Which do you think would be most effective in working with people in groups?

Take a few minutes to write down some notes about your thoughts and reflec-tions about these theoretical orientations and about how they might affect your work with groups. If you have an immediate affinity—or dislike—for any of these, please make note of that, and consider your reasons for this reaction.

When you've taken some time to reflect personally about the application of theory to group work, create another fishbowl experience with your student colleagues.

As in previous exercises, there should be two leaders, some group members (numbers will depend on the size of your overall group), with the remainder of your group as observers. Try to ensure that everyone in your group is trying on different roles for these fishbowl experiences.

The group should take 20 to 30 minutes to share ideas about the relevance of theory to their own group work. Members could be encouraged to talk about their own theoretical leanings and how that might affect their work with groups. The leaders should do their best to draw everyone into the discussion, in addition to sharing their own thoughts about the use of theory in groups.

When the allotted time is up, the observers should share their observations—again, focusing on what the leaders did best to facilitate discussion.

ESTABLISHING AN ETHICAL FOUNDATION FOR LEADING GROUPS: CONSIDERATIONS FOR LEADERS

Back in the heyday of the late 1960s and most of the 1970s, it was a no-holds-barred approach to working with groups. Leaders did all kinds of extraordinary and outlandish things with groups—using sleep deprivation, drugs, no clothing—you name it. All was done in the name of "helping" people become more authentic and honest.

Professionals in the field started to look more closely at what was happening to people in these groups. They started to look at outcomes, the aftermath of these group experiences, and what they found was troubling. Many of the people who were emerging from some of these more radical group experiments were worse off than when they'd started. In particular, the most psychologically vulnerable people seemed to be negatively affected by harmful group experiences. Thus, one of the basic assumptions of the group work of that day was challenged: that people couldn't be harmed by negative group experiences.

Professional group workers then decided to patrol the group work ethical landscape more effectively. The Association for Specialists in Group Work was formed, and with its formation, a set of ethical standards was established (Carroll & Levo, 1985; Ward, 2003). The standards addressed group leader training—including the need for leaders to be psychologically healthy, screening for member appropriateness for groups, the need for fair and equal treatment of people in groups, and, finally, for the ongoing need to assess the quality of group experiences. These ethical standards are now the foundation on which mental health professional training programs for group workers are built.

People will take some interpersonal risks, they will try on some new behaviors, and they will share a bit more about themselves when they feel safe. A little anxiety makes for a good learning environment. Too much anxiety prohibits new learning because people shut down. The mandate for group leaders is to find that right balance of anxiety, and, if anything, to err on the side of too little. Better that members be bored than hurt.

Your sound, ethical, group leadership creates safety in the group. The ground rules on which the group operates (e.g., confidentiality, informed consent, right to privacy) help create this safety, as does your relative health and the appropriateness of the fit of members within the group. When taken together, all of these safety precautions conspire to create a *containment* function. The group becomes surrounded by an emotional boundary, of sorts, within which you and your group members can take some appropriate risks with one another.

Your ethical responsibility in working with groups has three safety components: (1) to protect your members, (2) to protect yourself, and (3) to protect the field of group work and your profession (Meara, Schmidt, & Day, 1996). It is unfortunate that sometimes you may learn that other group leaders have done harmful things with people, as in engaging in inappropriate relationships with them. You may also hear of instances where a group member will try to victimize a group leader through slander or harmful innuendo. You may become a victim of unfair allegations yourself. Bad things happen to good group leaders, and bad things can also, unfortunately, happen to good group members.

Generally, your good-hearted instincts will serve you well as you make decisions about how to proceed ethically in your groups. Your own conduct in your personal affairs and your general approach to your relationships with others will dictate, to a large extent, how you deal with ethical dilemmas as they arise in your groups. The foundation of your group work ethical base is shaped by who you are as a person (Bertram, 2011; Colgan, Berthold, & Marinoff, 2009). The best and most ethical group leaders are people who are simply generally kind and fair in their attitudes and dealings with other people.

But there is more to becoming ethically competent than just being a good person. You also need to know the ethical rules by which group work is governed (Aveline, 2006). You will want to familiarize yourself with the Best Practice Standards of the Association for Specialists in Group Work (Capuzzi & Gross, 2013). This will help remind you of some of the principles and things you need to do as you approach a new group.

You'll want to couple your understanding of these principles of best practice with the code of ethical conduct of your particular professional affiliation. My own affiliation is with the counseling profession, so it is the American Counseling Association's (2005) code of ethical conduct that shapes my approach to ethical decision making in groups.

Additionally—and this is really important—you will want to find and consult with *a good supervisor, as well as other colleagues, with whom you can talk about your work with your group* (Kitchener, 1994; Puleo, Anderson, & Gillam, 2004). If you have a coleader in a group you're running, that will help. This is someone with whom you can discuss problem situations and possible intervention strategies for dealing with those situations. A good supervisor, meaning someone with group work experience and whose work you respect, can be invaluable in helping you negotiate difficult decisions about how to best proceed with tricky ethical dilemmas.

In the event that something unfortunate and damaging happens in your group (e.g., you are falsely accused of wrongdoing by someone in the group), you will be able to bring your supervisor into the conversation, suggesting that the decisions you made were only made in consultation with others. You can also work with your supervisor to create some helpful ways of *assessing group progress*. Evaluating your groups, both at the end and as they go, is a good practice and is also an ethical obligation.

Anyone who leads groups needs to view both the skills associated with group leadership and *personal self-awareness* as being of equal importance. This means that in addition to acquiring the *knowledge and training associated with working with people in groups*—typically by way of a professional training program and ongoing professional development and continuing education—we also need to pay attention to how we, as people, are using those skills. Professional knowledge is critical, but not sufficient.

If you are involved in any kind of helping profession or training program, you may have encountered individuals who seem to know a lot about their professional roles and responsibilities but who just don't seem to be able to connect very well with people. They have the academic tools but lack the self-awareness to put those tools successfully to good use. We need to ensure that we have both the professional knowledge and the personal awareness of our strengths and weaknesses to provide good service as group workers. Self-understanding can help ensure that we don't work out our own unfinished business through the people in our groups.

This is why most academic programs in counseling, social work, and psychology insist that students engage in personal growth work, in addition to their academic training. This is also why anyone who is doing group work should have a capable supervisor and colleagues with whom he or she can collaborate.

Part of your ongoing commitment to your own personal growth and expanded self-awareness should be your *appreciation for the diversity of the members you find in your groups*. We've already talked about the wide array of differences you'll encounter—the racial and ethnic differences, the class differences, the religious differences, and so on—but your growing appreciation and understanding of those is not just good group practice. This appreciation of diversity is also an ethical obligation. The people in our groups deserve an understanding of how they see the world.

Finally, there may be some situations that arise in your group that merit some *legal advice*. If you work in an agency or a school, there may be an affiliation with a lawyer who could help you with particularly problematic issues. You'll also want to make sure that the agency or school will assume legal responsibility for you in the unfortunate event of a lawsuit.

ETHICAL CONSIDERATIONS LEADERS HAVE FOR MEMBERS

We are ethically bound to conduct our work with groups in ways that help ensure that no one who is participating in a group experience will be hurt. Toward this end, we make sure that the following safeguards are in place.

Informed Consent

Everyone who participates in your groups need to know exactly what he or she is getting into. The overall goals for the experience should be explicit. Whenever possible, members may help fine-tune those. Finalizing the goals, then, becomes a shared endeavor.

Your members should know about your qualifications to lead the group and something about the ways it will be run. When I am teaching courses about group work, I usually take this as an opportunity to share something about myself—not just my professional background but also some personal details about what drew me to the profession of counseling and of my love of working with groups. I am clear about my desire to share a personal passion for working with groups and my hopes that this passion will be infectious. You could do something similar when you introduce yourself to groups—doing this also helps model some appropriate use of self-disclosure.

I also take this as an opportunity to talk about some of the activities, guests who might come in, or other details about the experience that will be helpful for people to know. I stress my belief in the importance of safety and the development of trusting relationships and my desire to get to know and be known by people in the group. People need to know that you can't guarantee that everyone will respond positively to them, that there is a certain amount of risk taking involved with group work. Articulate those risks as clearly as you can. These are the kinds of details—whatever your approach is—that you'll also want to share with your groups at the outset.

You'll also want to make sure that members know what will be expected of them in this experience. I assume you'll want them to show up for every session, to come on time, and to actively participate in the group. You may need to discuss fees. You'll want, in other words, to be very clear about what their, and your, responsibilities are (Shakoor, 2010).

Confidentiality

We've talked about confidentiality in previous chapters, but it merits emphasizing again, particularly as an ethical issue, because of its central importance in the potential success of your group. People need to know about how personal information will be managed. If you're working with kids in a school, what information will be shared with administrators or parents? If you're working in an agency, what kinds of information will be shared with other agencies? What are member's obligations regarding holding one another's information confidentially?

People need to know that there is no such thing as absolute confidentiality. If there are personal safety issues at stake, confidentiality might be violated. And sometimes people make mistakes, and confidentiality can be unwittingly compromised. Thus, people should be encouraged to think about what they share, and to avoid sharing things that would be potentially really harmful if confidentiality were to be broken.

Voluntary Membership

Everyone who participates in your group should be there voluntarily. No one should be absolutely forced into being in your groups. Furthermore, anyone should be able to get up and leave a group whenever the need is felt.

Now, let's clarify that. Sometimes people are told that they need to attend a group as part of a probation deal (to stay out of jail) or as part of a school discipline plan, or any other numbers of leveraged ways people can be coerced into participating. A judge can mandate group participation, as can a school administrator.

People should always know that they have a choice, however, to follow the mandate or not. The mandated person can opt for a jail cell instead, or with the school child, the detention room. There is always choice about participation. Sometimes the alternatives are unpleasant, but there is always choice.

Also, in each meeting you have, anyone has the right to leave. No one will be tied to a chair. Whenever someone does choose to leave, however, it creates a situation that merits your special attention. I've sometimes had people leave groups because they've become overwhelmed with difficult emotions—usually sadness or anger—and they need some time to personally regroup. Typically, this has involved my allowing them some personal space, then checking in to make sure that they'll be coming back, and inviting them to talk about what happened. You could do the same.

I've been involved in some group interventions. In these, generally, someone's difficult behavior has mobilized a group to confront the person about the behavior. In the planning for this meeting, if there is a thought that the person might be inclined to get up and leave, we'll talk about setting up the seating arrangement to minimize the flight risk (like putting myself between the person and the door)—but we would never physically stop someone from leaving. Participation in a group, including each session, is always voluntary. People can choose not to attend in the first place, and they can also choose to leave once things have started. They simply need to know that there may be consequences related to such a choice.

Member Screening

Not everyone who is referred to your group is appropriate to participate. You will want to devise some way of screening potential members to find those who are best suited to join (Tyson, Pérusse, & Whitledge, 2004). Even people who really want to be in the group might not be the right choice for the group. Some people may have a significant issue—personal or mental health, for example—which means they should be steered in some different direction. They may need more attention than a group can afford, or maybe another group with a different set of therapeutic goals and activities would be better for them.

When someone becomes involved with a group whose needs are larger than the group can manage, the person and the group will suffer. I've seen instances where a group will turn on someone who needs more attention than the group feels it's prepared to give. It's not pretty. The person who's been turned on can feel attacked, and the rest of the people in the group can feel that their experience has been compromised.

Your job, to the best of your ability, is to select people who are appropriate for your group. You might interview people or use some kind of written assessment process, like a questionnaire, to judge the right fit of people for your new group. This is really more about selecting out, rather than selecting in. You want to screen out people who need more, or something different, than this group can afford. While this screening process can take some time and extra effort, the pain that can be saved is worth the work.

Reflection and Discussion Exercise

Following are some problem/ethical dilemmas, any of which you might encounter in a group that you're leading. Consider each of these and decide a course of action. With each of these, what would you do?

When you've had a chance to consider these on your own, talk them over with one or two of your colleagues. If you have access to a course instructor or clinician with significant group experience, share your ideas with her.

1. One person in your group started out talking a lot but has gotten pretty quiet during the past few meetings. This person is racially different from the rest of the members.

2. Your coleader tells a racist (or sexist) joke in the group.

3. Someone in the group breaks confidentiality.

4. Someone in your group says that in a previous group she had "relations" (meaning a sexual relationship) with one of the leaders.

5. Someone in your group asks you out for coffee after group.

6. Someone in your group is monopolizing, talking far more than others.

7. You find out that one of your group members is being cyber-bullied by other members of the group.

(*Hint:* Consultation with a supervisor and/or colleagues should be a part of your response to each of these.)

CONCLUDING THOUGHTS

Hopefully, you're now convinced of the importance of becoming fluent with the theories of psychotherapy as they relate to groups. An understanding of these theories and your ability to utilize appropriate skills from those is an important part of becoming a proficient group leader.

What I really think underlies all of the theoretical approaches as the key to successful group work—and that is at least as important as the theories themselves—is the ability to form a therapeutic alliance with your group. Whether you want to teach your group some skills utilizing cognitive–behavioral techniques or help them understand their inner turmoils using an insight orientation—or whatever other theoretical orientation you might choose to use—your ability to form alliances, solid relationships, with your group members is what makes all the rest of what you want to do with the group possible.

Just as in any other kind of helping relationship, your ability to form an alliance, a connection, with people is key to success (Brodsky, 2011; Gelso, 2011). I would even probably agree with those who assert that these relationships you form in the group may be even more important than your theoretical approach (Horvath & Symonds,

1991; Orlinsky, Grawe, & Parks, 1994). That, however, is not a universally held position. Whether or not you agree with this extreme view, you can at least be assured that this ability to make connections is a critically important part of the equation (Gelso & Carter, 1985).

Bring everything you can to the groups you run—your knowledge of group dynamic theory, your understanding of theories of psychotherapy, and all your relationship-building skills. This combination of your theoretical knowledge and your interpersonal skills—plus your genuine interest, kindness, and enthusiasm (and grit)—should help ensure successful experiences with your groups.

FOR FURTHER THOUGHT

1. This chapter very briefly examined how selected theories about counseling and psychotherapy might be applied to group work. Examine (most likely in a textbook about counseling theory) other theoretical approaches not discussed in the chapter (e.g., narrative theory, solution-focused theory), and thoughtfully consider how those might be applied to work with groups.

2. Psychodrama is a theoretical approach to working with people that was specifically designed for group work. Investigate the work of Jacob and Zerka Moreno and this unique approach to group work. Also see if there are any psychodrama-trained professionals in your area. If there are, consider talking with them about their work.

3. There are a number of YouTube videos demonstrating different approaches to counseling and psychotherapy. Find and watch some of these, particularly those related to group work. Then think about which of these are most appealing to you.

4. Different state agencies or local mental health agencies offer trainings on theory-specific approaches to group work. Investigate what trainings might be offered in the region where you live, and consider whether you might want to become involved in any of those.

REFERENCES

American Counseling Association. (2005). *ACA code of ethics*. Alexandria, VA: Author.

Aveline, M. (2006). Group psychotherapy. In S. Bloch (Ed.), *An introduction to the psychotherapies* (pp. 237–263). New York, NY: Oxford University Press.

Berg, I. (1994). *Family-based services: A solution-focused approach.* New York, NY: W. W. Norton.

Bertram, B. (2011). Ethics and legal issues for group work. In T. Fitch & J. L. Marshall (Eds.), *Group work and outreach plans for college counselors* (pp. 9–17). Alexandria, VA: American Counseling Association.

Blackford, J., & Love, R. (2011). Dialectical behavior therapy group skills training in a community mental health setting: A pilot study. *International Journal of Group Psychotherapy, 61*(4), 645–657.

Brodsky, S. (2011). *Therapy with coerced and reluctant clients.* Washington, DC: American Psychological Association.

Bugental, E. K. (2008). Swimming together in a sea of loss: A group process for elders. In K. J. Schneider (Ed.), *Existential-integrative psychotherapy: Guideposts to the core of practice* (pp. 333–342). New York, NY: Taylor & Francis.

Capuzzi, D., & Gross, D. R. (2013). Group counseling. In D. Capuzzi & D. R. Gross (Eds.), *Introduction to the counselling profession* (6th ed., pp. 228–255). New York, NY: Taylor & Francis.

Carroll, M. R., & Levo, L. (1985). The Association for Specialists in Group Work. *Journal of Counseling & Development, 63*(7), 452–454.

Colgan, P., Berthold, T., & Marinoff, J. (2009). Group facilitation. In T. Berthold, J. Miller, & A. Avila-Esparza (Eds.), *Foundations for community health workers* (pp. 479–511). San Francisco, CA: Jossey-Bass.

Ellis, A. (2003). Early theories and practices of rational emotive behavior theory and how they have been augmented and revised during the last three decades. *Journal of Rational-Emotive & Cognitive-Behavior Therapy, 21,* 4.

Ellis, C. C., Peterson, M., Bufford, R., & Benson, J. (2014). The importance of group cohesion in inpatient treatment of combat-related PTSD. *International Journal of Group Psychotherapy, 64*(2), 180–206.

Enns, C. (2004). *Feminist theories and feminist psychotherapies: Origins, themes, and diversity* (2nd ed.). New York, NY: Haworth.

Fairfield, M. A. (2004). Gestalt groups revisited: A phenomenological approach. *Gestalt Review, 8*(3), 336–357.

Feldman, G., Harley, R., Kerrigan, M., Jacobo, M., & Fava, M. (2009). Change in emotional processing during a dialectical behavior therapy-based skills group for major depressive disorder. *Behaviour Research and Therapy, 47*(4), 316–321.

Frew, J. (1988). The practice of Gestalt therapy in groups. *Gestalt Journal, 11*(1), 77–96.

Gelso, C. (2011). *The real relationship in psychotherapy: The hidden foundation of change.* Washington, DC: American Psychological Association.

Gelso, C. J., & Carter, J. A. (1985). The relationship in counseling and psychotherapy: Components, consequences, and theoretical antecedents. *The Counseling Psychologist, 13,* 155–243.

Horvath, A., & Symonds, B. (1991). Relation between working alliance and outcome in psychotherapy: A meta-analysis. *Journal of Counseling Psychology, 38,* 138–149.

Horwitz, L. (2014). *Listening with the fourth ear: Unconscious dynamics in analytic group psychotherapy.* London, England: Karnac Books.

Hutchinson, D. (2014). *The essential counselor: Process, skills, and techniques* (3rd ed.). Thousand Oaks, CA: Sage.

Jones-Smith, E. (2014). *Strengths-based therapy: Connecting, theory, and skills.* Thousand Oaks, CA: Sage.

Khoo, A., Dent, M. T., & Oei, T. S. (2011). Group cognitive behaviour therapy for military service-related post-traumatic stress disorder: Effectiveness, sustainability and repeatability. *Australian and New Zealand Journal of Psychiatry, 45*(8), 663–672.

Kitchener, K. (May 1994). Doing good well: The wisdom behind ethical supervision. *Counseling and Human Development, 16*(9), 1–8.

Linehan, M., & Dimeff, L. (2001). Dialectical behavior therapy in a nutshell. *California Psychologist, 34,* 10–13.

Livingston, M. (January 1999). Vulnerability, tenderness, and the experience of self object relationship: A self psychological view of deepening curative process in group psychotherapy. *International Journal of Group Psychotherapy* [serial online], *49*(1), 19–40.

McEvoy, P. M., Burgess, M. M., & Nathan, P. (2013). The relationship between interpersonal problems, negative cognitions, and outcomes from cognitive behavioral group therapy for depression. *Journal of Affective Disorders, 150*(2), 266–275.

McGillivray, J. A., & Evert, H. T. (2014). Group cognitive behavioural therapy program shows potential in reducing symptoms of depression and stress among young people with ASD. *Journal of Autism and Developmental Disorders, 44*(8), 2041–2051.

Meara, N., Schmidt, L., & Day, J. (1996). Principles and virtues: A foundation for ethical decisions, policies, and character. *Counseling Psychologist, 24,* 4–77.

Orlinsky, D. E., Grawe, K., & Parks, B. K. (1994). Process and outcome in psychotherapy—Noch einmal. In A. E. Bergin & S. L. Garfield (Eds.), *Handbook of psychotherapy and behavior change* (4th ed., pp. 270–376). Oxford, England: Wiley.

Polster, E. (1995). *A population of selves: A therapeutic exploration of personality diversity.* San Francisco, CA: Jossey-Bass.

Provost, J. A. (1999). A dream focus for short-term growth groups. *Journal for Specialists in Group Work, 24*(1), 74–87.

Puleo, S. G., Anderson, M. L., & Gillam, S. L. (2004). Supervision issues: "I'll protect you." In L. E. Tyson, R. Pérusse, & J. Whitledge (Eds.), *Critical incidents in group counseling* (pp. 121–130). Alexandria, VA: American Counseling Association.

Rogers, C. (1970). *Carl Rogers on encounter groups.* New York, NY: Harper & Row.

Sayın, A., Candansayar, S., & Welkin, L. (2013). Group psychotherapy in women with a history of sexual abuse: What did they find helpful? *Journal of Clinical Nursing, 22*(23–24), 3249–3258.

Schoenberg, P., & Feder, B. (2005). Gestalt therapy in groups. In A. L. Woldt & S. M. Toman (Eds.), *Gestalt therapy: History, theory, and practice* (pp. 219–236). Thousand Oaks, CA: Sage.

Shakoor, M. (2010). *On becoming a group member: Personal growth and effectiveness in group counseling.* New York, NY: Taylor & Francis.

de Shazer, S. (1985). *Keys to solutions in brief therapy.* New York, NY: W. W. Norton.

St. Clair, M. (1996). *Object relations and self psychology: An introduction* (2nd ed.). Pacific Grove, CA: Brooks/Cole.

Strupp, H. (1992). The future of psychodynamic psychotherapy. *Psychotherapy, 29,* 21–27.

Sue, D., Ivey, A., & Pederson, P. (Eds.). (1996). *A theory of multicultural counseling and therapy.* Pacific Grove, CA: Brooks/Cole.

Tyson, L. E., Pérusse, R., & Whitledge, J. (2004). *Critical incidents in group counseling.* Alexandria, VA: American Counseling Association.

Ward, D. E. (2003). Reflections of the *Journal for Specialists in Group Work*'s past editors and the *Journal Today. Journal for Specialists in Group Work, 28*(4), 285–290.

White, M., & Epston, D. (1990). *Narrative means to therapeutic ends.* New York, NY: W. W. Norton.

Woods, J. (2013). Group analytic therapy for compulsive users of Internet pornography. *Psychoanalytic Psychotherapy, 27*(4), 306–318.

Yalom, I. (1980). *Existential psychotherapy.* New York, NY: Basic Books.

Zinker, J. (1978). *Creative process in gestalt therapy.* New York, NY: Vintage Books.

Chapter 6

Planning for a New Group

Meticulous planning will enable everything you do to appear spontaneous.

—Mark Caine

When I was in graduate school I was in three different groups. My program expected students to engage in personal growth activities, and most of us in the program saw involvement in groups as an economically viable and satisfying way to meet this requirement.

By the time I came to be working on my doctorate, I was coleading personal growth–type groups with students working toward their master's degrees. These were largely unstructured, unplanned experiences. My coleader and I did very little planning for these groups, but it didn't matter. The people in these groups knew what was expected, and they did what they needed to do to make the groups work.

Then I left school. My first job after graduate school was in a residential treatment center for adolescents with drug problems. I was expected to provide individual—and group—counseling services for the residents. I naively thought that I could approach these groups like I had the groups I'd run in graduate school, with a minimal amount of planning and preparation. I walked into my first group as the single leader without any kind of real game plan. I figured that we'd talk a bit about our goals and what we were going to do in the group, and then the members would take over.

My lack of preparation for this group was a big mistake. That first group meeting was filled with a great deal of awkward silence, some hostility, and even some direct appeals for more guidance. It was almost, but not quite, a total disaster. Fortunately, after the first meeting was over, I was able to confer with colleagues and my supervisor about how badly things had gone and was able to make corrections that eventually led to a salvaging of the experience. I got my planning act together and made sure that there was appropriate structure in place for each group that followed. Despite its rocky start, the group actually turned out to be quite a positive experience, both for the members and for me.

Don't make the same mistake I made. Plan, plan, plan—and think carefully about who your members will be and what kind of experience they've had with groups. Even with my groups of graduate students I should have prepared more carefully, but they were skillful enough to make up for my lack of planning—the group of adolescents wasn't.

THE NEW GROUP

There is a lot to do in getting ready for a new group. You will want to carefully match your planning for a new group to the overall goals of the group and the people who will be in it. Everything in your planning should support the things your group is supposed to do for the people in it and for the group's hoped-for outcomes (Kuechler, 2011; Thomas & Pender, 2008). When you ask people to join a group, they'll need to know what they are getting into (Rapin & Conyne, 1999; Young, 2013).

Putting a new group together is definitely not just a matter of rounding up a bunch of people and putting them in a room together. There are all the emotional and psychological variables of the people with whom you anticipate working that need to be considered and all the logistical details that then need to be taken into account. Naturally, you'll want your logistics to be able to optimally respond to the needs of the people your group will be serving.

When you are planning for a new group, the devil, as they say, is truly in the details (Tomasulo, 1998). Everything associated with getting a new group together—from where you hold it to how you recruit and screen people to be in it—will affect how well this group goes.

This chapter will help you appreciate the range of things that need to be done in planning for a new group.

Find a Coleader

Whenever you're setting up a new group, think about finding a coleader to share the experience with you. A coleader will share the responsibility for planning and

---

PLANNING FOR A NEW GROUP

- Finding a Coleader
- Establishing a Setting
- Defining Membership
- Setting Time/Length of Meeting
- Establishing Supervision
- Getting Permissions

- Setting Goals and Objectives
- Developing a Group Game Plan
- Member Recruitment
- Member Screening
- Pregroup Training
- Creating Ground Rules

- Evaluation

---

running the group, and he or she will be someone with whom you can regularly consult about how things are going in the group.

Having a coleader simply makes the whole experience more fun for you, and it also affords the people in your group the opportunity to watch two different leadership personalities in action.

When you're thinking about a new group, a coleader is someone who can help think through all the details involved in planning to ensure a successful start to the group. Then, when the group is up and running, he or she is someone who can share the leadership responsibilities—you can take turns being the active leader, with the less active one being more observant of the dynamics unfolding in the group. And when a group meeting has ended, the coleader is someone with whom you can debrief, process the experience, and do some troubleshooting.

Naturally, circumstances may dictate that working with a coleader will not be possible, but it's almost always preferable to work with someone else, if you can. If you're leading a mixed-gender group, it probably makes best sense to work with a coleader of the opposite sex—and with someone of the same sex for a single-gender group.

Goals and Objectives

As you begin to think about forming a new group, you will want to first consider why you're doing it. What are you meaning to accomplish by forming this group? How will it be good for people? Your group needs a reason for being, and this will translate into some broad, general statements about what your goals are for the people who will be engaged in this experience. Individuals may have their own specific goals, their reasons for joining this group (Wenzel, Liese, Beck, & Friedman-Wheeler, 2012), but there should additionally be some broad, overarching goals that are common to all who join.

Then you will also want to think about specific learning objectives within those broadly defined goals (Pitkala et al., 2004). What, specifically, would you want people to take away from this group experience? What will be the anticipated outcomes for individuals, either in terms of how people think and feel, or perhaps in terms of how their behavior will change?

These goals and learning objectives can help keep you on track as your group gets under way and then guide you along the way as it proceeds to develop. These are the directional compass, the reminder of what you are trying to accomplish with this experience. These are the things you can point to when you are talking with people who are interested in finding out more about whether they want to sign on for this group experience—these are the things people can hope to get out of being in the group.

You'll want to make sure that once you're comfortable with the goals and objectives that you've articulated, the relevant others are informed and afforded the opportunity for input about these, as well. If you work in a school or agency, you will want to make sure your administration is on board with these goals and objectives, and if you are working with a coleader, you'll certainly want to make sure that both of you are in sync with these.

Finally, you'll want to include these for discussion either before or during your group's first meeting to ensure that all of your members are also aware of what's in store for them. All this sharing of the goals and objectives can help ensure that you, your coleader, your group members—and whoever else needs to be involved—are moving ahead in the same direction.

Developing a Group Game Plan

The group game plan is your planned set of discussion topics, curriculum, exercises, and/or any other activities that you plan to use in the group. These activities you plan should be congruent with and support the goals and learning objectives that you've already outlined.

Sometimes your plan will very carefully plot out the activities that will be used in every group session for the lifetime of the group. These plans resemble a course curriculum and are typically used in psycho-educational groups, where the primary group intent is to teach specific skills.

Other groups will require that you do a lot of planning at the front end, but won't necessitate that you explicitly plan activities for the entire life of the group. The idea here is that the group will need to meet for a while before you can plot activities for its later sessions. Planning then becomes a continual part of your work, responding to the emerging needs of the group. You might plan activities for the first three or four sessions, and then reassess where to go from there, based on emerging group needs.

You will definitely want to create some activities or discussion points for your first meetings. These activities, also known as "structure," in group lingo, should be designed to get people talking and/or doing things together in a way that begins to make some connections between people, as well as to help reduce some early group jitters. Many of these structured activities, oftentimes called group exercises, have been designed for use with groups. You may want to look at and use some of these, or you may want to design your own. We'll look at the use of exercises in groups more thoroughly in the next chapter, and I'll make some recommendations about where you can go to find good exercises to use with your group.

I would suggest that if you are new to group work, you put a lot of structure into your groups. Have lots of activities planned, and then you can decide how many of these you want to use, depending on what transpires. It's always easier to let go of things you planned in order to respond to something that's come up in the group than it is to come up with something spontaneously when the group runs out of steam or when it stalls looking for something new to do. I strongly suggest that you'll always want more material than you can use—it's a comforting cushion against the anxiety of the dead space created by a group that doesn't know what to do or where to go next.

With experience, you'll be more comfortable with those long silences and periods of unplanned time and may even be able to deal with them productively with your own comments, for example, about the meaning of the silence. You'll experiment with the use of more *unstructured* time—maybe even entire sessions that are unstructured—as you develop your group leader legs under you. But in the beginning, have your bag of activities at your side.

You do want to make sure that the activities you plan are appropriate for your group. You want the activity to fit the developmental level of your group members, and you don't want the activity to be too much of a "stretch" for people. I once used an exercise that asked the undergraduates in my psychology class to act out favorite animal noises. This was early on in the class, and students didn't know one another well—the exercise bombed. You can avoid this kind of mistake by being smarter about the exercises you pick.

Defining Membership

How big is your group going to be? Will it be all one gender, or mixed? Are there some shared characteristics that members will all have in common, like some particular issue they are all working on, or not? Oftentimes, groups are built around these common issues that people share (O'Neill & Fry, 2013).

All these are questions you'll want to resolve before you actually start looking for group members. You'll want to once again think about your goals and overall intent for the purpose this group is to fulfill and then define and select members based on that assessment of who will work best in this group.

Think about the advantages, versus the drawbacks, of having a single-sex group, as well as the size of the group and the age of members. For some groups, like a group in which members are exploring sexual identity issues, you may want to maintain a same-sex membership (Morson & McInnis, 1983). For other groups, you may see advantages for having them run with mixed-sex membership.

Regarding the age of members in your group, particularly if you work with children and adolescents, there are obviously developmental differences to consider. In most adolescents between grades 9 and 12, for example, there are some very large social, physical, and emotional differences—what would be the advantages of having mixed-age levels as opposed to only a single, or perhaps two, ages?

All this needs to be thought out.

As a general rule, I think the range of 6 to 12 is a reasonable number of people to have in an adolescent or adult group, though some group theorists would argue for smaller numbers (Edelwich & Brodsky, 1992; Levine, 1979). Fewer than that can result in people feeling undue pressure to perform. A group that's larger than that can start to feel unwieldy for you, and intimidating for members. Naturally, special circumstances may dictate other sizes of groups with which you'll work. You'll simply accommodate your planning to those size differences.

Younger children or people with special issues (e.g., serious and persistent mental illness) will necessitate smaller group sizes. The youngest group I've worked with was 3-year-olds, and I think that group only had three members. A friend once told me that when having birthday parties for kids, base the number of invited children on the age of the child having the birthday—the age, plus one, defining the numbers to invite. For example, for a 6-year-old, seven kids. This seems like a pretty good guideline for numbers in a group for children, as well.

After you've figured out how many people you want to have in this group, you'll want to decide whether membership will be *open* or *closed*. The term *open* suggests that people can come and go (like an Open Speaker meeting of Alcoholics Anonymous), and *closed* means that the membership is fixed week to week, or perhaps with some variation, where specific members are replaced if they leave at some point during the life of the group. While there may be some particular reasons for having open membership in some of the groups you run, generally open membership makes it significantly more difficult for members to develop any sense of group cohesion or interpersonal trust, for obvious reasons.

Time: Number of Sessions and Length of Each Session

Oftentimes, the number of times a group will meet is defined by some already-defined time boundaries, like the length of a semester, or an academic school year.

The group simply meets as long as that time frame allows. Or you may decide that for 8 weeks, or some fixed length of time, meeting once a week makes sense.

Other groups, like intensive outpatient groups (e.g., for people with substance abuse problems), may meet more than once a week, and sometimes for longer periods of time. And still other groups may have no fixed endpoint. I know of one group that was formed as a support group for widows and widowers who had experienced the recent loss of partners and that is still continuing after 12 years. The group morphed from its original support group roots into a social support system. They continue to meet to talk with and support one another, as well as go bowling, share meals, and even travel together.

The length of each session will depend on your membership and the time constraints imposed by the organization within which you work. In a school, your session might be defined by a class period or by a lunch break. In an agency, you may be given a specific block of time with which to work. Generally, 1 to 2 hours seem to work best for groups of adolescents and adults, shorter time spans for younger children or people with special attention issues.

You might eventually, as you've gained some experience, experiment with alternative time formats. I've found, for example, with many of the groups I've run that staying and living together, where we also prepare and share meals together, promotes a sense of group community in a way that is difficult to do in a once a week format. This, of course, necessitates a look at the ground rules for how such an experience will be conducted, as you want to ensure an emotionally safe experience for everyone. If, for example, this is to be a multiple-day group and people can stay overnight in the space where you're holding the group, you'll want to ensure that people maintain their own private sleeping space. We'll talk more in later chapters about the risks involved in group work where members become romantically entangled—but for now, do what you can to make sure that these entanglements don't happen on your watch.

The Setting

I think that where you decide to meet with your group is one of the most important planning decisions you'll make. The space you choose sets the tone for the work you'll all do together. Your group space is your "office" for the group, and just like the office you maintain for seeing individuals, this group space should be similarly comfortable, intimacy promoting (without being overly intimate—so think about whether you really want a couch in there), and aesthetically pleasing.

Do the best with what you have, and think consciously about the space you pick and what you can do with it to make it appealing. The setting you choose communicates a lot to your group about what you think about them, and about the work you'll all do together. Many schools and agencies do not have great space for group meetings—the available space is oftentimes neither comfortable nor aesthetically pleasing, but you might be able to do something with it to make it more appealing. Maybe even some simple tinkering with the space, like the addition of a couple of floor lamps that you bring in yourself (what can be less appealing than overhead, fluorescent lighting?), might help.

Try to ensure that, at the least, the room is private and soundproof, so that what members share with one another cannot be overheard. You want to be working with your group in a place that communicates safety (Suzuki, 2003). If you wind up in a space that is not private—like a school cafeteria at lunchtime—try to ensure that the sharing that people do is appropriate to the setting.

I have the good fortune to teach many of my courses—including ones related to working with groups—at a beautiful retreat center surrounded by fields and woods. There are huge windows that let in ample light, a woodstove that creates a great atmosphere on cold, winter days, and lots of space for movement. It took many years of experimenting with group spaces to find what works best for the groups I lead. I know of the frustration of dealing with space that is not conducive to group work, and have spent many hours trying to compensate for space that is inadequate.

You've got a tremendous advantage if you've got access to good, aesthetically pleasing space. Aesthetics play a large role in helping a group work well, I believe. The space you pick reflects the degree of respect you have for the people with whom you work. If you can, do your group work in space that appeals to you.

Get creative in your thinking about the space for your group. If you are able, even think about having some of your group meetings outside. Going for walks, integrating the outdoors with what you're doing in your group, can be a great way to go. Some groups (e.g., Adventure, or Wilderness Therapy groups) may even spend the bulk of their time outside (Williams, 2000). One residential treatment center I worked in was located on a 300-acre working farm, and some of our best groups were those that spent time working in the gardens and with the animals.

You might not have ready access to a farm, but you can still think about how you might do something safely with your groups outside.

Recruiting Members

This can be one of the most challenging aspects of group work. Getting people into your group, and then maintaining their presence through the life of the group, can be a daunting task. It's not easy to get people to commit to coming to a group, particularly given how busy most people's lives are.

Naturally, the recruitment process is simplified when people are leveraged into your group, as by a Department of Probation and Parole or—as was the possible case with the group you were putting together for the earlier group vignette—by a school administration. While you always want to be working with a group of volunteer members, sometimes the options provided to people coming to your group (like going back to jail) can make attendance seem almost mandatory.

This kind of leveraged member "invitation" to participate in your group makes the recruitment process simpler, but it makes the initial work once the group gets started more complex. You will inevitably then have to deal with some resentment and reluctance, some of it passive (as with silence), some of it active (as with, "This group stuff stinks, and I don't want to be here."). I would suggest that, if you have the choice, it would be better to start your group-leading experience with groups full of people who really want to be there. We'll talk about these other groups, working with reluctant members, in later chapters.

If your group isn't going to have members leveraged into it, how will you recruit people? You have to think this through as carefully as any other planning aspect, with the full knowledge that even if you have a spectacular plan in place for what will happen in a group, it won't mean anything if you can't get people to come. The familiar adage, "If you build it, they will come," does not apply to group work.

This is all about marketing. When you're recruiting people for a new group, you have to think like someone in the sales world. What positive incentives can you create, and how can you make this experience really attractive for potential members?

Here are a number of things you could consider doing as part of your recruitment plan.

Name Your Group Strategically

If you were starting a new group for children whose families were going through the tumultuous changes associated with divorce and separation, would you really want to call this a "Children of Divorce" group?

Probably not. While technically accurate, the name is stigmatizing and unappealing. It will be better to find a name that suggests a bit about what the group will do, but is also engaging. A common name for middle school–aged children who are dealing with changing families, for example, is "The Banana Splits."

Use Incentives

What kinds of rewards can you use to entice people into your group (Cox & Klinger, 2011)? You believe, of course, that the experience itself will be inherently rewarding, and while that may be the case once people are involved, that might not be enough to get them to sign up for the group. Thus, what else is there that might appeal to potential group members?

Food is usually a helpful tool in attracting people, and not just young people. While pizza or ice cream might do the trick for adolescents, more sophisticated

Figure 6.1   Food Can Be Useful in Attracting New Members to a Group as It Has Been
for This Men's Group

culinary delights might attract an older crowd. I have been intrigued by and attracted
to any number of groups by the descriptions of the food that will be provided
(Figure 6.1).

If you're working with high school, college, or even graduate school students,
academic credit may be another appealing incentive you might be able to offer. Can
you offer your group experience for credit, either as a stand-alone or as an extra
credit for a relevant course? I've often worked with instructor colleagues who are
more than willing to offer extra credit for their students who have agreed to participate in my groups. Think about whether this is a strategy that might work for you.
Think really creatively about the incentives that might appeal to the people who
you serve. What could entice your target population into a group?

Training as Treatment

Sometimes people are more willing to get involved with a group if they expect
that they will receive training to help others. I have often worked with groups
of high school and college students who are interested in becoming peer counselors or prevention program directors. These students will sign up for training
opportunities—which function as groups where they learn a lot about themselves
in interaction with others—in ways that they would be reluctant to do if they
thought the focus would only be on receiving help for themselves.

Similarly, mental health agencies often offer training to help community volunteers identify and intervene with neighbors suffering from mental health crises. Here too, the volunteers learn a lot about their own interpersonal behavior in these training groups.

In a sense, all of the group "treatment" we do is a kind of training. We would hope that the people who complete our groups will take what they learn about effective interpersonal skills into their lives beyond the group. Not only will they be able to personally interact more effectively with others, but others will be positively influenced, as well. This ripple effect of human relations is part of the beauty of group work.

OTHER PLANNING CONCERNS

In addition to the planning concerns just reviewed, there are some other issues you'll need to consider. Some of these are not directly related to the actual work of the group but are important supports that will affect its well-being.

Supervision

Whenever you're working with people in some kind of helping role, supervision is important. Any time you are working as a counselor, social worker, or psychologist in any helping capacity, whether it's in a group or individual capacity, you will want to receive supervision. This is not the same thing as supervision in another kind of job setting, where oftentimes evaluation is the focus of supervision activity.

A supervisor in group work is someone who will help protect you and the people with whom you are working by providing another, usually more experienced, set of eyes and ears on what transpires with your group (DeLucia-Waack & Fauth, 2004). A supervisor will help you sort through some of the dynamics that are evolving in your group and help you strategize about best ways to proceed as the group grows and evolves. A good supervisor will help you come to grips with some of the reasons individuals in your groups trigger your strong reactions (countertransference). This is someone you should be able to trust, someone with whom you can share your fears about your own inadequacies, someone who can serve as a mentor and guide. Ideally, this is someone who shares your theoretical approach to group work. If you are pursuing some kind of practitioner license (e.g., clinical mental health counseling, clinical social work), you'll want to make sure that your supervisor has the necessary credentials to assist you.

A good supervisor may be hard to find. Finding someone whom you like, someone with whom you can feel comfortable being vulnerable about your perceptions of your group-leading faults, and someone whose work you admire is of a tall order. You may have to search your community for the right person, and you may have to pay for supervision.

If you work in an agency or school, your work to find a supervisor may be simplified. You may be simply assigned a supervisor. With a little luck, this person will have the right combination of skills and personality that fit your needs. Be assertive about what you need from your supervisor, and remember that your supervisory support is only as worthwhile as your ability to be open to suggestion. Try to maintain an attitude of openness to the feedback you're given about your work.

If your agency or school does not automatically provide supervision, seek it out on your own. If supervision is not available on-site, consider teaming with people in other schools or agencies to provide it for one another in peer supervision fashion.

Member Screening and Informed Consent

You want to ensure that the people coming into your group are appropriate and ready for the experience you're planning (MacNair-Semands, 1998). This means that you will most likely want to interview people before deciding whether they will be able to benefit from and contribute to this group experience. Naturally, some deciding factors will be easy: age, sex, issues that someone wants to examine (particularly if this is to be an issue-specific group, like our high school group with kids dealing with divorce).

Other factors, however, may be a bit more challenging, and this may be a bit more like deselecting people, rather than selecting potential members. Some people may be suffering from some kind of emotional or mental disorder that may make them inappropriate for your group, some people may simply have really poor impulse control, and some others may have so great a need to talk about themselves that you fear they would monopolize group discussions. In these cases, either another kind of group or perhaps individual counseling or attention would be more appropriate for them (Corey, Corey, Callahan, & Russell, 2004). You will be invested in finding the best experience that can help these individuals, knowing that the well-being of the group you have planned could be jeopardized by their presence, and that the group might not treat them well if they are allowed to participate. Of course, when you tell people of your decision about not being selected for this group, you want to put a positive spin on the other experience you've found for them. You don't want this to be experienced as a rejection.

Once you've invited members to participate in your group, based on whatever criteria you've deemed important, you may want to do some pregroup training, particularly with people who have never been in a group before (Zimpfer, 1991). This, in part, helps people decide whether this group you're inviting them into is right for them. This kind of pregroup discussion can be a great asset in helping guarantee the success of your group, particularly when you are dealing with people who have had little group experience (Bowman & DeLucia, 1993).

People need to have some idea of what to expect and of how to behave. They need to be briefed about informed consent guidelines for involvement in the group. This informed consent consists of a number of pieces of information that are important for people to know (Association for Specialists in Group Work, 1998). They need to know, for example, about your credentials and experience in leading groups, and about how you'll approach working with this group. They'll need to know about the goals of the group and about the confidentiality guidelines that the group will encompass. They'll need to know that once they get involved in the group, you won't have other kinds of relationships (e.g., friendships) with them. Informed consent defines the responsibilities each of you, member and leader, will have.

An example of a form you might use for this, which you would have new members sign, is included in the For Further Thought section at the end of this chapter.

Another Informed Consent Concern: Defining Ground Rules

Good things, even great things, happen in groups where people feel safe taking risks with one another. Part of the process of describing informed consent issues involves a discussion of the group's ground rules. Ground rules, some basic assumptions about how you will all operate, help make for safe group experiences (Rife, 1997). Before your group meets for the first time, you will want to give some consideration to some basic ground rules that you think are critical, given the characteristics of the group you'll be leading.

Once your group gets started, you'll want to go over ground rules with everyone. You'll share the ones you think are critical, and you'll ask other people what other ground rules would help to make this a safe experience for them. Safety in groups is key, and ground rules help ensure this safety (Corey, 2011; Korda & Pancrazio, 1989).

Most of the groups I lead now are with groups of graduate students, people who have good social skills and usually know a bit about groups and ground rules. Thus, the list of ground rules is short, what I call my "big three." Confidentiality is the biggest one (Plotkin, 1978), followed closely by "right to privacy," meaning that people have the right to not answer personal questions. The last of my three is borrowed from Project Adventure, a program that is a leader in adventure-based experiential education. They tell all of their program participants that any challenge that they choose to undertake is a personal challenge, a "challenge by choice." This means that no one will be coerced or pressured by the group into trying anything he or she doesn't want to—it's all about challenging oneself. I incorporate this same ethic, this same ground rule, into the groups I run. You may want to do the same.

Each of these ground rules will need to be discussed and negotiated with the new group. Confidentiality, in particular, is a multifaceted issue, and it will take some time to make sure that everyone fully understands it—and its limits—and it is brought on board with its fundamental tenets. We'll talk more of this when we discuss actually meeting for the first time with a group.

If you are planning on working with younger, or less sophisticated, groups of people, you will most likely want to add some more ground rules. With younger children, for example, who might be doing a lot of active physical exercises in groups, you might want to include rules about no running or body checks or you might want to address whatever other kinds of physical problems you might guess will develop. You might include a "one person speaking at a time" ground rule—or anything else that ensures a safe, relatively orderly experience for everyone.

I'm sure you get the idea—think about what kinds of things might happen in this group you've got and then determine what kinds of ground rules suit it best.

Permissions

In almost all situations where you are working with children under the age of 18, or with people who are under the guardianship of someone else, you'll need permission from the parents or guardian for those kids to participate in your groups (Decker, 2010). Parents, or guardians, have the right to refuse, for whatever reason they want. These reasons might be religious or personal, or—as is possibly the case with the hypothetical group of teens you considered putting together earlier in this chapter—they may be simply suspicious of the kinds of information that might be shared in the group. Families with secrets might be reluctant to have their children participate in groups, so getting their permission can be tricky.

School counselors I know will oftentimes deal with this permissions issue by sending out a notice to parents at the beginning of a school year, saying something like, "Your child may be invited to participate in any number of personal growth experiences during this coming academic year. Please let us know if you would prefer that your child not participate." This, then, puts the onus of responsibility on the parent for saying "no," as opposed to having to get a "yes" from every parent every time you want to start a new group.

That being said, you want to see yourself as an ally of the child's parents. It is the rare parent who doesn't want the best for his or her child, so you'll be able to work with them as a partner in the child's best interests. Even—or perhaps especially—parents in desperate circumstances almost always want their children to be healthy and happy. I've worked with children of drug-addicted parents, for example, who wanted the children to be involved in groups so that these children could be helped to understand that the addiction in the family was not their fault.

You'll want to assure the parent that you'll be letting them know if there is anything that gets shared that is potentially dangerous (e.g., threats of self or other harm), and other specifics as defined by both you and the child. The parents need to know that you are not taking over their job. We'll talk more about this sharing with parents and confidentiality guidelines in a later section of this chapter, as well as in Chapter 7, which discusses first group meetings.

In some cases, you may be working with children in a setting where parental permission is not required and may even be discouraged. These are situations in which children, aged 12 and above, are looking to you for services for so-called adult problems, like drug use or sexual behavior. In organizations that provide these services, you are allowed to serve children without parental permission. If you work in an agency that provides these kinds of services, you'll want to get very clear about what the permission and confidentiality guidelines are.

Evaluation

How will you know if your group has done what you intended it to do? How will you know if people have either enjoyed the experience or changed in any way because of it? The only way you'll have a sense of what impact a group has had on people's lives will be if you devise some way of evaluating the experience (Little, 2011; Pender, 2012).

There are a variety of ways you can approach evaluating group experiences, some of which are very informal—like simply asking the group how things have gone—and some of which take a more formal written approach (Trotzer, 1999). When we look later at how to end a group, we'll discuss ways the informal talking evaluations can be handled in the context of wrapping things up. Talking at the end about what has happened in the group both serves as a good way to terminate the group and also serves a rough evaluation purpose.

Sometimes you might want to get a sense of whether people have changed attitudes or behaviors or gained knowledge about specific things you've been teaching about in your groups. In this case, you'll want to do some kind of pre- and postgroup evaluation or assessment. You might put this assessment package together yourself, or if you are using some kind of packaged group curriculum (as in some psycho-educational group experiences), assessment tools might be a part of the package. Alternatively, you might be working in an agency or school where you will be asked to use assessment tools that are used for all group experiences there. In the evaluations I do for my courses, for example, I use the same evaluation form that is used by all other instructors at my college, and I supplement that with discussion about things specific to this experience.

You may do periodic evaluative check-ins during the life of the group, mostly to see how things are going. Generally, however, evaluation of a group experience comes at the end of the group. You will want to know, whether you are designing your own evaluation device, or using one that is given to you, how the group has influenced people. How have they liked the experience, and what would they do to change it next time around? What have they learned, and how will their behaviors change, or not?

There are a variety of ways that you can do this evaluation. You can use questionnaires or checklists, or you can do personal interviews, or have the entire group discuss the experience. Whether you evaluate formally or informally, or with written assessment tools or in personal discussion, it's important that somehow you do it. This is the only way you will know about whether your group has in any way had any effect (Young, Reysen, Eskridge, & Ohrt, 2013).

It may be helpful for you to actually put a list together of all the planning details involved for creating a new group. This checklist may help.

GROUP PLANNING CHECKLIST

Have You

- developed a clearly articulated set of goals and learning objectives?
- developed a plan of action and activities you want to use?
- defined your group membership—how many you'd like, what characteristics they share, and whether the group will be open or closed?
- decided how many meetings you'll hold, and how long each will be?
- thought about where you'll meet?
- strategized about how you'll get people to join the group?
- considered whether you'll have a coleader, and who that person will be?
- found a good supervisor?
- screened potential members and provided them with information about what to expect in the group?
- clearly articulated informed consent concerns and had them sign appropriate forms?
- gotten necessary permissions from parents/guardians?
- defined preliminary ground rules?
- established a way you'll evaluate the group experience?

Are there any other concerns? List.

PLANNING FOR THE *NEW DIRECTIONS* GROUP

A couple of years ago, two of my former students, both of whom are now working as counselors in an area high school, came to me for some advice about a new group they were going to set up and run. Vanessa and Gary were both counselors in the school. Vanessa was a school counselor, and Gary was the school-based mental health clinician. He'd been placed to work there by the area's community mental health agency.

The school's principal had requested that Vanessa and Gary work together to design and implement a semester-long group for some students who were having difficulty because of family problems. The principal gave them a list of 15 names of students he thought could benefit from some kind of group experience. All of these students had parents who were going through a process of separation or divorce.

Gary and Vanessa knew a number of these students on the list, and they agreed that these kids were struggling, both emotionally and academically. They also agreed with their principal that by helping make some connections between these students, as well as by teaching them some skills for coping with their family situations, a group experience could be helpful.

I suggested that they begin by brainstorming a list of all the emotional/ psychological and behavioral "issues" that these students might be bringing into such a group. They said that they knew some of the kids quite well and that they knew about some of the thoughts, feelings, and behaviors that would be at play in this new group. Some of the other students they knew less well. With these others, they had to make some assumptions about how they were doing. Vanessa and Gary considered how these young people might be thinking and behaving in reaction to their changing families. Some of them might be doing quite well, seemingly unfazed by the changes in their families, but others, they thought, would undoubtedly be struggling. By the time they finished their brainstorming, they had quite a list of possible "issues," a long list that included possible feelings of abandonment, depression, anger, anxiety, and behaviors such as the potential for drug and alcohol abuse and other kinds of acting out.

Then, with their long list of issues in hand, I asked that they begin to consider all those things they needed to do before the group was to meet for the first time. "What," I asked, "do you need to put in place to ensure that this group will get off on the right foot? Considering the issues—all of the thoughts, feelings, and behaviors—that your students will be coming in with, how can you effectively plan in a way that almost certainly guarantees that this group will be successful? How can you plan for all the details that will help make this a great group?"

Put together a list, I suggested, of all the big things you need to plan—starting with the group's goals and objectives, for example—as well as all the other things—like where you'll meet and how you'll decide who will be in this group—that anticipate the issues that these students will bring to the experience.

And then, as they were to begin to put together their planning list, I asked them to consider a name for the group, mostly so they could call it something other than "the new group" in our discussions. After trying out and rejecting a number of alternatives, they settled on *New Directions*, a name they thought might be appealing to this group of high school students. I went along with this thinking that, at least, it didn't suggest any stigma.

REFLECTION EXERCISE: PLANNING FOR A NEW GROUP

Here's a situation to consider. Assume that you work in a community social service agency that deals with families and children. Your program director has asked you to put together and run a group for new parents of young children. These people all have children who have been identified as being at risk of removal from the home because of the parents' suspected abuse and/or neglect.

You'll want to design your group with the intent of helping people talk with one another about the struggles of being a parent, while also helping them develop some positive parenting skills. The group, then, will be a mixed process (talking about personal parenting difficulties) and content (the psycho-educational skills training) experience.

Begin to think about how you would go about constructing a new group for these parents. Just as you saw was done in the group vignette at the beginning of the chapter, first consider all the potential issues and concerns—the thoughts, feelings, and behaviors—that these people might be bringing in to a new group experience. Once you've considered this thoroughly, think about all the things you'd want to have in place, all the things you'd want to do, before the group meets for the first time. You don't need to be overly specific about these plans at this point. Thus, while you think a series of parenting skills training sessions might be important, for example, you don't need to specify here exactly what those would be. Check your plan carefully to make sure that it contains all those things that need to be done to ensure that this group will get off to a good start.

How well does your plan anticipate the details that were articulated in what you've just read about planning for a new group? What gaps do you see in your plans, and where might difficulties arise because of these? Again, make some notes about these.

GROUP FISHBOWL LAB PRACTICE EXERCISE: PLANNING

For this exercise, it will be helpful if you have markers and an easel with a flip pad, or something equivalent, that you can make notes on that everyone can see.

Following the example of group fishbowls described in earlier chapters, assemble a group of your colleagues, all of whom have just completed the previous Reflection Exercise, with two of you as the designated coleaders. A group of 7 to 10 members, including the coleaders, would be a good number of people for this. This group will sit in a circle, with others watching, as observers. The observers will sit silently during the exercise and will take notes on what they see and hear, being prepared to give feedback about the proceedings at the end of the exercise. The observers should, in particular, be watching for those leader behaviors (things that are said or done) that seem to promote productive member interaction. The observers should also keep time, ending the discussion after the allocated time for this—20 to 30 minutes is probably sufficient.

The leaders' job is to initiate and facilitate a conversation—lasting perhaps 20 to 30 minutes—among the members about their planning ideas for the new group they were instructed to plan for in the preceding Reflection Exercise. The leaders, or someone designated, could make two lists on the flip pad: one of potential "issues" that the new group might encounter and the second of all the things that need to be done before the group meets for the first time. The leaders will want to do what they can to make sure that everyone is involved in the discussion. They should feel free to add their own ideas about these potential issues and planning concerns.

When this discussion is over, the observers can share their observations and ideas about what has transpired, again, focusing on those leader skills that seemed to move the conversation in positive directions. This feedback session should be supportive and positive, while at the same time highlighting things that might have been done differently.

CONCLUDING THOUGHTS: SOME FINAL PLANNING ADVICE

If there's any single piece of advice I can give you in your planning efforts to begin a new group, it's to overplan. Try to anticipate as many details as you can, all the little logistical things that can help your group go well, and all those things that could potentially derail it. Don't rely solely on the planning suggestions made in this chapter. Utilize a variety of source materials in your group-planning efforts (Rosenthal, 1998).

There have been times when I've planned some activities for a group and wound up running out of activities well before the end of the group. Don't let this happen to you. Always have at least as much activity planned as you think will be needed, or even more. You're not compelled to use all the activities you plan, and oftentimes, you might want to drop any and all activities to deal with material that comes up in the group. Experience, supervision, and consultation with coleaders will help you gain the sense of when and how to do this. But remember, you can always drop and not use your overloaded activity—it's much more difficult to create it when you're in the midst of the group.

The other primary piece of advice I can offer is to plan for ample time for your group to talk about an exercise after it's completed. Remember that the primary purpose of the activity is not the activity itself; rather it is the purpose it serves for the group. Talking about the exercise and what it's meant to the group will most likely be more valuable than the exercise itself.

In any new group, expect the unexpected. You won't be able to totally control all the events that will affect your group, but you should be able to anticipate some of them. The more of these you can incorporate into your plan, the more secure you'll feel about starting the new group.

Planning for a new group is fun. It's like traveling, where a third of the fun of a trip is in the planning, a third is in the actual trip, and a third is in talking and reflecting about it afterward.

Plan well, and have a great group!

FOR FURTHER THOUGHT

1. Think about some kind of group that you might want to lead, or that you might be asked to lead in a place where you work. This might be an agency, a school, or a private setting. Then consider who you might work with as a coleader. Finally, put together a plan for this group, utilizing all the planning details outlined in this chapter.

   Make a list of all the incentives you think you could offer to make this group attractive to potential members.

2. Take a list of your planning items—use either your own or the ones described in this chapter—to someone you know who regularly leads groups. Ask this person to take a look at your list, and ask him or her what items he or she thinks should be changed, and what he or she would add.

3. Come up with three or four different names for the group that you were asked to plan in the Reflection and Discussion Exercise in this chapter.

4. Following is an example of a form that could be used to confirm that a potential group member understands informed consent. This is the kind of informed consent form you might ask a new member to read and sign before participating in a new group. (Thanks to Chuck Roberts of the Center for Biblical Counseling, McKinney, Texas, for the use of this form.)

INFORMED CONSENT: GROUP COUNSELING

Welcome to Your Group Experience!

Group counseling can be a powerful and valuable venue for healing and growth. It is the desire of your group facilitator(s) that you reap all the benefits a group has to offer. To help this occur, groups are structured to include the following elements:

- A safe environment in which you are able to feel respected and valued as you work—an understanding of group goals and group norms

- Investment by both your facilitator(s) and members to produce a consistent group experience

A Safe Environment

A safe environment is created and maintained by both the facilitator(s) of a group and its members. Primary ingredients are mutual respect and a chance to create trust. Another primary ingredient for a safe environment has to do with confidentiality. Your group facilitator(s) are bound by law to maintain confidentiality, as group members are bound by honor to keep what is said in the group in the group. We realize that you may want to share what you are learning about yourself in group with a significant other. This is fine as long as you remember not to talk about how events unfold in group or in any other way compromise the confidentiality of other group members.

The facilitator(s) of your group will ask you to sign a release form so that they can talk with your individual therapist. This is a safeguard for you that allows consultation between group leaders and your individual therapist should the need arise. This also provides you with extra support should a difficult issue come up in group that may need more individual attention.

Limits of Confidentiality

- If you are a threat to yourself or others (showing suicidal or homicidal intent), your facilitator(s) may need to report your statements and/or behaviors to your family, your therapist, or other appropriate mental health or law enforcement professionals in order to keep you and others safe.

- There are a broad range of events that are reportable under child protection statues. Physical or sexual abuse of a child will be reported to Child Protective Services. When the victim of child abuse is older than age 18, reporting is not mandatory unless there are minors still living with the abuser, who may be in danger. Elder abuse is also required to be reported to the appropriate authorities.

(Continued)

(Continued)

- If a court of law orders a subpoena of case records or testimony, your facilitator(s) will first assert "privilege" (which is your right to deny the release of your records although this is not available in all states for group discussions). Your facilitator(s) will release records if a court denies the assertion of privilege and orders the release of records. Records may also be released with your written permission. Records will include only your personal progress in group—not information about other group members.

- Facilitators may consult with other professionals regarding group interactions. This allows a freedom to gain other perspectives and ideas concerning how best to help you reach your goals in group. No identifying information is shared in such consultations unless a release has been obtained from you as a group member.

Other Safety Factors

- Members of a group may not use drugs or alcohol before or during group
- Members of a group should not engage in discussion of group issues outside of group
- Members of group should remember that keeping confidentiality allows for an environment where trust can be built and all members may benefit from the group experience
- Your group facilitator(s) will monitor discussions and maintain a respectful environment to keep safety and trust a priority

Attendance

Your presence in group is highly important. A group dynamic is formed that helps create an environment for growth and change. If you are absent from the group, this dynamic suffers and affects the experience of you and other members of the group. Therefore, your facilitator(s) would ask that you make this commitment a top priority for the duration of the group. It is understood that occasionally an emergency may occur that will prevent you from attending group. If you are faced with an emergency or sudden illness, please contact your facilitator(s) before group begins to let them know you will not be present.

Because it usually takes several group sessions for clients to "settle in" and receive the full benefits a therapy group provides, we ask incoming members to make a 10-week commitment when they join a group (except for time-limited groups). We also ask members to give a 3-week notice when they decide to leave a group. We ask this because each member of a group is important—your presence and your absence affects members and facilitators—and we want to allow time for members to process when members choose to leave.

What to Expect

Group time consists of both teaching and processing time. Processing may revolve around an issue one member of the group is working on with time for structured feedback and reactions by other members of the group. At times, the group may focus on a topic with all members verbally participating. In either case, the group dynamic offers a place where you can experience support, give support, understand more clearly how you relate to others, and examine your own beliefs about yourself, God, and the world around you. These dynamics provide a very powerful environment for change.

(Continued)

Remember, the more you give of yourself during the sessions, the more you will receive. The more honest and open you are, the more you allow for insight and growth.

Fees

The fee for this group is $_____ per 90 minute session. (You must sign a release form for your individual therapist to participate in this group.) You are responsible to pay for each session except in the case of a true emergency. When a client is a minor, counseling fees are the responsibility of the parent/parents or legal guardian.

REFERENCES

Association for Specialists in Group Work. (1998). Best practice guidelines. *Journal for Specialists in Group Work, 23*(3), 237–244.

Bowman, V., & DeLucia, L. (1993). Preparation for group therapy: The effects of preparer and modality on group process and individual functioning. *Journal for Specialists in Group Work, 18,* 67–79.

Corey, G. (2011). Doing it by the book: Ethical issues in teaching a group didactically and experientially. In W. Johnson & G. P. Koocher (Eds.), *Ethical conundrums, quandaries, and predicaments in mental health practice: A casebook from the files of experts* (pp. 277–285). New York, NY: Oxford University Press.

Corey, G., Corey, M., Callahan, P., & Russell, J. (2004). *Group techniques* (3rd ed.). Pacific Grove, CA: Brooks/Cole.

Cox, W., & Klinger, E. (2011). Systematic motivational counseling: From motivational assessment to motivational change. In W. Cox & E. Klinger (Eds.), *Handbook of motivational counseling: Goal-based approaches to assessment and intervention with addiction and other problems* (2nd ed., pp. 275–302). Hoboken, NJ: Wiley.

Decker, E. (2010). Modeling a nondefensive and empathic acceptance of group resistance in a school-based anger management group with urban adolescents. In S. Fehr (Ed.), *101 Interventions in group therapy* (Rev. ed., pp. 237–241). New York, NY: Taylor & Francis.

DeLucia-Waack, J. L., & Fauth, J. (2004). Effective supervision of group leaders: Current theory, research, and implications for practice. In J. L. DeLucia-Waack, D. A. Gerrity, C. R. Kalodner, & M. T. Riva (Eds.), *Handbook of group counseling and psychotherapy* (pp. 136–150). Thousand Oaks, CA: Sage.

Edelwich, J., & Brodsky, A. (1992). *Group counseling for the resistant client.* New York, NY: Lexington Books.

Gelso, C. J., & Carter, J. A. (1985). The relationship in counseling and psychotherapy: Components, consequences, and theoretical antecedents. *The Counseling Psychologist, 13*(2), 155–243.

Korda, L. J., & Pancrazio, J. J. (1989). Limiting negative outcome in group practice. *Journal for Specialists in Group Work, 14*(2), 112–120.

Kuechler, C. F. (2011). Review of dynamics and skills of group counseling. *Social work with groups: A Journal of Community and Clinical Practice, 34*(2), 210–212.

Levine, B. (1979). *Group psychotherapy: Practice and development.* Englewood Cliffs, NJ: Prentice Hall.

Little, N. (2011). Review of group process guidelines for leading groups and classes. *Psychiatric Rehabilitation Journal, 34*(4), 337–338.

MacNair-Semands, R. (1998). Encompassing the complexity of group work. *Journal for Specialists in Group Work, 23,* 208–214.

Morson, T., & McInnis, R. (1983). Sexual identity issues in group work: Gender, social sex role, and sexual orientation considerations. *Social Work With Groups: A Journal of Community and Clinical Practice, 6*(3–4), 67–77.

O'Neill, D., & Fry, M. (2013). The grief group: A university and hospice collaboration. *Journal of College Student Development, 54*(4), 430–432.

Pender, R. L. (2012). ASGW best practice guidelines: An evaluation of the Duluth model. *Journal for Specialists in Group Work, 37*(3), 218–231.

Pitkala, K. H., Blomquist, L. L., Routasalo, P. P., Saarenheimo, M. M., Karvinen, E. E., Oikarinen, U. U., & Mantyranta, T. T. (2004). Leading groups of older people: A description and evaluation of the education of professionals. *Educational Gerontology, 30*(10), 821–833.

Plotkin, R. (1978). Confidentiality in group counseling. *APA Monitor, March,* 14.

Rapin, L., & Conyne, R. (1999). Best practices in group counseling. In J. Trotzer (Ed.), *The counselor and the group: Integrating, theory, training, and practice* (pp. 253–276). Philadelphia, PA: Accelerated Development.

Rife, J. C. (1997). Group counseling model for helping older women secure employment. *Clinical Gerontologist: Journal of Aging and Mental Health, 18*(1), 43–47.

Rosenthal, H. (1998). *Favorite counseling and therapy techniques.* Philadelphia, PA: Accelerated Development.

Suzuki, A. (2003). The intervention for the group of juvenile delinquents by the school counselor: Providing the place where they felt a sense of relief in the school. *Japanese Journal of Counseling Science, 36*(4), 464–472.

Thomas, R., & Pender, D. (2008). Association for specialists in group work: Best practice guidelines 2007 revisions. *Journal for Specialists in Group Work, 33,* 111–117.

Tomasulo, D. (1998). *Action methods in group psychotherapy.* Philadelphia, PA: Accelerated Development.

Trotzer, J. (1999). *The counselor and the group* (4th ed.). Philadelphia, PA: Accelerated Development.

Wenzel, A., Liese, B. S., Beck, A. T., & Friedman-Wheeler, D. G. (2012). *Group cognitive therapy for addictions.* New York, NY: Guilford Press.

Williams, B. (2000). The treatment of adolescent populations: An institutional vs. a wilderness setting. *Journal of Child & Adolescent Group Therapy, 10*(1), 47–56.

Young, T. L. (2013). Using motivational interviewing within the early stages of group development. *Journal for Specialists in Group Work, 38*(2), 169–181.

Young, T. L., Reysen, R., Eskridge, T., & Ohrt, J. H. (2013). Personal growth groups: Measuring outcome and evaluating impact. *Journal for Specialists in Group Work, 38*(1), 52–67.

Zimpfer, D. (1991). Pre-training for group work: A review. *Journal for Specialists in Group Work, 16,* 264–269.

Chapter 7

Getting Your Group Started

First comes thought; then organization of that thought, into ideas and plans—then transformation of those plans into reality. The beginning, as you will observe, is in your imagination.

—Napoleon Hill

Some years ago, I led a group comprising widows and widowers. This was a group designed for people dealing with issues of death and loss. Each of these people had been married or partnered to someone who had died within the past year. Each of them had gone through periods of shock and some denial in reaction to the death, and now they were in a "what now" period of their coming to grips with their loss.

I remember some of the folks in this group quite well, and one in particular. Alisha was very depressed and sad. She missed her husband, Alan, bitterly. He had been a strong and virile kind of guy, a man's man, and they had gone together on a number of adventurous hiking expeditions in different, remote sites around the world. They had enjoyed each other's company so much that they had decided not to have children, for they thought that children might interfere with their closeness. This reliance on only each other meant that they didn't have many friends outside of their relationship with each other, as well.

Additionally, Alan had generally, as she put it, "taken care of everything." He had paid the bills, taken care of the house repairs, and even maintained the yard. He had also provided well for his family as the Chief Financial Officer of a successful local business, which had allowed Alisha to stay at home and concentrate on her artwork, her painting. The fact that his death was sudden, a heart attack while shoveling snow, was particularly difficult for her. She hadn't had an opportunity to say good-bye.

Alisha had recently made a decision to stop using antidepressant medications. The medications had dulled her depression, but they had also dulled her ability to feel. She said that she was ready to deal with the pain of the death and that she was alternately very sad and very angry. How, she asked, could he leave her with all these responsibilities and without her best friend? The savings account they had planned on using for retirement was running low, and she was going to have to find a job, not to mention learning how to do all those things he'd taken care of for both of them. She was not happy about any of these.

We were at the end of our first meeting. We had done our rounds of introductions, and people had shared some fairly intimate information about their current situations and about their lives with their spouses before and during the illnesses that had taken them away. The group had listened patiently as Alisha had taken more than her share of the group's time to talk about her life, her loss, and her feelings about it all. Her pain about her loss, as well as about the implications the loss had for her new life, was palpable.

As we came to the last few minutes of this first meeting, Alisha said, "I really appreciate you listening to me. I must sound like such a whiner. . . . I'm just so lost and sad." She sobbed quietly.

We all sat there for a bit, and then I said, "This is just really, really hard. Your husband has died, and not only have you lost your best friend, but now you've also got to relearn how to do your life." She kept on crying.

Then someone in the group said, "I'm really looking forward to hearing more stories about all the trips you two did together. He must have been quite a guy."

At this, Alisha actually stopped crying and looked up. She said, "That's great. There's lots to tell. He was wonderful."

And then someone else said, "Yep, and I bet there's some stuff that wasn't all hunky dory, too. I bet he wasn't Mr. Fantastic all the time. That's what I want to hear about." In response to this, Alisha actually kind of laughed, saying, "You got it."

"And maybe," said yet someone else, "we can help you learn how to balance a checkbook and get ready for a job."

That comment ended our first group together. Taken together, these last three remarks seemed a fitting way of capturing the essence of our future work with Alisha and about our potential work together. We would encourage her to talk about her pain of loss, to experience the sadness and anger of her husband's death, and also to help her see him and their relationship in a realistic, human—not idealized—way. Finally, we could help her develop the skills necessary to live a new life, a life without Alan.

We had done, at least for Alisha, what a first group can optimally do for anyone—provide some support, begin to create some authentic connections with other people, and hold out some hope that this will be a productive and useful experience where something new can be learned.

This had the potential to be a great group.

STARTING A NEW GROUP

Starting a new group can really be an exciting experience. All the planning and thought that have gone into getting ready are now about to pay off as you actually begin.

This chapter talks about the tasks new groups need to accomplish and the skills you'll need to have with you to successfully help a new group get off the ground. Some of the skills discussed here will be exactly like the skills you'd use in individual helping relationships, and some are unique to group work.

All these skills will be supported by the genuine interest you have in these people, your natural kindness as you think about and respond to them, and your enthusiasm for leading this new experience.

This chapter will help you gain a better understanding of what to expect in a new group. It will help you understand the skills you'll need and the things that need to be accomplished to ensure that everything gets off to a good start.

The Dynamics of a New Group

There will be lots of anticipatory anxiety in the room as your group meets for the first time. You'll most likely be wondering if you've prepared adequately for all that is to come (Counselman, 2012). This simply comes with the territory; it's all a natural

---

STARTING A NEW GROUP

- New Group Dynamics: The Group as Family and Hidden Agendas
- How to Observe a Group Using Different Levels of Observation
- Essential Tasks: What Needs to Happen in a New Group
- Essential Skills for Starting a New Group
- Pitfalls to Avoid in Starting a New Group

part of being a group leader. It's a little bit like being an actor in a live theater, getting ready to go out on stage. Some stage fright can actually make for a better performance—too much, naturally, is not helpful.

Some of what will help you deal with these little doubts will be knowledge that you have some natural and learned skills that you will be able to put in motion once things begin. The more you can think consciously about and practice these skills before you're in a leadership position, the more you'll trust that you'll be able to use them in new group experiences. As you gain some experience, the skill set you utilize will feel more natural, and you will simply have more confidence in your ability to use these skills well.

You won't be the only one in your group who is experiencing some anxiety. Most of your members will also be at least a little nervous. For some, this anxiety won't be a big deal—for others, it will be huge (Vassilopoulos, 2005). You, at least, know the game plan, what activities, what kind of structure these first meetings will utilize. Unless you've talked about this with your members already, they have no knowledge of this, and some of these people might be quite anxious about not knowing what's to come.

The activities you've planned will help deal with some of this early anxiety, once things get under way. Your good will and interest in finding out about people will also help diminish this anxiety somewhat (Huang, Zhang, Liu, & Zhu, 2012). Certainly, the skills you bring to this experience, as well as your understanding of your new members' developmental needs, will also serve to make people feel more comfortable (Rasmussen, 1999). Most people want to be liked and accepted, and some of your members will have concerns about how they'll do with this new group of people. Sometimes, the nervousness is simply related to not knowing what's going to happen.

There may be more to it than this, however. I've come to see that it's not always just a fear of the unknown, or uncertainty about what is going to come. Additionally, for many people, there have actually been negative experiences in groups, times when they've been judged, or ignored, or even ridiculed (Nesdale et al., 2010). Sometimes, these slights have been unintentional but have nevertheless been hurtful. Thus, for some of the people in your groups, there will not only be the fear of the unknown but also the fear that this group experience will repeat some past group abuse. Additionally, some people may be extremely shy and may have studiously avoided group situations (Marmarosh, Markin, & Spiegel, 2013). This new experience may be pushing them far away from their comfort zones.

This anxiety can take different forms. Some people may express it directly and talk about being anxious or afraid. Some other people express it actively but indirectly, by being belligerent or by challenging your authority. Still other people may express it more passively, by being silent. Mostly, I think, it is our job to understand that the anxiety is present and to also understand that behind the anxiety—no matter how difficult the outside behavior—there is someone yearning for contact and desiring to be known and accepted.

This is critically important for anyone acting in a helping role—the capacity to see the person behind the behavior. It is our job to find the beauty of the person hidden behind the wall of defenses.

Don't get me wrong—sometimes that yearning for contact is really hidden, and sometimes you may be dealing with people in groups who have histories of having not only experienced, but also perpetrated, some pretty awful stuff. Nevertheless, you need to maintain a belief that the people whom you're dealing with are capable of looking at and changing behaviors in a way that will more successfully help them meet some basic needs for affection and acceptance.

The Group as Family

In a sense, your group is a replication of the first group any of your members were in, their family. Everyone in the group—your members, your coleader, and you—bring your own family histories into this new group experience. With good fortune, this group will also come to feel like a new family, with cohesive, close attachments among members.

This new group is a recapitulation, a subtle reminder (perhaps even unconscious, in psychoanalytic terms), of each person's experience of his or her family (Rippa, Rippa, & Moss, 2013). Some of these family histories may have been positive, some not. You may be able to detect, even this early on, some of the roles that people played in their own families, the roles we discussed earlier—the hero, mascot, lost child, or scapegoat—being played out in this new "family" group.

All of this cumulative history is, on some level, at play as this new group gets under way. It is our job, as savvy group leaders, to look behind the obvious and to think more critically about these hidden personal and family histories (Greene, 2012).

Families today, of course, take all kinds of forms, but there is generally always at least one parent or guardian at the helm, and then there are the kids. In your new group, you symbolically represent a parent, and if there's a coleader with whom you're working, he or she is the other parent.

The people in your group will expect you—the symbolic parent—to provide direction. If you don't provide direction, they will probably get even more anxious and act out. This will not be much fun for you, or for them. Hence, best to plan some activities and act as the ringmaster. While you will be looking for the group to eventually assume more responsibility for itself, and not rely so much on your direction, in the beginning you'll want act as the responsible "parent."

Individual members may also be looking at and dealing with you in some of the same ways they have dealt with other people "in charge," like their real parents. I—and I am not alone in this—have come to believe that this *transference* is a very real phenomenon in group work, and as a group member personally; sometimes it's not about you but rather about someone from the past (Dwivedi, 1993; Sheehy & Commerford, 2006).

By way of example, I once had someone in a first group complain about the way I was dressed, about my "preppy shirt and tie." This was clearly not about my clothing, but rather about what the clothing—and I—represented: authority. Before he had any personal knowledge of me, I simply appeared to be an extension of all the people in his life who had told him what to do—his parents, his teachers, his probation officer. He had *transferred* his feelings about those people and situation onto me. Thus, there was no reason for me to get defensive about his comments, and I could instead begin a speculation with him about what the clothes represented.

Your job, and your supervisor can help with this, is to separate out what is about you and what you're doing specifically, and what is simply transference. Then, if need be, you can make the reasonable changes that need to be made.

Hidden Agendas

Then there are the hidden agendas some people may be harboring. You may have people in your group who know one another, either in good ways (e.g., they worked together) or in ways that are not so great (e.g., they dealt in drugs together). You may also have individuals who simply have a personal agenda, which can be either constructive (a strong need to see things in the group go well) or destructive (a strong need to block productive activity).

Some of these behaviors, these hidden agendas, may have been originally learned and used in their families (Barrett, 2012), and when people bring them into your group, it is simply one more way in which old family issues are at play. These agendas can really complicate things. Certainly, the more you can find out about these hidden agendas before the group begins, and then perhaps use this information to aid your member selection decisions, the better. You will inevitably not be able to unearth all of them beforehand, and some of these hidden agendas may remain hidden for the entire life of the group.

All this is to suggest that there is a lot going on with a new group. While you can be aware of some of the anxieties and hidden material that people are bringing into a new group, this doesn't mean that you need to know what all that is. You can simply appreciate the complexity, respond to some of the obvious issues that will come up, and plan on being active and directive as a way of minimizing the silent space in which the anxieties would multiply.

Observing the New Group: Different Levels of Observation

One of your primary tasks, in addition to actually getting the group going, will be to observe how individuals in the group behave. How comfortable are people with one another, and how do they express that? Are there people who seem really troubled and who will need extra attention? Are there any people who will be problematic because of their lack of interpersonal skill, because of their reluctance about being in the group, or because of some other reason? Are there quiet, even silent, people?

The better you can manage your own anxiety about how you're doing as a group leader, the better you'll be able to accurately observe what's happening in your group. The more focused you are on yourself, the less you'll be able to pay attention to what's going on around you.

This is tricky, because you also want to be aware of what you're thinking and feeling about what's happening around and within you: being able to check in with yourself, taking stock of what's happening inside you (your own thoughts and feelings—your *intrapersonal world*), while not being preoccupied with that, as well as observing the interactions between individuals in the group (the *interpersonal world*) and the group as a whole (the *group or collective world*). The ability to swiftly shift back and forth in observing these different realities is a skill that you'll develop as you gain experience. Your increased ability to accurately observe and respond from these different perspectives will translate directly into your effectiveness as a group leader.

Reflection and Discussion Exercise: Observing a Group

To do this exercise, you'll need a group to observe, preferably one that doesn't know you're actively observing it. This group might be a work/task committee in which you're a member. It might be a class, a sports team, or any other group where you are a participant.

CHECKLIST: OBSERVING THE STARTING OF A NEW GROUP

Are you able to see

- the dynamics of the new group?
- the group as a replication of the family?
- hidden agendas?
- the intrapersonal, the interpersonal, and the collective?

At some point during one of this group's meetings, silently check out of the activity of the group for a minute or two, and then check in with your internal (the intrapersonal) world. What are you thinking about? What are you feeling? Are any of your thoughts, and particularly your feelings, connected to anything that's happening in the group? If so, what's that about? What would happen—and I'm not suggesting that you do this as part of the exercise—if you gave voice to some of these thoughts and feelings?

Then shift your attention back to the group. What do you notice about the dynamics between individuals in the group (the interpersonal)? Are there people who appear to be friends, or are there others who appear to be antagonistic with one another? Do you sense any kind of romantic "chemistry" between people in this group? What about your own relationships with individuals in this group? Are there some people you feel more comfortable with than others? What would happen— and, again, I am not suggesting that you do this—if you shared these observations with these individuals or with the group as a whole?

Finally, what observations would you make about the group as a whole (the collective)? Does it seem to be working productively? Or have things gotten stagnant, or even worse, is there out-and-out fighting and unpleasantness? And, again—and, please really don't do this—what would happen if you shared your observations with the group?

After you had sufficient time to make and think about all these observations, sit and talk with a colleague about what you've observed. In particular, focus on the "What would happen if you shared . . ." part of these observations. This relates directly to choices you'll make when leading groups—how much of what you observe within and around you could and should be shared. Sometimes, for example, it might be helpful to share observations from your internal world, sometimes not. Such is also the case with your other observations. We'll talk more of this in the next chapter.

ESSENTIAL TASKS: WHAT NEEDS TO HAPPEN IN A NEW GROUP

There are some specific things you'll want to make sure happen early on in your new group. The first couple of group meetings will set the tone for how the group will develop and grow, so it's important that you make sure that you get off on the right foot.

In addition to the things you need to do in getting a new group started, like going over goals and ground rules and creating activities for the group, there are skills you'll need to employ to help all of this go smoothly. These skills, in addition to your personal characteristics that you naturally bring in to this group, will help get things moving in a productive fashion. Some of these skills are the same you'd employ in any helping relationship, and some are exclusive to group work.

Making Connections: The Role of Introductions

The major function of a group's first meeting, or few meetings, is to help people feel comfortable with one another and to get everyone on board with the general goals and purpose of what the group's about. You'll want to create some way for people to introduce themselves to the group, and to do this in a way that is congruent with the group's goals. In a task group, for example, you'll want people to share their relevant background experience that may be helpful in getting the work of the group accomplished.

In a group where people are primarily there to learn about themselves in relationship with others, or some variation of this, you'll want the ways in which people introduce themselves to be personal and interpersonally engaging. The process of talking can serve a double purpose—sharing some personal information and also reducing anxiety. The more quickly people get started in this talking about themselves and to one another, the more quickly they'll most likely feel comfortable in the group.

While you don't want people to go on too long about themselves, you do want them to say something brief that begins to give the group a beginning sense of who they are. Structured exercises, which we'll discuss in a moment, can help with this.

You may have had the experience of being in groups where people, when asked to introduce themselves, give out some well-rehearsed and well-worn information that may be accurate but doesn't really capture anything of the essence of who these people are. You can help avoid this kind of introducing by naming it at the front end and inviting people to do it differently, saying something like,

> You know, I've been in—and I'll bet you've been in—lots of groups where people just tell the basics about themselves when they introduce themselves, and it's almost like they're bored to say it again. So this time, as each of us introduce ourselves, let's try to do it in a way that's different, maybe even personal—not just rank, file, and serial number. Maybe something about your likes and dislikes, your nickname, something that really tells us a short bit about who you are.

Finally, it helps create some way for people to remember one another's names. There are some name recognition exercises that can help with this. One of these exercises is included later in this chapter.

Giving Direction and Using Exercises

Your slate of planned activities will help ensure that things move along smoothly. As important as the planning you've put into the exercises is the way in which you introduce and orchestrate them. Try to be clear about the directions, and communicate your interest in doing this together with your group. Whenever possible, and when it makes sense, involve yourself in the activity as a director-participant.

Oftentimes, simply paying attention to the language you use in introducing an exercise can help get things moving more smoothly. It's probably better, for example, to say, "Who would like to begin?" as opposed to, "Would anyone like to start?" The first question assumes that things are already under way, and the second makes it all sound more tentative. Your language communicates your confidence in the activity.

The exercises you'll use in starting a new group will generally be designed to get people interacting with one another in ways that help them become more comfortable with one another. These kinds of exercises, oftentimes called "icebreakers," should be nonthreatening and engaging, but also gently push the group toward more personal sharing.

Exercises you use later in the life of the group may be designed to help people learn new skills (Fall & Howard, 2012), in addition to helping them look at their interactions with others (McAllister, 2010).

When you use these exercises, think about what would work well for you, if you were a member of this group. If it works for you, it'll most likely work for the group. I think that the best exercises are the ones that require minimal outside materials (e.g., art supplies, blocks, etc.), are simple, and are gauged to match the needs of a particular group. You'll gain facility for skillfully matching exercises to groups with experience.

Remember that each exercise you use has a function, a goal. It's not activity for activity's sake, and you'll always want to reserve time at the end for talking with people about their perceptions of what's transpired—both their observations about what's happened in the group as well as their personal reactions and feelings about the experience. This discussion of the activity, including the members' personal responses, is as important as the activity itself.

Group Fishbowl Lab Practice Exercise: Using Exercises

For this fishbowl exercise, you'll need six people to volunteer to be group members, two people to volunteer to be group leaders. The rest of the people will be silent observers, taking note of how the fishbowl exercise goes, particularly focusing on the leaders' interactions with the group. The observers should be prepared to give feedback to the leaders at the end of the experience.

The group leaders' job is to introduce and conduct a group exercise. There are two exercises provided in the For Further Thought section at the end of this chapter. One of these could be used. Each of these exercises is a so-called icebreaker, designed to get people talking with one another. Alternatively, the leaders could choose to use an exercise from some other source or they could create one of their own.

Paying attention to all the things that this chapter has discussed regarding starting a new group, the leaders should talk about which of these exercises they'd like to use, and why. They should then run this exercise with the group for the amount of time allotted by the exercise's description. Observers should pay attention to how all of this goes and then should give feedback, primarily to the leaders, about their perceptions of the process.

Feedback to the leaders should be specific, behavioral, and supportive. Focus primarily on the things you think that the leaders did well.

Following their feedback, the leaders and the group members should talk about their own participation and observation of the exercise. In particular, what was seen as particularly helpful in moving the group in productive directions were the things that happened that might have been done differently. If there is time, you could all talk about how this group might proceed if it were to continue as an actual working group.

Including Everyone

When you have your first few meetings of a new group, you'll want to pay close attention to making sure that everyone is involved in discussions and activities. While, on the one hand, you want to respect individual differences regarding a desire to talk in the group, you want to have everyone engaged and involved on some level in the talking and activity that is planned for these first meetings.

The best way to make sure that everyone participates is to orchestrate activities or exercises that include everyone. I'll sometimes say to a group, for example, "As we talk about this (whatever it is), we don't need to just go around the circle in turn, but I do want to hear from everyone." I have group leader colleagues who will use talking sticks (when you have the stick, you talk, and the stick is passed to everyone), or other tools, to the same effect.

Some people will be shy and need to be nudged a bit to participate, so you might want to think about how people can be included while responding only briefly. Some of the people in your group might easily slide into a pattern of nonparticipation, if they are not encouraged to talk early on. In the event that this happens, your skill at *drawing out*, which we'll talk more of in the next chapter, will help rectify this.

You want to make sure that if you "nudge" someone to participate, it doesn't embarrass or single someone out as being too quiet. This would most likely only serve to make her or him feel even more isolated.

Defining Goals and Ground Rules

Your first meeting will always include a review of the essential reasons why people have come together for this group experience, the goals (and, perhaps, learning objectives) that are the group's reason for being. If you and your coleader have been the ones who have constructed these goals, you'll want to make sure that there is consensus that these work for everyone.

You might consider including an invitation to people, as they introduce themselves, to talk about any specific things they are looking to get from or learn in this group. Given what people say when invited to share their own "wants" for the group experience, you could then negotiate some revisions in the group goals.

This is also the time to discuss the ground rules that will help make this a safe experience. While you and your coleader have outlined your ideas about appropriate ground rules for the group during the planning process, as was discussed in the last chapter, you now need to go over these with the group. Ground rules that are clearly and effectively articulated at the beginning of a group can help ensure a safe and productive experience for everyone in the group (Peterson, 2012). Confidentiality, right to privacy, and challenge by choice are my typical favorites, as were reviewed in the last chapter. You could invite people in the group to make suggestions about other ground rules that could help ensure a safe experience for them. This can serve to make the process more collaborative.

You'll want to spend some time talking about confidentiality and its limits. You'll want people to know when it's appropriate to break confidentiality—to protect someone—and that safety trumps confidentiality. People need to know that if there are certain things they share, then you will necessarily be taking appropriate action (e.g., reporting child abuse). You will want to be clear about agency or school policy about this before meeting with the group.

You'll also want people to know that there is no such thing as unbreakable confidentiality. Sometimes, people slip and let information out unwittingly. Or worse, on rare occasions, someone will share information as a way of getting back at someone in the group. Thus, people should always be cautioned not to share anything that would have devastating consequences if word about that were to leak out of the group. People can be encouraged to share, but thoughtfully. Self-monitored self-disclosure is the optimal kind of sharing.

You'll want to think carefully about other concerns you might want to create ground rules around. With many of the addictions treatment groups I ran, for

Figure 7.1 Romantic Relationships Between Group Members Can Divide a Group

example, there was a ground rule against group members becoming romantically involved with one another as long as the group was running (see Figure 7.1). We wanted individuals to focus on their own recovery without becoming entangled with another person's issues.

Educating About How to Use the Group and Informed Consent

If you're running a psycho-educational, content-oriented group, much of your time with the group will be structured and planned. A curriculum of planned activities will most likely be available to help you orchestrate the beginning of the group. You'll be instructing people as to what to do and how to interact with one another as a part of this planned regimen. This instruction will include a review of the informed consent concerns that we discussed in the last chapter, if you haven't already done this individually with people before the group started.

Other groups you lead may be less structured, may be more process oriented, and are primarily designed to help people look at how they relate with others. Depending on how much group experience your members have had, you may need to help people understand how they can best use the group to learn more about themselves and their interactions with other people. This will be particularly important if there was no pregroup training.

CHECKLIST: TASKS FOR STARTING A NEW GROUP

- Handling Introductions
- Helping People Remember Names
- Reviewing Ground Rules and Group Goals
- Educating About How to Use the Group and Informed Consent
- Using Introductory Exercises
- Assessment
- Remembering to Include Everyone
- Providing Time for Group Reflection and Discussion

Assessment of Members' and the Group's Progress

While you will have done what you can during your time of selecting members for your group to ensure that people are a "good fit" for this experience, you will also want to monitor their progress throughout the life of the group (Cox & Klinger, 2011; Gaw & Smyk, 2011). This will be a time when you'll also want to introduce any written assessment tools you'll be using to evaluate the experience.

As the group begins, you'll want to take stock of particular behaviors and issues that may be problematic, either for the person himself or herself, or for the group. You'll want to assess the ways in which people interact with one another. Who seems to be shy and reluctant to participate? Who's angry and reluctant to be here? Is there anyone who has some serious personal issues that could impair his or her ability to function well in the group? Who will emerge as a leader in the group (not as a challenger to your authority but as an ally), and who might actively resist the group's efforts to do positive work?

All your perceptions of these kinds of issues can help you—in consultation with your coleader—make adjustments to your future group planning. You can plot ways to include shy members, strategize about how to deal with hostile behaviors, and think about mechanisms for capitalizing on the positive contributions that some members make. We'll talk more of these specific strategies in future chapters.

ESSENTIAL SKILLS FOR STARTING A NEW GROUP

You'll need to have some specific skills at your disposal in order to accomplish the tasks for your new group that we've just outlined. Most of these skills are tools that you'd use in developing any counseling relationship—or friendship, for that matter. You use, in other words, many of the same skills you use in your individual relationships to work with groups. In the next two chapters, we'll also review some additional skills that are used specifically in working with groups. These two chapters will also introduce a number of other tools, additional skills, you can use, in addition to those that follow here.

You may have already had an introductory counseling, social work, or human services course that covered and encouraged your use of these skills. If not, I could recommend reading and using the skills practice sessions in any good counseling skills text.

Breaking Into Smaller Groups

Because large groups, even groups of 10 to 12 people, can intimidate many people, it can often be helpful to break the group into smaller groups, especially when getting started. You could ask the group to divide into groups of two, three, or four (dyads, triads, or "quadrads") and then initiate an exercise. You'll see an example of this later in the chapter, with the beginning of Vanessa and Gary's *New Directions* group.

Take care to ensure that information that is shared in the smaller groups stays in the small groups unless everyone says that it's appropriate to share that with the larger group. Also, try to follow this small group work with something that the large group does together. While it's helpful for people to begin to make connections with others via the small groups, it's important that the larger group connect again. Again, you'll see an example of how this can be done with the *New Directions* group.

Using Questions

There is a real skill in being able to use questions in a way that helps engage people with one another in a group. The best questions are brief and open ended and imply that a longer response is requested. "How would you describe the town where you grew up?" and "What do you see yourself doing 5 years from now?" are examples of these.

There may be times when you'll want tight, specific answers, and then, more closed questions are appropriate: "Where do you live?" and "Where do you work?" are examples of these. The best questions build on what has come before, are not overly invasive, and are intelligent. There is no point, after all, in asking questions that are irrelevant.

Observing Nonverbal Behavior

Watching and carefully observing your new group members' nonverbal behavior can tell you legions about who these people are. The clothes they wear, the way they sit or walk, and where they sit or stand in relation to one another—and to you—give you some immediate initial clues about how these people will act and interact with one another. Learning how to studiously observe and understand this kind of behavior is as important as learning how to listen well to the verbal interchanges that people have (Crowell & Conyne, 2008). Pay attention to voice tone, how people make eye contact (or avoid it), and how they carry themselves in their bodies. Pay attention to these things in yourself, as well.

As with any kind of communication, you will want to become more sensitive to cultural differences in this communication arena (Ringel, 2005).

Using Simple Prompts

Sometimes all you need to say, in response to what has been said, is "Go on."

Or, "Tell us more." Even an encouraging hand gesture, or nod of the head, can be enough of a prompt to help someone continue. Silence, as well, can suggest that you won't be the one to fill the void with a question or comment but that the space exists for someone else to say something. A bit of silence, coupled with an encouraging smile, head nod, and hand gesture, can be a prompt to the entire group—a suggestion that the floor is open for someone to jump in.

Modeling: Your Energy, Confidence, and Enthusiasm

I can't emphasize enough the importance of your approach in setting a positive tone for a new group. Your general attitude and demeanor will have a huge effect on your members' perceptions of the group experience. If you come into the experience acting tired, listless, bored, or preoccupied with other matters, this will communicate itself to your group, and your group will respond in kind.

If, on the other hand, you are genuinely excited about getting to know people and getting things started, this will have an infectious effect. This general demeanor will communicate itself to your group as much as anything you say (Jayakody, 2008). Your level of enthusiasm will have a tremendous effect on the group and how well everything comes together (Caperchione, Mummery, & Duncan, 2011)

Similarly, your level of confidence in what you're doing and how you handle yourself will communicate itself to the group. It will certainly be natural for you not to be feeling overly confident as you first begin work as a group leader, but it's probably not a bad idea to hide how insecure you might be feeling. You can at least feel secure in the knowledge that your intention of doing a good job and in being fully present for your group is absolutely there, even though you may not have a lot of experience in this.

Even when there are a lot of other things going on in your life that may be distracting you, and even though you may be feeling inexperienced and new to group work, it's probably best to act otherwise. Sometimes we do need, as they say, to

---

PRIMARY SKILLS FOR USE IN STARTING A NEW GROUP

- Breaking Into Smaller Groups
- Using Questions
- Observing Nonverbal Behavior
- Using Simple Prompts
- Modeling
- Managing Time and Giving Clear Directions

"fake it until we make it." You may be surprised to find that you can sometimes even fake yourself out; you may automatically become less distracted and feel more on top of things as you simply act that way.

Managing Time

You'll want to keep an eye on the clock as you're working your way through these first group sessions. While I've encouraged you to think about planning more activities than you'll actually need, you also want the pace of things to not feel rushed. Make sure that you have enough time left in a group meeting to finish an exercise and try to clue your group in when the session is coming toward the end, saying something like, "We've only got a few minutes left, just enough time for some final reflections." Be as clear as you can in giving directions about how to go about using an exercise. That will help you make the most efficient use of the time you have.

Try to avoid cutting anyone off too abruptly. We'll talk about "*cutting off*" skillfully in the next chapter. If someone brings up something toward the end of the group that you think will take a lot of time, you can always say, "This is really interesting, and I'm wondering if it will be OK to take this up first thing next time we meet. . . . We want to make sure this gets the time it deserves."

STARTING THE *NEW DIRECTIONS* GROUP

Let's take a look now at Vanessa and Gary's *New Directions* group—the group of high school students with families in transition we began to plan in the last chapter. We'll see how some of the tasks and skills needed in helping a new group getting up and running are actually put into play. The skills are identified in parentheses; some have been talked about here, and some will be reviewed in the next chapter.

Gary and Vanessa are now meeting for the first time with their new group. They have selected nine high school students for the group, all of them experiencing significant changes in their families. There are five young women and four young men. They are all juniors or seniors, 11th or 12th graders. People have arrived early, and they've begun to interact informally. A few people know one another. The leaders take note of how people are interacting, or not (*observing nonverbal behavior*).

Eventually, they begin. Seats are arranged in a circle, so that everyone can see everyone else's face. Vanessa and Gary sit across from each other, allowing each to see the other's eyes and facial expressions. This seating arrangement also helps distribute the power of the leadership positions equally around the room (*paying attention to nonverbal behavior*). Vanessa explains how this meeting will work—how long it will be and other logistical details (*giving directions*). She invites questions about this and answers them as they come.

Then Gary asks what has brought people to this experience (*using questions and simple prompts*). What special things, in other words, are they hoping to learn? Inevitably, this draws an interesting mix of responses, some personal (e.g., "I want to learn to be more comfortable talking about myself.") and some more noncommittal (e.g., "My mother told me I should come."). This conversation segues nicely into people talking more about themselves, introducing themselves to the group. Gary shares in this, being the first to more fully introduce himself. He highlights some of his professional and personal background, talking about his love of group work, and he also shares some edgier personal background material (addiction in his family of origin, some other emotional difficulties in the family). He shares these things in way of talking about his personal connection to this kind of group, and he's cautious not to overshare (*modeling self-disclosure*).

When introductions are finished, they talk about things they can do to get extra credit for a course that is related to the group (*use of incentives*). Vanessa suggests that their participation in this experience should be as a participant-observer and that they should not only immerse themselves in the process fully but also occasionally step back to look more objectively at what transpires. And then they go over ground rules, particularly the "big three": (1) confidentiality, and its limits; (2) the right to privacy; and (3) challenge by choice. Vanessa and Gary stress the need for mutual respect.

Having laid out the framework of how this will go, including reviewing group goals and expectations (*defining goals and ground rules*)—what these students can expect to get out of this—the group then completes some initial introducing by introducing a simple name-remembering game (*using exercises*).

Vanessa breaks the group into small groups of three or four (*use of smaller groups*), trying to make sure that the people who know one another aren't in the same small group. Gary and Vanessa know that for many people, it is easier to begin talking more personally with smaller, as opposed to larger, groups. They assume that when people begin to make connections via the small group, they will then carry those connections back to the larger group, making it easier to talk with everyone.

Gary encourages them to find a relatively private place to sit together, and then he gives them a series of specific questions each of them is to answer, such as "What is some beautiful aesthetic experience you've had?" and "What is some embarrassing thing that's happened to you?" The questions are never overly charged, pushing for too much self-disclosure, and they stimulate a good deal of spirited discussion and good-natured humor (*using exercises*).

Vanessa and Gary split up and move between the small groups, serving as silent observers in this particular exercise. They then get together briefly as the small groups are working to discuss specific members, privately trying to identify possible problem issues or behaviors, as well as talking about members who they think will be strong assets in moving the group in positive directions (*assessment*). This is a conversation they will continue after the group has ended for the day.

Eventually, all come back as a large group and talk about (or "process," in group talk) what has transpired. Vanessa asks them to share observations—and related personal feelings—about the differences between talking in the large group and in the small group. She makes the observation that people generally feel more comfortable taking some interpersonal risks when they feel personally safe.

While the benefit of creating the smaller groups has helped create some safety for people to begin to make some connections with others, the deficit is that information has been shared that is privy to a few but not to the whole group. Thus, now that they are all back together, Vanessa poses one final question that each person will answer: "What is one thing about yourself that you can share with us that you don't typically share in groups?"

This generates a really interesting mix of funny, a few superficial, and some very personal disclosures. Gary discourages further discussion of what's been shared, opting at this point to have the material simply put out there, knowing that these are things that they may want to come back to, or not, at some point in the future.

Finally, Vanessa asks people for their observations about what's transpired during this time spent together. People talk about the richness of material, the diversity of experience and background, and about the potential to do some good work together. The group ends on a high note, with a sense that people have made some good initial contacts and a notion that this will be a productive experience.

This, Vanessa and Gary agree, could become a great group.

REFLECTION AND DISCUSSION EXERCISE: HOW WOULD YOU START THIS NEW GROUP?

In this description of how Vanessa and Gary started this new group, you can see that they played an active and directive role in getting things started. They needed to share some information, and they also wanted to create an atmosphere that invites some personal sharing. In a new group, people need to feel that this will be a productive experience and that they will learn some things about themselves, about others, and about groups.

There is nothing sacred about this, however. Different group leaders start groups in different ways. Following are some questions designed to stimulate your thoughts about how you might start a group similarly or differently.

- Which of the activities described appeal to you, and which don't? What kinds of activities might you use when working with a first group you might be leading?
- How would these activities be altered if you are working with children, or with adults? What if you were leading a group that was going to meet outdoors—what kinds of activities would you plan then?
- What do you think would happen in the small groups if no questions were provided for them to discuss—if they were told to just talk?
- What ground rules might you want to create if you were leading a group of young children?
- Think about a group you might want to create, and then imagine yourself with this collection of people at your first meeting. What kinds of feelings do you have, or anticipate that you would have, as you sit there waiting for things to begin?

Now discuss any ideas you have about all of this with some of your colleagues.

PITFALLS TO AVOID IN STARTING A NEW GROUP

Just as there are some guidelines for things to do, and skills needed, to start a new group, there are also some things I would suggest you avoid, if at all possible. There are certain things—pitfalls—that can happen in these early meetings, which can seriously hinder a group's ability to move forward productively (Alvarez, 2002; Sturkie & Hanson, 1992).

Too Much Content, Not Enough Process

There can be a tendency for new group leaders to get so enamored with the activities they've planned that they forget that the real essence of the activity is how people are reacting to it. Try to ensure that there is time taken for discussion of how people have responded to an exercise or other activity. You can sometimes get this discussion going with some preprepared questions about the activity that can help people begin to talk about it.

Remember, the activity is simply a vehicle for talking, at least with a verbally oriented group. Always be prepared to drop the activity when some important talking begins. Knowing how and when to do this is a skill you will learn with experience and with good supervision and dialogue with your coleader.

Member Oversharing

Sometimes, people will divulge some very personal information about themselves very early on in a group. Despite all of your warnings about the limits of confidentiality, some people will nevertheless go, at least to your way of thinking, overboard in how much they share. This can even happen with groups of sophisticated graduate students (Shumaker, Ortiz, & Brenninkmeyer, 2011).

Some people may do oversharing for attention-seeking purposes; others simply may have poor "boundary" management skills. Whatever the reason, this can cause some problems. It can make other people really uncomfortable, and it can also jeopardize the individual's future in the group. I've often seen that when someone shares something particularly personal, this can be followed by a backing off, a retreat, or, rarely, an exit from the group.

I once had a group member share some grisly details about some crimes he'd committed and the jail time he'd served during our introductions in a first group. The group was stunned into a long silence when he finished. I think he recognized that he'd gone too far, and he never came back. My sense is that he was so embarrassed about the things he'd said that he didn't want to face the group again. Perhaps there were other reasons, as well, but we never had the opportunity to find out.

Thus, do what you can to help people understand that self-monitored self-disclosure is the best kind of sharing. Personal sharing is a good thing but only when done thoughtfully.

In the next chapter, we'll be talking about skills you can use to cut people off when they're going on for too long or too far, and those may help you with these situations, too.

Not Including Everyone

Try to ensure that everyone participates, if only minimally, during the first couple of times your group meets. Some people will be shy or reluctant to say much, particularly when they feel culturally or in some other way different from the majority of people in the group, so it's important that you do all you can to involve them, whether through the exercises you use or by personally drawing them out (Westwood, Mak, Barker, & Ishiyama, 2000). Some of the people in your group may be used to being excluded from participation in many of the groups in which they've participated (Thomas & Hard, 2011); thus, you'll want to do all you can to ensure that this group isn't a repeat of those exclusions.

If they are allowed to be silent for a meeting or two, it will be very easy for them to slide into simply being quiet in all the groups that follow (see Figure 7.2). That's a normative behavior you'd want to help them avoid.

Being "Out of Sync" With a Coleader

In my first formal group-leading experience, I was paired with a coleader who had a great deal more experience than I had. Moreover, she had been leading the group for a number of months alone, and I was invited to join it well after it had already experienced a number of the developmental challenges we've discussed earlier. While she and the group were generous in the ways they included me, I always felt like a junior partner. It's better if you can avoid this kind of experience disparity and feel like an equal with a coleader.

Also, try to work with a coleader who will complement your personal style. It helps if the two of you know each other well and have a sense that you will work well together. The last thing you want is a situation in which the two of you are

Figure 7.2   Include Everyone to Avoid Isolation

CHECKLIST: PITFALLS TO AVOID IN STARTING A NEW GROUP

Is There Too Much Content but Not Enough Attention Paid to Process? Or Is There Too Much Time Spent With Process, Not Enough Content?

- Are Any Members Oversharing?
- Is Everyone Included?
- Are My Coleader and I Having Problems With Each Other?
- Have I Talked Too Much?

---

at odds, or—even worse—competing with each other for leadership of the group (Gabriel, 1993).

You won't be able to avoid these pitfalls 100% of the time, and there will be other problems not covered here that you'll discover on your own. All of us who lead groups continue to rethink what we've done and how we'd do it differently next time. Hopefully, we learn from our mistakes and adjust accordingly.

CONCLUDING THOUGHTS

Starting a new group can generate a really interesting mix of feelings of excitement and anxiety—both for you and for your group members. As long as the anxiety is held at reasonable levels, it can help promote the feelings of excitement and anticipation.

How the group gets started sets the tone for how the experience will unfold. If this is seen as a safe place to share personal information and it is seen that there are possibilities for important contact with others, this will help promote a hope and an expectation that this will be a positive, productive experience. And that can be truly exciting!

FOR FURTHER THOUGHT

1. Examine and critically review five different exercises designed to help with getting groups started. Typically, these exercises will be of the "icebreaker" variety.

2. Talk with counselors, clinical social workers, or psychologists who lead groups, and ask them about the specifics of how they start groups. Compare and contrast their strategies, and think about which of these most appeal to you.

3. Design and write up an exercise for use in starting a new group. Include all the ingredients (title, goals, materials, etc.) in the exercise, and write it up in the same format as was used in the sample exercises included in this chapter.

4. There are many books of exercises for groups that have been compiled by experienced group leaders. While I would certainly encourage you to think about designing some exercises yourself, you can always draw on the experience of others and utilize the exercises that they have put together. Any exercise you design or use should comprise the following elements: a title; the overall goal or goals of the exercise; the target population; group size; the setting required; time required; materials required; and the procedures to be followed in conducting the exercise. Then there may be some directions included for varying the exercise, for use with a different population or time frame, for example.

Following are collections of exercises for groups that you might find useful:

Belmont, J. (2006). *103 group activities and tips (treatment ideas & practical strategies)*. Eau Claire, WI: PESI.

Carrell, S. (1993). *Group exercises for adolescents: A manual for therapists*. Newbury Park, CA: Sage.

Jones, A. (2013). *Team-building activities for every group*. Richland, WA: Rec Room.

Kraus, K. (2002). *Exercises in group work*. Boston, MA: Pearson.

Miller, G. (2012). *Group exercises for addictions counseling*. New York, NY: Wiley.

5. Graduate students in my courses about working with groups have created simple—but effective—group exercises, and two of them have graciously agreed to have theirs included here (below). While they have done their best to create original exercises, there are undoubtedly "icebreakers" already in existence that are very similar to these.

THE INTERVIEW

—Angel Roy

Goal: Icebreaker to use as group introductions

Target Population: Any group of people

Group Size: 4 to 12

Materials: None

Space: Any space where the group can be divided up into two to four smaller groups

Time: 20 to 30 minutes

Procedure: Depending on the group size, the instructor will divide the group up into two to four smaller groups. Each individual will be given three interview questions to use to interview one member from the smaller group. The small groups will be given 10 minutes to conduct their interviews.

Interview questions:

1. What is your name?

2. What adjective describes you best?

3. Name one hobby that you have.

When the larger group convenes, each individual will be responsible for introducing the individual that they interviewed to the larger group by using the three answers to the interview questions as the person's name. For example: This is Interesting Biking Kate.

Variations: Interview questions can be altered depending on the age of the group. "What is your favorite color or animal?" may be a more appropriate question when working with younger children.

DON'T DROP THE BALL

—Lesley Robinson

Goal: This exercise can be used as an icebreaker or to explain the idea of being present while in the group sessions.

Target Population: Middle school age and up

Group Size: Six to eight (more than eight, and the group will be too big and you will have to toss the item too far away; less than six and there are not enough people to make it challenging)

Materials: Five different balls

Setting: Can be done indoors or outdoors. (If done inside, please make sure nothing can be spilled or broken.)

Procedure: Stand in a circle, shoulder width apart. Have one person begin with the first ball by calling out the name of another group member and tossing the ball to him or her. That person will then call out a new name (one that has not been called yet) and toss the item to him or her and so on. The ball should be tossed to a new person every time until the only person left is the group member who began. Do this round again tossing to exactly the same person you did in the first round. Continue this process for one more round so everyone becomes relaxed with who they received the ball from and who they tossed it to. Then add a second ball into the rotation. Continue this until the second ball has made it back to the original person, and add a third ball. Continue this until you have added up to all five balls.

After reaching the desired number of balls being tossed in the circle, continue for a few rounds and then stop the group. If the activity has worked as desired, much of the group will be laughing at dropping items, remembering who they need to toss it to, and having items back up in the tossing rotation. This should loosen up the group and relax everyone. Ask everyone what was going through their minds as the activity was happening. Ask if anyone was thinking of their grocery list or what homework they had due, and so on. Group members should share that they were only thinking about who was tossing to them and who they need to toss to. Explain how this activity showed the importance of staying in the present moment, that if you thought of something else you would forget who you needed to throw to or forget to look at the person tossing to you. By not being present during the activity, you could distract or disrupt the process. Explain the importance of being present in group sessions. Anyone distracted or disruptive will hinder the growth of the group as a whole.

Variation: By changing the number of items or the items themselves, this activity could be used with a younger crowd as an icebreaker, as a way to learn names, and to work on motor skills.

REFERENCES

Alvarez, A. (2002). Pitfalls, pratfalls, shortfalls and windfalls: Reflections on forming and being formed by groups. *Social Work With Groups: A Journal of Community and Clinical Practice, 25*(1), 93–105.

Barrett, M. (2012). Family dynamics and the educational experience. In H. High (Ed.), *Why can't I help this child to learn? Understanding emotional barriers to learning* (pp. 85–102). London, England: Karnac Books.

Caperchione, C., Mummery, W. K., & Duncan, M. (2011). Investigating the relationship between leader behaviours and group cohesion within women's walking groups. *Journal of Science and Medicine in Sport, 14*(4), 325–330.

Counselman, E. F. (2012). Beginning a group with beginner's mind. *International Journal of Group Psychotherapy, 62*(3), 375–379.

Cox, W., & Klinger, E. (2011). Systematic motivational counseling: From motivational assessment to motivational change. In W. Cox & E. Klinger (Eds.), *Handbook of motivational counseling: Goal-based approaches to assessment and intervention with addiction and other problems* (2nd ed., pp. 275–302). Hoboken, NJ: Wiley-Blackwell.

Crowell, J. L., & Conyne, R. K. (2008). Advanced training in using group techniques. In G. R. Walz, J. C. Bleuer, & R. K. Yep (Eds.), *Compelling counseling interventions: Celebrating VISTAS' fifth anniversary* (pp. 273–281). Ann Arbor, MI: Counseling Outfitters.

Dwivedi, K. (1993). Conceptual frameworks. In K. Dwivedi (Ed.), *Group work with children and adolescents: A handbook* (pp. 28–45). London, England: Jessica Kingsley.

Fall, K. A., & Howard, S. (2012). *Alternatives to domestic violence: A homework manual for battering intervention groups* (3rd ed.). New York, NY: Routledge/Taylor & Francis.

Gabriel, M. A. (1993). The cotherapy relationship: Special issues and problems in AIDS therapy groups. *Group, 17*(1), 33–42.

Gaw, K., & Smyk, S. (2011). Gaining perspective series: A career group for college students. In T. Fitch & J. L. Marshall (Eds.), *Group work and outreach plans for college counsellors* (pp. 43–48). Alexandria, VA: American Counseling Association.

Greene, L. R. (2012). On becoming and being a group therapist. *Group, 36*(4), 333–337.

Huang, W., Zhang, R., Liu, Y., & Zhu, W. (2012). Effect of group counseling on graduate students' mental health-based on positive psychology. *Chinese Journal of Clinical Psychology, 20*(4), 527–529.

Jayakody, J. K. (2008). Charisma as a cognitive-affective phenomenon: A follower-centric approach. *Management Decision, 46*(6), 832–845.

Marmarosh, C. L., Markin, R. D., & Spiegel, E. B. (2013). Assembling the group: Screening, placing, and preparing group members. In *Attachment in group psychotherapy* (pp. 67–95). Washington, DC: American Psychological Association.

McAllister, E. C. (2010).The rope exercise to experience process in the group. In S. Fehr (Ed.), *101 interventions in group therapy* (Rev. ed., pp. 269–274). New York, NY: Routledge/Taylor & Francis.

Nesdale, D., Durkin, K., Maass, A., Kiesner, J., Griffiths, J., Daly, J., & McKenzie, D. (2010). Peer group rejection and children's outgroup prejudice. *Journal of Applied Developmental Psychology, 31*(2), 134–144.

Peterson, C. (2012). The individual regulation component of group emotional intelligence: Measure development and validation. *Journal for Specialists in Group Work, 37*(3), 232–251.

Rasmussen, B. (1999). Joining group psychotherapy: Developmental considerations. *International Journal of Group Psychotherapy, 49*(4), 513–528.

Ringel, S. (2005). Group work with Asian-American immigrants: A cross-cultural perspective. In G. L. Greif & P. H. Ephross (Eds.), *Group work with populations at risk* (2nd ed., pp. 181–194). New York, NY: Oxford University Press.

Rippa, B., Rippa, B., & Moss, E. (2013). Interpersonal communication at the internal group level. *Group Analysis, 46*(4), 415–425.

Sheehy, J., & Commerford, M. (2006). Eating disorders. In P. A. Grayson & P. W. Meilman (Eds.), *College mental health practice* (pp. 261–280). New York, NY: Routledge.

Shumaker, D., Ortiz, C., & Brenninkmeyer, L. (2011). Revisiting experiential group training in counselor education: A survey of master's-level programs. *Journal for Specialists in Group Work, 36*(2), 111–128.

Sturkie, J., & Hanson, C. (1992). *Leadership skills for peer group facilitators*. San Jose, CA: Resource.

Thomas, M., & Hard, P. F. (2011). Support group for gay and lesbian students. In T. Fitch & J. L. Marshall (Eds.), *Group work and outreach plans for college counselors* (pp. 123–135). Alexandria, VA: American Counseling Association.

Vassilopoulos, S. H. (2005). Anticipatory processing plays a role in maintaining social anxiety. *Anxiety, Stress & Coping: An International Journal, 18*(4), 321–332.

Westwood, M. J., Mak, A., Barker, M., & Ishiyama, F. (2000). Group procedures and applications for developing sociocultural competencies among immigrants. *International Journal for the Advancement of Counselling, 22*(4), 317–330.

Chapter 8

Your Group Is Engaging

The well-run group is not a battlefield of egos.

—Lao Tzu

Mr. Tzu clearly knows a thing or two about groups. Groups that are cohesive and work productively have members who work together cooperatively. These are groups where people are able to see the importance of the "we" and can backburner the "me" for at least a while. Here there are no egos doing battle.

The road to this "we" can be bumpy, however. Early on in a new group, there can be a time when egos do, in fact, bump up against one another. While this might not be an actual "storming," there can be a period of some honest and direct exchange between people. I call this the period of direct exchange, this time before the group has coalesced into a cohesive working unit, a period of "engaging."

I recall a group experience of mine that might provide some illustration. I had been meeting with a relatively new group for just a few weeks, and already the group was starting to work together pretty well. People talked freely, and some personal material was being divulged. We seemed to be off to a good start. Some very distinct, strong, personalities had also begun to emerge. It had become clear that some of these individual differences would start to rub up against one another.

Three people, in particular, stood out as dominant forces in these early meetings. The first of these, Alvero, was an ebullient presence in the group, always cheerful, helpful, and positive about virtually everything that came up for discussion and about any activity that we did together. He was a veritable fountain of good cheer.

On the other end of the spectrum was Matt, a wisecracking, cynical, and generally negative voice in our midst. He was the kind of guy who could take lemonade and make lemons. Every time someone would tell some kind of sad story about his or her life, Matt would either make subtle fun of it or slyly tell the person to stop whining. That the group had persevered and proceeded to become more personal and close was certainly no fault of his. Most people simply shrugged off his cynicism.

And then there was Renate, a tough-talking, no-nonsense kind of woman who just wanted people to get along. As she put it, "I've had enough fighting and bulls— in my life. I didn't come here for more of that. I want to make some friends!" She had surmounted a number of difficulties in her life, including a bout of breast cancer and the recent loss of her parents. Renate had set her sights on what she believed were her top priorities, developing good relationships. She was looking to connect with people in this group and wasn't interested in wasting a lot of time on what she called "inconsequentials."

At that night's meeting, it became clear that Alvero and Matt would lock horns and that their very different styles would finally begin to seriously clash. I think that everyone knew that the storm was about to break. It was only a matter of how it would unfold.

Very quickly after we finished our original round of check-ins, the clashing began. Alvero had enthusiastically responded to everyone's brief recounting of their week, and Matt had simply scowled with every positive remark that Alvero made. Then he openly complained about Alvero's upbeat attitude. "I'm getting pretty sick of this Mr. Pollyanna always sucking up to everything everybody says. I've never seen such a suck-up brownnoser."

Predictably, this upset Alvero. He quickly jumped to his own defense, saying, "I'm no brownnoser. . . . I just happen to like people and what's going on. And, for my part, I'm getting pretty sick of this negativity. People should just say decent things to one another or keep to themselves."

They went on this way for awhile, each complaining about the other's style of interaction, without really dealing with each other. They talked in abstractions about "people" who talk negatively or positively.

After a few minutes of this, Renate looked at me and said, "Sheesh, what kind of leader are you, anyway? Aren't you going to do anything about this? Are we all going to have to sit here and listen to this baloney for the rest of the night?"

"Well," I said, "clearly you think I should be taking a more active role in intervening."

"Duh!" she said. "You bet I think you should be 'taking a more active role,' as you put it. That's why you're making the big money," she smirked.

The group started laughing. Momentarily, the focus had shifted away from the conflict between Alvero and Matt, and had landed squarely on me. Renate had successfully, whether it was intentional or not, put me on the spot.

Then I sat back, thought for a bit about what was going on, and contemplated about what to do and where to go next.

LEADING THE ENGAGING GROUP

My dilemma in this group I've just described is the dilemma of every group leader who deals with a new group with members who are beginning to be more honest and direct with one another and with the leader. The initial veneer of politeness and social appropriateness is beginning to peel away, exposing more true expression of thoughts and feelings.

Leading a group that's moving into the engaging stage is like driving a car with a manual transmission. In this analogy, you're shifting from first into second gear, and while the car—or group—isn't really running at full speed, it's gaining traction and momentum. While you're shifting, particularly if you're just learning how to drive, there can be a few grinding crunches and jolts if the clutch doesn't engage properly. Similarly, the engaging group can have a few jolts as it moves toward a smoother working time.

Some theories of group development—most notably Tuckman's (1965) enduring model of group growth—label this movement of a group into more honest dialogue as a "storming" (Bonebright, 2010; Maples, 1988). Others, and I would include myself in this, prefer to think of this more as a kind of "engagement," in that oftentimes there is no apparent conflict or fighting, rather simply a more direct kind of communication (Kelly, Lowndes, & Tolson, 2005). I always look forward to this developmental milestone, kind of like how you, as a parent might look forward to your child moving into adolescence. Even though you know that this might become tumultuous, and that it could be a wild ride getting through those years, this time is important and necessary. There are unique opportunities, either for a child moving through those teenage years, or for a group moving through its own adolescence—or its engaging—for learning and growth.

This is a critically important time for a group. It sets the stage for successful movement toward becoming a really productive working group. If things are handled well

LEADING THE ENGAGING GROUP

- The Hallmarks of the Engaging Group
- Essential Tasks for the Engaging Group
- Essential Skills for Working With the Engaging Group

here, the group will feel empowered and capable of tackling important material. If things don't go well here, however, the group may flounder and never become very cohesive. It will be helpful for you if you know what to look for in a group that is beginning to seriously engage, the things that need to happen as the group engages and the skills you'll need to have to help the group successfully move forward.

THE HALLMARKS OF THE ENGAGING GROUP: ANXIETY, RESISTANCE, AND PROBLEM BEHAVIORS

I don't want to overstate the negative things that can happen when a group begins to seriously engage. Some groups appear to hit the ground running and proceed with ease into a fully productive working mode. Remembering the car's manual transmission analogy, this group, like the car, can shift smoothly into second gear if the clutch is engaged properly. These groups look like they move seamlessly from their beginnings, where there simply seems to be a good deal of camaraderie and goodwill at the outset, and then very quickly into productively working. There doesn't appear to be much anxiety or resistance in these groups.

In most groups, however, there is a more obvious shifting from an initial tentativeness into a period where people, the members, simply start to act more honestly with one another. Sometimes people are cooperative and helpful as this starts to unfold, and sometimes they aren't. The group, like the manual transmission car, can sometimes sputter as it tries to find its way into the next gear.

You can assume that your group will have some bumps and grinds as it finds its way toward a more effective working mode. Much of this will have to do with the continuing *anxiety* some people are feeling, either about themselves being in contact with others, or about the structure—the activity—(or lack of it) in the group. A certain amount of anxiety in the group is natural and should be welcomed, as you would welcome it in any learning situation. When there is no anxiety, things get stagnant and the group becomes boring. If there is too much anxiety, however, people have difficulty taking in new information and certainly don't feel safe in taking interpersonal risks. They turn inward and outwardly shut down.

The right amount of anxiety promotes some risk taking and generates possibilities for new learning, just as some anxiety promotes performance in sports or the arts (Rowell & Martin, 2004). Maintaining just the right tension and tolerating a certain amount of anxiety is one of the great challenges of group leadership (Donigian & Malnati, 1997).

There is no substitute for experience in helping you learn how to gauge this tension level and aiding you in designing personal strategies to manage this well, so you'll need to be patient with yourself as you construct and lead new groups.

There are some characteristics of this anxiety in groups, however, that you can know about at the outset, so at least you'll be prepared for what might happen.

This anxiety in the group might be related to one or more factors about individuals in the group or about their feelings specifically related to being in the group. Some members may have substantial fears about simply being in close proximity to other people, particularly when they think that others may see them as they really are. Some people in your group may have had difficulties making close friends and relationships generally in life, and this difficulty, with its accompanying anxiety, will most certainly be carried over into this group experience (Boccato & Capozza, 2011).

Many of us have aspects of ourselves, things that we've experienced, for which we carry some shame and possibly even some guilt. If you have such people in your group, there may be some fear that others will judge them if they show too much of themselves. Additionally, some people in your group may have some emotional or mental problems that are triggered by other people. They may be made unusually anxious by seemingly innocuous behavior of others. One of your ultra-sensitive members, for example, might be really disturbed by another member who is unusually quiet. She might fantasize all kinds of things about the quiet and about what the person is thinking, most usually assuming that the other's thoughts are critical and judgmental.

Then there is the anxiety related to differences between people. There may be racial, ethnic, religious, gender, or other kinds of differences in your group that may cause anxiety for some. People are oftentimes afraid of that which they are not familiar, and these differences may cause difficulty for some.

Paradoxically, the opposite can also cause anxiety. People who are quite familiar with other people in the group may also be nervous. They may harbor unspoken—or sometimes spoken—concerns about things about them that might be shared by these other people inside or outside the group.

And then there is simply the natural anxiety of being in a group. The anxiety we talked about in the last chapter, the anxiety associated with being in a new group, continues into this engaging stage. People are still concerned about being judged, about doing the "right" things in the group, and about being liked and accepted by the group. Depending on how well the structured activities you've provided have worked in the group, this kind of anxiety will either be less or greater than when the group first began.

The anxiety that is present in the group, whether it is specific to individuals or more of a general group characteristic, may show itself openly or in more indirect ways. There may be a pervasive *resistance* (or reluctance) to move forward in positive directions. While you may be invested, for example, in people becoming more personal and self-disclosing in your group, individuals in the group—or even the whole group—may dig in their heels and hold back. People may be afraid to risk becoming more personal, more vulnerable, because of that same old fear of judgment: "If I show too much of myself, people won't like what they see, and then they won't like me."

In this "engaging" stage of your group, some members' resistance may become more up front, more palpable. While at the start of your group you may have had some inkling that some people might be reluctant to share about themselves, now that reluctance has blossomed in full view of everyone. You can assume that the resistance you see—and it can take many forms—is usually all about the anxiety simmering below the surface.

The resistance to becoming more personal and connected with others in the group might be expressed in either *active or passive* ways (O'Reilly & Parker, 2013). When the resistance is active, it's obvious. Some people may come late or try to leave early. Others may actively undermine group activities and discussions with inappropriate behavior and talk. Some may joke around during times when you're trying to get something serious going. Two or three people may form a subgroup and strive to undermine the activity of the large group. If people have been coerced into being in your group (e.g., as an alternative to incarceration), their resistance may be escalating beyond the initial disgruntlement displayed in the group's early meetings (Rabinowitz, 2014).

Other ways of expressing resistance may be more passive, less obvious. Some people may simply be silent, and not participate. Some may be outwardly helpful, even talking about how much they like the group, but are not really engaging with others in productive ways (Figure 8.1).

There are some *common problem behaviors* that are typically related to resistance in groups that are in this engaging stage and will need your attention. I'll simply list and describe them here, and then in the next section of the chapter, we'll talk about the things that should happen and the skills you'll need to deal with these behaviors.

Some of the problem behaviors you might encounter in the engaging group include the following:

Advice Giving

This is a common problem encountered in many relatively new groups. Sometimes, even inexperienced group leaders can engage in this (Stone & Waters, 1991), despite the fact that generally poorer outcomes are associated with group leaders giving advice to individuals in the group (Crits-Christoph, Johnson, Connolly Gibbons, & Gallop, 2013). When one person talks about a difficulty, one or more other members try to offer quick-fix solutions. Instead of simply listening and reflecting on the dilemma that's been described, people will offer band-aid suggestions about what should be done. There are two problems with this kind of advice

Figure 8.1   Resistance Can Come in a Variety of Forms

giving: It is rarely what is really needed, and it also suggests that the person with the dilemma is incapable of making his or her own decisions.

Conflicts Between Members

Personality clashes, as we saw in the vignette that started this chapter, or competing for attention and control are the two most common ways conflict might emerge in the group.

One or More Members May Become Silent, Seemingly Disengaged

Silence is not always a sign of resistance (Yildirim, 2012). Some people are simply vicarious learners, and they learn by watching others. Usually, however, you can assume that silence is a problematic sign of resistance. Sometimes a member might be typically silent, and only break silence by making occasional critical or sarcastic remarks about other individuals or the group's activities. This is never productive.

Storytelling

Instead of talking personally in the group, some people may take the opportunity to talk to tell lengthy tales of their experiences. This is oftentimes used as way of avoiding talking more personally (Hetzel, Barton, & Davenport, 1994). As a variation on this, some may talk about personal situations of concern, but only in an intellectual, disconnected fashion. I've found this kind of storytelling particularly unhelpful in substance abuse treatment groups, where people may want to share their drug-dealing or drug-using horror stories.

Challenge to Your Authority

Someone in the group may think that he or she has more expertise or good ideas about how things should go in the group than you do. In some cases, he or she might.

Personal Attacks on Another Member or the Leader

Sometimes one member may be acting in ways that prompts others to respond negatively. This person may be monopolizing discussion or simply behaving in ways that others find distasteful.

There may also be dissatisfaction or anger related to what is or isn't happening in the group. Some people may be upset with how the group is going, and this may have more to do with being angry than anxious. Renate, for example, in the vignette that started this chapter, was expressing frustration that the group wasn't moving more smoothly in directions she wanted it to go. Others might mirror her frustration with the group, or it might be hers alone.

This "attack the leader" game puts you directly on the spot. It's not much fun when a group is aiming its dissatisfaction directly at you, but it's an important, potentially very productive time for the group. We'll talk about how you can deal with this momentarily.

Reflection and Discussion Exercise: Resistance and Problem Behaviors

You've just read about how resistance in a group, whether it's that of an individual or of the group as a whole, can result in some problem behaviors that will require some management by you, the leader. You will undoubtedly have to deal with these when you lead groups, and some of these behaviors will give you more trouble than others.

Look at these problem behaviors and consider the strategies you might use to deal with them. Each one will take some thought and consideration. Remember, you want the group to move on without becoming bogged down in one person's problem behavior, and yet you don't want to humiliate or embarrass anyone. How you deal with people in these situations communicates volumes to everyone in the group. How you handle conflict and problems tells people, either directly or indirectly, how safe a space this is. Make some notes about each of these situations.

Next, check those problem behaviors that you think will be most personally challenging for you as a group leader. Some of those behaviors might have been listed here, but you might be able to add some that you could anticipate would cause difficulty for you. What is it about these that you think would make them particularly difficult for you? What kinds of thoughts—and feelings—might you have as these problem behaviors are unfolding in your group? Take a few minutes to visualize the behaviors, and try to imagine your feelings that would be triggered by these.

If you are doing this exercise as part of a study group, take a few minutes to share your thoughts with some of your colleagues.

ESSENTIAL TASKS FOR THE ENGAGING GROUP

Helping your group negotiate this interesting stage in its development primarily involves helping it maintain itself as a safe place for people to share about themselves while also managing to encourage honest expression with others, even if that means some conflict between people. You want your members to see and experience this group as a place where they can feel safe—meaning being heard and respected—while also sometimes disagreeing, even strongly, with others.

This means that there are a couple of critical things you'll want to do here. One of these is to teach people how to deal honestly, even be in conflict with one another, while also being respectful. You want to teach people how to fight fairly, in other words. I have a pretty effective way of doing this that has served me well over the years, and I'll share that with you here. You can feel free to use this strategy and see if it works for you. Essentially, what I do is teach people how to give and receive feedback to one another and how to be assertive with others in the group. Most people who work with groups see this as a critical skill for members to learn (Crits-Christoph et al., 2013; Hsu, 2011; Kivlighan & Luiza, 2005). I put my own particular spin on how this lesson is delivered. Instead of teaching people in the group how to confront one another directly, I first use myself as an example as to how to best confront another. In addition to modeling how to deal with confrontation, this also serves to make the experience more immediate.

Remember the group vignette that started this chapter, where two of the men in the group, Matt and Alvero, were in conflict, and Renate was demanding that I step in and resolve things? Here's what I did, and would do similarly in most other groups at this stage of their development.

Teaching a Group About Dealing With Conflict: A Demonstration in Receiving and Giving Effective Feedback

First, when conflict begins to emerge in a group, I call a time-out. Then I suggest that the best way to proceed will be to do a small demonstration. I offer myself up, as a model, as an example of how people in the group might want to think about dealing with conflict. The initial part of this, I go on to say, involves learning how to receive difficult information (feedback) from others. This is a critical group skill, I tell them, that can help resolve conflicts in groups. Rather than talk about this, I suggest, let's demonstrate how this works here. "I invite you," I tell the group, "to take a little time to criticize me—how I've been leading the group, what I'm wearing, whatever. Feel free to make stuff up."

Typically there's some nervous laughter that follows this invitation (my groups these days are typically composed of usually polite graduate students). Then somebody will take the first shot: "You dress funny. You look like you walked out of a catalog from 1965." Then, after the laughter dies down, I'll say, "Yeah, I'm a real fashion plate. But can you tell me, specifically, what 'funny' means?" Then the person will make some comments about my socks, or shirt, or something. But people begin to get it—that my response is nondefensive, even a little self-deprecating, and asks for specificity.

Eventually, after a few of these inconsequential comments and jabs, there may be more substantive comments: "I thought that activity we did last week was really lame." Again, I force specificity: "What, exactly, does 'lame' mean?" And then, after the person has clarified exactly what the criticism is, I turn to the group and ask them how many feel similarly. I take a quick poll to see how much dissatisfaction with that activity there was.

Finally, someone might blurt out, "You're just such a jerk! (And then he will generally follow with a disclaimer—"But I don't really mean it, I'm just saying that for the exercise.") "No," I reply.

Stay with this . . . but you can't call me a jerk. No one in here can call me—or anyone else—names. I won't allow that. But there's something I'm doing here that you don't like, something that you find "jerky." Tell me, specifically, what that is.

After a few minutes of the group lobbing insults my way, and of my responding, we then talk about what they've observed happening. The group distills some observations and thoughts about this process, and then together we list some guidelines for dealing with—primarily in receiving—feedback, particularly when it's negative.

GUIDELINES FOR RECEIVING CRITICAL FEEDBACK

- Be nondefensive. Think of yourself as a martial artist when critical feedback is coming your way. Let the criticism flow around you; go with it—don't fight it.

- Force behavioral specificity and clarity. Exactly what does the other person want?

- When a person in the group is challenging you in what you're doing, check in with the rest of the group to see how widespread the dissatisfaction is. If nothing else, this process buys you some time to think and regroup.

- Express appreciation for the feedback, even though you might add that it was tough to hear. Tell the others that you'll seriously consider what's been said.

- View this "receiving feedback" session as a real opportunity to make the relationship (or group, if it's directed at you, as leader) deeper, better.

- Seriously consider whether there are things you can do to accommodate the feedback—while still maintaining your integrity and bottom line of what you hold important.

- Don't allow personal insults to you as a person. Name calling should not be tolerated. What, again, are the specific things that the others might find troubling?

All these guidelines that have just been listed for receiving feedback have to do with when the feedback is negative. Naturally, there is also *positive feedback*. This kind of feedback can give you a sense that what you're doing is being received well. When given positive feedback, you can simply acknowledge it, thank the person who has given it to you, and move on. Even here you might ask for specificity.

The ability to receive feedback, whether critical or positive, is a skill that you can hone with practice and experience. Your ability to model this as a group leader will be the best way you can instruct people in your groups—in addition to actually spelling out the mechanics of receiving feedback, as we've done here—how they can receive feedback themselves.

Once I've discussed ways people can receive feedback, using myself as an example, I work with a group to define the best ways feedback can be given.

Once again, now that you've used yourself as a model for how to receive— and give—feedback, you can begin to deal with the conflicts that come up between your group members as they arise. While you may be encouraging your group members to be honest with one another, and to share difficult information with one another, you may also need to remind people occasionally about these guidelines to make sure that disagreements are managed well. Some conflict in your group can be tolerated, even welcomed—as long as people fight fair.

GUIDELINES FOR GIVING FEEDBACK

Think of the feedback you're sharing as information that will be helpful for the person receiving it to know about.

The information should be directly related to some piece of behavior that has been observed (or heard).

- Keep it short, simple, and specific.
- Avoid judgmental comments.
- If you can, share how you feel and what you want.

Example: "When I heard you talking about your kids, with so much obvious pride about them and their achievements, I felt really wonderful, glad about it all, and for you. I'd love to hear more about them."

Example: "You just spoke to her in a really loud voice—I don't know how she took it, but I felt pretty scared. I'd really appreciate it if you could tone it down a little."

ESSENTIAL SKILLS FOR WORKING WITH THE ENGAGING GROUP

In addition to the skills introduced in the last chapter, there are some effective strategies that you can use in dealing with the engaging group, and particularly for dealing with problem behaviors. While you will continue to utilize those skills you've used to get the group up and running, these new skills will most likely come into play once your group has begun to get its legs under itself. These are the skills you'll want to use to deal with the anxiety, reluctance, and problem behaviors that might have emerged.

In addition to teaching people how to give and receive difficult feedback to one another, you can use this set of skills to address whatever negative behaviors are hindering group progress. Keep in mind that while you want to minimize these distracting problem behaviors, you want to proceed in a way that doesn't so unduly embarrass or, even worse, humiliate someone. You and your coleader have significantly more power, if only because of your position as designated leaders, than anyone else in the group. You never want to abuse this power or use it in ways that are destructive.

Following are descriptions of some of these skills you'll want to have at your disposal as you deal with your engaging group. You'll see that some of these skills are the same skills you'd use in any counseling or other kind of helping relationship. Three of these—linking, drawing out, and cutting off—are specific to work with groups.

It will be helpful for you to have some familiarity with and skill in using these skills before you embark on leading groups. You might consider reading books that review these skills and practicing the use of these skills with colleagues or friends. Also, please bear in mind that while these skills are listed here as for use with engaging groups, they are certainly also available for you to use with groups at other stages of development. Similarly, you may want to use skills listed in other chapters for use with groups that are engaging.

Reflecting

The ability to respond empathically to people is the hallmark of any good helping professional. You can best demonstrate your empathic interest by astutely listening to what someone says and responding back to them in a way that accurately captures the content and feeling of what has been said. This kind of intervention, when done skillfully and immediately, can do a lot to help a group move forward (Raviv, 2010).

Example: When, an eighth grade boy is telling you at length about being bullied, you might respond with, "It's really tough having a bunch of guys on your case . . . scary and really frustrating." The more accurately your reflection can capture the meaning—and feelings—of what has been said, the more clearly heard the other person will feel.

These kinds of reflections can also be very useful in dealing with someone who is challenging you or something that is happening in the group. Instead of becoming defensive, you can use a reflection to indicate your understanding of their dissatisfaction. In doing this, the person knows that, while you might not be in agreement, you at least are willing to try to understand his position.

Example: Someone in the group has just told you that he or she is upset that the group has been spending a lot of time talking about war and disease in Africa. You might say, "There is something about this discussion that's either not personally relevant for you—or maybe too personally relevant, and hitting close to home— that's really troubling." You could then encourage the person to talk more about this.

Using a Hunch (or Speculation)

A variation on reflection is the hunch. With this skill, you are speculating with someone about his or her reason for thinking, feeling, or behaving in some way. This is really adding some of your own thought to a reflection you're making. It's an extension of the reflection. This hunch—or you could call it speculation— invites the person you're talking with to consider the meaning of what she has been saying. Oftentimes, such a speculation will start with "I wonder what . . . ," or "It's interesting that. . . ."

Thus, with the previous example of reflection where the boy is being bullied, you might add to the reflection about it being a scary experience—"It's interesting that they single you out as a target." This invites him, in a way that is more effective than a question, to consider this whole bullying business.

Linking

Your ability to track the themes of what different individuals talk about in your group and then to tie those together cohesively with some kind of comment, usually a kind of reflection, will be a helpful tool in helping your group become more cohesive (Hsu & Woo, 2010; Morran, Stockton, & Whittingham, 2004). By tying these themes together, you help people to understand their commonalities and to connect them to one another.

Example: "It's interesting that three of us, in three different stories we've related about our parents, all seem to have the same kinds of issues with our dads."

Using Silence

Sometimes the best thing to say is nothing at all. It's almost always best to let someone else in the group come up with whatever solution, comment, or suggestion is needed. Your job is to provide the comment when you think the group is not ready or able to do it for itself. The younger the group (either in age or in stage of development), the less silence you'll want to tolerate. When you think the group does have the wherewithal to do and say what's needed, you can always make some kind of process comment about the silence: "There's a lot on the table, and we're not exactly sure where to go next." This kind of comment speaks about the silence, without you having to take responsibility or plot the direction for where the group will go.

Experience will be your best teacher as you figure out exactly how much silence is appropriate. You'll learn to discriminate different kinds of silence. There are silences that are comfortable, quiet reflection moments, and then there are silences that are filled with anxiety. Sometimes you can even reflect on this kind silence, maybe saying something like, "My sense is that this time of quiet, on the heels of all that we've been talking about, is really OK . . . that we're all chewing over what this all means for each of us, personally."

Dealing With Conflict

Learning how to give and receive accurate feedback, as we discussed earlier in this chapter, goes a long way in setting the stage for helping people in your group know how to deal with interpersonal differences of opinion or style. After modeling how to receive and give feedback yourself, you'll be in a good position to help others do that with one another. Your role, then, in helping people work out conflicts, will be to see that they play by the rules—no name calling, being behaviorally specific, and listening nondefensively to information that is shared. You can even have people in conflict practice reflective listening, where they try to accurately paraphrase what has been said to them.

Drawing Out and Cutting Off

You'll want to be able to encourage shy, quiet people in your group to talk, to draw them out. Sometimes people are quiet because of some past negative experiences, and drawing them out will require some care and sensitivity (Kieffer, 2006).

At the other extreme are people who are talking too much, or inappropriately. Sometimes you'll want to short-circuit someone who is giving inappropriate feedback to another person in the group (Morran, Stockton, Cline, & Teed, 1998). Not cutting off this kind of behavior can sometimes result in some serious harm being done to the group (Gillam, Coker, & Trippany, 2004).

You'll also want to shut off "blowviators" (people who just love to hear themselves talk) and people who can't stop themselves, for whatever reason, from speaking.

You never want to embarrass someone or unnecessarily put someone on the spot, so usually the best way to deal with this is to conduct some inclusive group activity, where there are distinct guidelines for participation and specified times for talking.

Cutting someone off who has been talking for an inordinate amount of time can be tricky. Again, you don't want to embarrass someone by simply shutting them down. Oftentimes saying something like, "These are some wonderful ideas you've tossed out. It'd be great to hear what other people think about this," can serve to shift the focus away from the overtalkative person. You can reinforce this by then turning your face and body toward others, inviting them to participate.

When inclusive activities don't succeed in either drawing out a quiet member (and, remember, some people will just want to remain very quiet) or cutting off someone who is talking too much, you might want to have a private conversation with that person before or after the group. We'll talk more of these skills of drawing out and cutting off in the next chapter.

Focusing

Different people in your group will bring up different things to discuss. You'll have to make choices about which of these things merit response. The ways you *selectively respond* to some of this material, and not other aspects of it, can serve to focus the group. You will want to selectively respond to the material that can help steer the group toward the goals and objectives that have been identified as of most interest to this group.

This can be particularly effective when it highlights material that is most personally and immediately relevant (Ormont, 2001).

I would also encourage you to think about using this skill of focusing, using your selective attention to some material that people bring up, to move your group into deeper reflection. Focusing can serve the purpose of helping a group to avoid skating on the surface and delve more deeply into material.

Example: Suppose you have a group of eight people. In one of your group meetings three or four people talk about the events of their week, and one of them talks about the loss of a job. This particular person and his job-loss issue seem to be the most significant event of the things that have been talked about. Moreover, you have a sense that this issue is laden with meaning for this man: His identity is wrapped up in his work; his sense of economic stability is threatened, the impact this will have on his family, and so on.

Thus, you might choose to respond to this person and his job-loss issue over the other things that have been brought up. Moreover, you might want to think about responding to him with reflections and speculation that invite moving into the issue with more depth, with something like, "Oh sheesh, losing a job can be really difficult. Really hard. And I have a sense that there's a whole lot of meaning attached to this event for you."

Observing

You'll want to continue to observe the overt and covert behaviors of people in the group, as well as keep track of your own reactions to all of this. Where do people sit, who do different people talk with most, who seems to be emerging as a leader? All of these things, and more, are indicators of how things are going in the group. This observation will also give you a rough sense of how individuals are doing, particularly with regard to their relationships with one another (Lucas, 2000). You'll want to continue to observe on three levels: (1) the intrapersonal (your own feelings and thoughts), (2) the interpersonal (relationships between individuals), and (3) the group, or collective.

Using Humor

The skillful use of humor can go a long way to lighten the mood of a group that has gotten heavy or bogged down (Cooperberg, 2010; Grover, 2010). The best kinds of humor are those quick reflections on something that has transpired in the group, including gentle self-deprecating remarks you might make about yourself

ESSENTIAL SKILLS FOR WORKING WITH THE ENGAGING GROUP

- Reflecting
- Silence
- Focusing
- Hunch/Speculation
- Dealing With Conflict
- Observing
- Linking
- Drawing Out and Cutting Off
- Using Humor

or your own contributions to the group. Humor should never be used in a way that might embarrass someone in the group.

SOME SPECIFIC SUGGESTIONS ON USING SKILLS FOR PROBLEM BEHAVIORS

Three of the problem behaviors listed earlier are quite common in engaging groups, and the application of some specific skills we've just discussed can usually go a long way toward eliminating or minimizing those.

The first two of these behaviors are storytelling and advice giving. When one or more people start telling stories, instead of asking them to become more personal and stop the storytelling, you can try to turn your attention to someone who is talking more personally and relevantly in the ways you'd like to see the group move. This selective attention, which is really a kind of behavioral shaping, can serve to focus the group in ways that you think will be most productive.

With the advice giver, you can make some cogent reflections about the advice, again shaping it in ways that you'd prefer people begin to talk with one another. In way of example, consider the person who advises another to leave a job she really doesn't like, mostly because of a difficult supervisor. Instead of telling the person to quit giving advice, you might say, "You really feel for the position she's in with her boss. It must be really hard for someone to consider giving up a good situation, and a good salary, just because of someone who's a real pain." Again, you're modeling how you think people can best respond to one another (e.g., using reflections instead of giving advice), and once you've done this a number of times, people will generally begin to catch on.

Failing this, you could make some oblique comments about the function of advice: that it's not usually taken, and when it is taken and goes wrong, it invariably comes back to bite the adviser.

Finally, there may be the person who challenges your authority. This is someone in your group who thinks he or she knows more than you. Try to avoid getting into a struggle for power with him or her. Why not power share by giving him or her a piece of the action? When, for example, I have a student who claims to know about a specific subject more than I do, I invite him or her to prepare a mini-lesson for the group, freely acknowledging that I might not be an expert on that topic. You can do similarly with someone who challenges your authority.

THE *NEW DIRECTIONS* GROUP ENGAGES

Let's revisit our school-based group of kids with changing families. Vanessa and Gary, coleaders, had been working with their group of teens, the *New Directions* group, for 3 weeks. Things had generally been going well, but they were becoming concerned about two group members. One of these kids, Amy, was silent and withdrawn. The other, Ted, was talking too much. He had a steady stream of complaints about the fact that the group was meeting during a time that he was scheduled to have a study period. Mostly, he complained about the fact that he was missing out on the prime time to get his homework done.

The group's first two meetings had been primarily devoted to introductions, a review of the group's goals, and some instruction about how people could best use the group. Vanessa had used some of the final moments of the second group meeting to do a short lesson on *giving and receiving feedback.*

As the third meeting of the group began, Gary and Vanessa both *observed* that Amy was sitting a little more removed than she had been in the previous two meetings. While most of the group sat fairly close to one another, her seat was set back a couple of feet, just off center with the rest of the group. Then, before anyone else started talking, Ted started in once again, on his not being able to use this time to study for an important test.

Vanessa noted that Ted's complaining was starting to make some people in the group angry, and she was concerned that the group would turn on Ted, and in their criticism of him perhaps even provide Ted with the excuse he needed to leave the group.

Gary decided that some kind of intervention was necessary. He then went around the group, checking in with each person, asking about the timing of the group meeting, and whether it was problematic for anyone else. This only took about 5 minutes, and while a couple of people said the time wasn't ideal, everyone—excepting Ted—said the time was OK.

Gary then told the group that, had there been widespread dissatisfaction with the meeting time, they would have tried to find an alternate time. "But," he said, this time directly to Ted, "there really doesn't seem to be anyone else besides you who has too much of a problem with this time." And then Gary went on, trying to make some kind of a *reflection* about the meaning of all this for Ted. "Naturally, Ted," he said,

> if this time is really no good, you could decide that your study hall is where you need to be, and you could quit the group. But maybe there's more to this than meets the eye; maybe it's not all about what time this group is meeting . . . You sound like you're under a lot of pressure.

With this comment, Mark was taking an educated stab at the issue of time, making a kind of *hunch* about what the real issue of the timing of the group was about for Ted.

To his credit, Ted got very thoughtful about Gary's reflection. He then went on to say that, yes, he was experiencing a lot of pressure, some of it internal, but lots of it coming from his parents. He talked about his parents' impending divorce, their own stresses at home, and their striving to ensure that Ted was successful at school. "Maybe they don't even know about how much they're stressing me out," said Ted, "but it's huge!"

Vanessa could see that others in the group were reacting to Ted's comments about stress. "I can tell," she said, "that Ted's dilemma has struck a chord with others here. Let's take a little time to talk about this business of stress in our lives—and it would be good to hear, at least a bit, from everyone." In this invitation to talk about stress, Vanessa was looking to *link* Ted's personal story to the experiences of others in the group. She was also hoping that by asking everyone to participate in the discussion about stress, Amy might be *drawn out.*

By utilizing these effective strategies—their abilities to observe and accurately reflect the meaning of what was going on beneath the problematic behavior and to link an individual's emotional difficulties to those of others—Vanessa and Gary helped the group to move forward.

GROUP FISHBOWL LAB PRACTICE EXERCISE

This practice exercise will take some preparation time. You might even want to allow a day or more to plan for this.

Consider the exercises (all of which were designed by graduate students) that are included in #5 of the For Further Thought section at the end of this chapter. You can pick one of these for your practice purposes. Any of these exercises might be used after a group has gotten past its initial beginnings. Alternatively, you could use an exercise that you create, or one that you find from some other source. An ideal exercise would be one that is designed to manage conflict situations.

In this group fishbowl exercise, designate two members of your group as coleaders, four to six as members, and the rest as observers.

If you are one of the designated leaders, spend some time talking this over with your coleader and plan about how you'll want to approach this. You might want to change/adapt the exercise you've chosen in ways that best suit your own group's needs. Then, when the time comes for the group to begin, introduce and conduct the exercise, just as you might if you were really running this group over time. Do what you can to include everyone, drawing on the skills we've talked about thus far.

If you are a member in this group fishbowl exercise, you should role-play a person who might be involved in this exercise (e.g., a middle school child for the career exploration exercise). Adapt your own personality to the role you are playing.

If you are an observer in this exercise, you should silently watch the group interaction and take note of how people are interacting and of how the leaders are responding. Think about what seemed to be particularly useful in moving the group along. When the fishbowl exercise has been completed, share your observations. As you do this, remember the guidelines for giving feedback—you want the information you share to be helpful.

Take perhaps 30 minutes to conduct this group exercise. Then take a few minutes to incorporate feedback from observers and to discuss the experience.

CONCLUDING THOUGHTS

The group that has matured to the point where people are engaging with one another more honestly and directly is doing exactly what it should be doing. This is a development that you should look forward to and embrace. Like the adolescent who rebels and tests limits, so too the group struggles out of its childhood, through this engaging period, toward some kind of more adult status.

Whatever the dissension is about, it is most likely not all about you and dissatisfaction with what you're doing. There may be some things that you're doing with the group, however, that need to be examined and modified. Your job is to sort out what should be seen as simply a group testing its muscles and what really needs to be adjusted on your part.

Remember, the group that can successfully engage and challenge one another—and you—and successfully work through those issues, will feel more powerful and responsible for itself. You can think of the transition like this:

Engagement → Empowerment → Cohesion

Disagreement among members is fine, as long as some basic rules of respect are followed. Teaching people how to effectively give and receive feedback will go a long way to help establish this foundation of respect.

As you work your way through this interesting phase of your group's developmental life, think like the parent of a rebellious adolescent. Have faith that with your skillful leadership skills—including your grit and patience—this, too, shall pass.

FOR FURTHER THOUGHT

1. Locate and examine structured exercises for dealing with conflict. These might be called exercises for "conflict resolution." A suggestion would be to use the books of exercises listed in the previous chapter.

2. Create an exercise designed to help people who are in conflict or to resolve a dispute. Consider creating a group fishbowl practice session to try the exercise out.

3. Examine a structured lesson plan for teaching people how to be more assertive. Compare that plan with the discussion in this chapter about the best ways people can give and receive feedback in groups.

4. Examine the literature related to conflict, or "storming," in groups. Compare and contrast what you read—and perhaps your own experience—with what has been discussed as "engagement" in this chapter.

5. Following is an exercise that might be used with an engaging group. You can use this for your group fishbowl lab practice exercise, or alternatively, you could use an exercise from another source or create one of your own.

YANKEE CAREER SWAP

—Brenda Logee

Goal: Career exploration

Target Population: 5th- to 8th-grade students

Size of Group: Minimum five participants, no maximum

Materials: Twenty or more large index cards displaying picture and description of different careers with a mixture of "blue-collar" and "white-collar" jobs.

Setting: Classroom or after-school activity room

Procedure: Students stand or sit on chairs in a circle with cards placed face down on floor in the middle of the circle. The first student selects a card randomly, returns to seat, reads aloud the job description, and shows the group the career picture. The next student (similar to Yankee gift swap) may choose the career card of the first student or may select a card from the pile and read it to the group. One at a time, each student chooses a career card, either one that has already been selected or drawing from the pile. If someone loses his or her card to another player, he draws a new card from the pile. When everyone has a card, the first person to start the activity gets to take another by either keeping the card he or she is holding or selecting a new one from the pile. Then everyone takes turns stating what career card they ended up with. This should generate a discussion of the "fit" of the card each person has drawn. It could also serve as the basis for research projects that might be assigned regarding these careers.

REFERENCES

Boccato, G., & Capozza, D. (2011). Attachment styles and social groups: Review of a decade. *TPM-Testing, Psychometrics, Methodology in Applied Psychology, 18*(1), 19–30.

Bonebright, D. A. (2010). 40 Years of storming: A historical review of Tuckman's model of small group development. *Human Resource Development International, 13*(1), 111–120.

Cooperberg, D. M. (2010). Using humor to advance group work. In S. S. Fehr (Ed.), *101 Interventions in group therapy* (Rev. ed., pp. 443–447). New York, NY: Routledge/Taylor & Francis.

Crits-Christoph, P., Johnson, J. E., Connolly Gibbons, M., & Gallop, R. (2013). Process predictors of the outcome of group drug counseling. *Journal of Consulting and Clinical Psychology, 81*(1), 23–34.

Donigian, J., & Malnati, R. (1997). *Systemic group therapy: A triadic model.* Belmont, CA: Thomson Brooks/Cole.

Gillam, S. L., Coker, A. D., & Trippany, R. L. (2004). Cutting off: "It just feels impolite." In L. E. Tyson, R. Pérusse, & J. Whitledge (Eds.), *Critical incidents in group counseling* (pp. 259–264). Alexandria, VA: American Counseling Association.

Grover, S. (2010). "What's so funny?" The group leader's use of humor in adolescent groups. In S. S. Fehr (Ed.), *101 Interventions in group therapy* (Rev. ed., pp. 87–91). New York, NY: Routledge/Taylor & Francis.

Hetzel, R. D., Barton, D. A., & Davenport, D. S. (1994). Helping men change: A group counseling model for male clients. *Journal for Specialists in Group Work, 19*(2), 52–64.

Hsu, Y. (2011). Practicum school counselors' concerns, learning, and experiences in group supervision. *Chinese Journal of Guidance and Counseling, 31,* 61–100.

Hsu, K., & Woo, S. (2010). Dealing with instances of heightened emotionality: Intervention strategies in the group counseling. *Chinese Journal of Guidance and Counseling, 27,* 245–284.

Kelly, T. B., Lowndes, A., & Tolson, D. (2005). Advancing stages of group development: The case of a virtual nursing community of practice groups. *Groupwork: An Interdisciplinary Journal for Working With Groups, 15*(2), 17–38.

Kieffer, C. C. (2006). Review of interactive group therapy in addiction: Intervention for dynamic groups. *Journal of Groups in Addiction & Recovery, 1*(1), 129–131.

Kivlighan, D., Jr., & Luiza, J. W. (2005). Examining the credibility gap and the mum effect: Rex Stockton's contributions to research on feedback in counseling groups. *Journal for Specialists in Group Work, 30*(3), 253–269.

Lucas, P. (2000). A consultant-led group for in-patients in a medium secure unit. *Psychiatric Bulletin, 24*(7), 269–271.

Maples, M. F. (1988). Group development: Extending Tuckman's theory. *Journal for Specialists in Group Work, 13*(1), 17–23.

Morran, D. K., Stockton, R., Cline, R. J., & Teed, C. (1998). Facilitating feedback exchange in groups: Leader interventions. *Journal for Specialists in Group Work, 23*(3), 257–268.

Morran, D. K., Stockton, R., & Whittingham, M. H. (2004). Effective leader interventions for counseling and psychotherapy groups. In J. L. DeLucia-Waack, D. A. Gerrity, C. R. Kalodner, & M. T. Riva (Eds.), *Handbook of group counseling and psychotherapy* (pp. 91–103). Thousand Oaks, CA: Sage.

O'Reilly, M., & Parker, N. (2013). "You can take a horse to water but you can't make it drink": Exploring children's engagement and resistance in family therapy. *Contemporary Family Therapy: An International Journal, 35*(3), 491–507.

Ormont, L. R. (2001). Bringing life into the group experience: The power of immediacy. In L. B. Furgeri (Ed.), *The technique of group treatment: The collected papers of Louis R. Ormont* (pp. 355–371). Madison, CT: Psychosocial Press.

Rabinowitz, F. E. (2014). Counseling men in groups. In *A counselor's guide to working with men* (pp. 55–70). Alexandria, VA: American Counseling Association.

Raviv, D. (2010). Using the group power for interpretation. In S. S. Fehr (Ed.), *101 Interventions in group therapy* (Rev. ed., pp. 255–258). New York, NY: Routledge/Taylor & Francis.

Rowell, C. J., & Martin, S. B. (2004). Review of sport psychology: From theory to practice. *Sport Psychologist, 18*(1), 112–113.

Stone, M. L., & Waters, E. (1991). Accentuate the positive: A peer group counseling program for older adults. *Journal for Specialists in Group Work, 16*(3), 159–166.

Tuckman, B. W. (1965). Developmental sequence in small groups. *Psychological Bulletin, 65*(6), 384–399.

Yildirim, T. (2012). The unheard voices in group counseling: QUIETNESS. *Kuram ve Uygulamada Eğitim Bilimleri, 12*(1), 129–134.

Chapter 9

Leading the Working (Norming–Performing) Group

The way a team plays as a whole determines its success. You may have the greatest bunch of individual stars in the world, but if they don't play together, the club won't be worth a dime.

—Babe Ruth

GREAT GROUPS IN ACTION: A GROUP VIGNETTE

Some groups seem to work better than others. This book, naturally, aims to help you work with groups in a way that ensures that they will go well. You will find, however, that even though your preparations and work for one group are pretty much the same as that for another, one group may simply seem to coalesce and work together better than the other.

There are good groups, groups where people get along well, where they share details of their lives, and where they get feedback from others about how they are perceived. And then there are great groups, where there is a significant level of trust and intimacy and where people take significant—but contained—risks with one another.

I recall one of these great groups and one particular day at one of our meetings. We had been meeting weekly, and things had been going pretty well. People in the group seemed to enjoy one another's company while accepting their differences.

They were talkative and not reluctant to share personal material, and some were reporting that coming to the group was having a positive impact on their lives at home and at work.

This was a group that had come together around issues related to grief and bereavement. I had put the word out to my contacts in schools and to the human service and medical communities that this was to be a group for people who had lost friends or family through some kind of death. I had received 20 inquiry calls, 12 had shown up for initial interviews to hear more about the group, and we now had a group of eight people who were coming regularly. This was a closed group, meaning that this same group of eight people met every week.

Each of our meetings had been filled with stories about the people who had died. Some of the deaths had been of natural causes, some had been by suicide, and one had been from a drug overdose. While there were eight people in the group, each with distinct stories and personalities, four stand out in memory.

Jessica talked bitterly about her husband and his slow death resulting from his chronic alcoholism. She had divorced him years before his death, yet she cared for him in his final months, the time when he was at his sickest. She regaled the group with stories about what an awful person her ex was. I began to experience her as something of a whiner, a chronic complainer, and found myself wondering what it might have been like for the ex-husband to live with her during his last days on the planet. Additionally, she was a one upper, always coming up with a problem that was worse than what another person in the group would describe.

Gabriel was a man's man—a truck driver by profession, stoic, and not very therapy-wise. He loved to listen to stories about others' situations, their losses, and then give them some piece of advice to make things better. He was a fixer. I had seen my role as trying to teach him to modify his need to make everything better and to help him learn some basic listening and responding skills. Different group members had generally reinforced this by telling him that what they really wanted from him was simply to be heard and understood. His wife had died of cancer, and though the death had occurred 10 years previously, her presence was still very much a part of his life.

Caitlyn was the group mother. Her response to loss was to care for others. She had lost a child to a heroin overdose and was heroically struggling to cope with his death by involving herself in a variety of drug abuse prevention programs (not an atypical response to tragedy—an attempt to somehow transform the loss). Her pain was palpable, and her stories about her attempts to thwart his drug use were hard to hear. Despite her own pain, she was always emotionally "there" for other group members when difficulties were discussed. She even brought home-baked bread and cookies to group meetings.

And then there was Gene. Gene's father had died 1 year ago, and on the day we were meeting, it was the anniversary of his dad's death. Gene had just been to the cemetery to visit his dad's grave. Gene's father had been very religious, a devout Roman Catholic, and Gene had come to share this devotion. But the dad had also been something of a bully, had ruled the home with an iron fist, and had sometimes been cruel with Gene, his brothers, and their mother. Gene's mother, he said, had seemed almost relieved when he died.

I experienced Gene as tightly controlled and out of touch with his inner world. He usually looked miserable, despite his claims of how well he'd been doing. When he talked about his dad, he used platitudes like "He's in a better place" and "It was God's will" to explain his response to his father's death. He described his home life with his family as idyllic—problem free. Being a naturally suspicious person (a decent clinician never takes what is said at face value), I never accept such sweeping characterizations as being wholly accurate. While in no way did I want to challenge his spiritual beliefs, I did want the group to help him dig below the surface of that perfect persona a bit. I thought that if he could loosen his grip on himself, he might not continue to appear quite so unhappy. In short, I wanted "Clean Gene" to rough it up.

On this particular Wednesday, we did our usual check-ins, where we briefly went around the group, each person talking briefly about the highlights of his or her week and how things were going. When we got to Gene, he said, "So you know that this is the day my dad died last year." "Yes," we said, "we remember."

He paused, and then, he said, "And I told you what he was like." "Yes," we said in unison, "we remember."

"Well, I've been thinking . . . ," and here he took a very long pause. The room got very quiet, and this lasted for quite some time. "Uh oh," I thought, "here we go. Clean Gene's about to take the lid off, and things are about to get really interesting."

The group, bless its collective heart, remained silent through these pauses, as Gene gathered himself to talk. No one jumped in with questions. It takes a while for a group to be able to suffer periods of silence, and thankfully, this was one the group didn't break. It kept the focus squarely on Gene.

"I've been thinking I'm turning out just like him." There was another long pause. The group maintained its silence, but many in the group were nodding in encouragement for him to go on. I was loving their silence and their nonverbal encouragement.

Finally, he spoke, and this time, it came out in a torrent. "I look in the mirror and I see his face. I look in my kids' eyes and I see myself when I was their age. I see their fear, their mistrust, their anger."

He continued,

I took care of the old man when he was sick. I managed his business affairs when he couldn't do it. I even washed him when he was too sick to do it himself. I was the dutiful son . . . and I hated every minute of it. I hated how he still controlled me; I hated how sick he got; I hated having to touch him. It got so bad sometimes I even almost threw up.

The group sat in a stunned silence as Gene recounted all this and more. I sensed that they felt as much as I did that this was a huge turnaround, a confession of immense proportions. For Gene to talk about these thoughts and feelings about his father, I imagined, was a betrayal of all that he supposed himself to be. He was shattering his image of himself as the dutifully loving son, of being something other than a fully loving, accepting person.

I really wanted to say something to Gene, to reassure him that these complicated feelings are normal and acceptable, particularly given what he'd been through in his history with his father—yet even greater than my desire to respond was my desire for someone else in the group to respond. Never do for the group, I thought, what the group can do for itself. So I hung on to my impulse to speak and held out, waiting for someone else to step up to the plate. I knew that this was a magic moment in our group, and that this was a wonderful opportunity for someone to respond with empathy and understanding. I continued to wait it out while Gene started to tear up and then to openly cry.

And then it came. "It can be really tough to have this idea about who and how you're supposed to be, and then all these feelings you have just don't line up. It sucks!" I was stunned. This response, this reflection of thoughts and feelings, was almost exactly what I could have said, and it came from a most unlikely source— Jessica. No whining here, no one-upmanship, nothing other than an intelligent and heartfelt response to this all-too-human dilemma of Gene's. She had avoided making suggestions or telling something about herself, and instead, she had accurately captured the essence of his dilemma—and the feelings surrounding it—and handed it back to him. I was sincerely moved, as I think most of us were, by this simple act of generosity. This brief interchange clearly demonstrated the healing capacity of groups—both for those who choose to take reasonable risks of self-disclosure as well as for those who respond.

Gene responded immediately to Jessica's comments. He continued crying freely and started banging his fists against his thighs. His feelings were fully engaged, and now, it did seem like a good time for a "leaderly" intervention, so I stepped in. "There's so much here, so much feeling, so many contradictions, and you've been beating yourself up for so long."

Now, the tears really came, not only from Gene but from others in the group as well. Gabriel, the stoic trucker, was weeping silently. Caitlyn simply sat quietly, one of the few times she didn't try to offer help. Others sat with their own personal thoughts about what Gene's admissions meant for them. All our own thoughts and feelings were being triggered by Gene's disclosures and emotionality. Gene—and

Jessica—had given the group permission to go deeper, and now, we had the opportunity to help Gene sort out the meaning of his tears, as well as begin to work with others about the meanings of theirs.

Gene had taken the risk of letting go of the known, the predictable, and allowed himself to show a side of himself rarely, if ever, shown to others. He had allowed himself to experience and show feelings in a way that gave others the permission to show theirs as well.

Furthermore, Jessica had modeled a way of responding that showed true understanding, a way of being present with Gene that was without judgment. She became, at least at this moment in time, the point person for a group that was demonstrating that it could hear and handle strong emotion and that people within the group could swim with one another through deep and difficult waters.

These few interchanges did, in fact, constitute a magical moment in this group. There was a current of feeling, an almost tangible electric connection between us, filling the room. I sensed that in this risk of disclosure and genuinely helpful responding lay the beginning of real work that we could do together. Gene would be able to explore the complexities of his relationship with his dad, with all of his family, including all of its contradictions. I hoped that the group would help him be more accepting of these contradictions, help him let go of some of his self-condemnation.

In the process of helping Gene continue to talk about and explore these thoughts and feelings—as well as in helping others who would inevitably step forward to take similar risks, now that Gene had broken the ice—we could all learn more about how to give responsively to another's pain and suffering.

This is the beauty of great groups: the giving, the risking, and the giving back again. The great group can be a place where one can let oneself out, and show parts not often seen, parts of a self that are too often filled with shame and regret. Moreover, it is a place where people can learn how to reach out to reassure and give sustenance to one another in a way that can be taken in and integrated. At its best, the group is a training ground for experimenting with new ways of being with people, for learning some new interpersonal skills, and for learning more about oneself.

These are some of the reasons why I love working with groups, and this is what I hope you come to love about them as well. The groups that I've enjoyed the most are like this one, groups where people like Gene choose to take the risk of becoming more vulnerable. These are groups in which people talk about things that are important and personal, and in a way that is heartfelt and with feeling, and where others witness and receive those disclosures with respect and concern. These are the truly great groups.

Groups create a space where people can not only learn more about themselves but also learn more about others and about themselves in relationship with others.

Groups, and perhaps everything that is important in life, are all about relationships. This book is about helping you lay the groundwork for groups that will work well and for creating the possibility that some will be truly great.

Reflection and Discussion Exercise

Following are some questions you could contemplate after thinking about this case vignette you've just read:

1. What are your overall reactions to this group interaction? What are your reactions and thoughts about the different members of this group?

2. How far along do you suppose this group to be? How many times has it met? Could Gene's disclosure have happened earlier in this group?

3. Is it the role of groups to encourage this kind of personal disclosure? Why or why not?

4. Would encouraging younger people to reveal themselves, like Gene has done here, be a good thing? Would you set any guidelines about age and self-disclosure in your groups?

5. What are your ideas about what might happen next (over the next few weeks) in this group?

Finally, if you are working on this exercise with other people, take a few minutes to discuss your thoughts with them.

This chapter will help you recognize and understand some of the dynamics of the group that has become fully productive and engaged. It will highlight some of the characteristics and features of the group at this stage of its developmental life and will provide you with some information about the skills you'll need to help work with this group. It will also provide you with ample opportunity to reflect on

---

LEADING THE WORKING GROUP

- Norms and Roles: Positive and Negative
- Strategies to Promote Positive Roles and Norms
- The Hallmarks of the Productive Working Group
- Skills for Leading the Working Group
- What to Do When It's Not Working

your ideas about these groups and practice some of your own leadership skills with a "norming and performing" group.

THE GROUP SETTLES INTO SOME REGULAR NORMS AND ROLES

As your group grows and gets it feet under it, there will be certain unspoken rules, or *norms*, that develop by which it will operate. People, for example, may sit in the same places, get quiet before the group starts, develop some routine jokes, or repeatedly have the same reactions to what you initiate. These and any other number of typical group behavior patterns may become regular occurrences in the group.

Relatedly, individuals may play specific *roles*, or parts, in this unfolding little drama. Their regular, somewhat predictable behaviors will typically support the norms that have developed in the group. You may be able to easily spot and name some of these—the monopolizer, the clown, the silent one, and so on. Some of these roles may be helpful, or *facilitative*, and some may be negative, or *obstructing*.

We talked earlier about how these norms and roles can theoretically affect how your group develops. We talked about how these norms, and particularly the kinds of roles that people adopt, can oftentimes be a replication of the ways in which they behave in most groups and of the ways in which they may have behaved in their families while growing up.

When you are in the midst of your developing group, all this becomes less theoretical and more of a real-life set of issues with which you'll have to deal. You'll most likely come to appreciate and value the facilitative roles that some play. They will mimic the kinds of skills you are trying to model—the reflective listening to others, the empathic understanding of the concerns shared by other group members, or the positive enthusiasm for the work of the group. They'll generally be hopeful and enthusiastic about the directions in which the group is moving. You will experience the ways in which they interact as supportive and in synch with what you are trying to do for the group.

Others may be playing less positive, obstructing roles. Some of these may pose minimal problems, like just being quiet, but one or more of these may be operating in roles that are really distracting, openly resentful, or reluctant to "get with the program." These can present you with some real challenges.

PROMOTING POSITIVE NORMS AND ROLES: MOVING TOWARD COHESION

When confronted with negative attitudes and behaviors, I would encourage you to think strategically. Start thinking—and strategize with your supervisor and/or your coleader—about the ways in which you can support the positive, facilitating things that happen in the group and minimize the obstructing behaviors. This can be a little tricky, because while you want to obviously throw your energy behind those who are acting in ways that promote the group goals, you also don't want to embarrass, or subtly shame, those who are more negative.

One of the best ways to funnel energy into positive directions is to *selectively attend* to those member statements that are operating in a facilitating manner. Simply respond more to the positive things that are said, while directing less energy toward obstructing commentary. You can even make affirming and supporting responses for the positive contributions the people make, perhaps not saying much—or anything—about the negative. This is a subtle *behavioral shaping* of your group, steering it in the positive, cohesion-building directions you want it to move.

When one or more persons are being particularly vocal in their obstruction, use your best *reflective listening* skills. Avoid becoming defensive, and roll with their resistance. Remember the martial arts analogy, and let their negativity flow around you. You can show that you understand what their complaints are without agreeing with them. Then, as we discussed earlier in strategizing how to deal with conflict in the group, you can check in with others to see how widespread the discontent is. If others share the concern, you can always nondefensively make some adjustments in what you're doing.

If one individual is alone in her or his complaints and negativity—and you've already found out that no one else shares that individual's perspectives—you could always have a *private conversation* with her or him, outside the group. Try to ascertain what it is that individual is really looking for (typically, some variation of affection or control) behind the obstructing behaviors. You can see if there are some things that you could let her or him do, or do for her or him, that would make the situation better. I wouldn't suggest having this conversation in the group,

---

TIPS FOR PROMOTING COHESION IN THE GROUP

Model the kinds of behaviors you want your members to emulate: empathy for others, enthusiasm, and a positive, hopeful attitude. Selectively attend to the positive, facilitating things the people say, giving less attention and responses to the negative.

In dealing with obstructive behavior or direct criticism, be nondefensive. Try to make reasonable accommodations that might empower the person who's being obstructive.

Use drawing out skills to encourage the quiet people to talk and cutting off skills to help the overtalkative people become more observant. Use inclusive activities, games, and exercises to promote total group engagement.

When someone is quietly subverting the group (e.g., showing up late, making negative aside comments, sulking), it might merit a private conversation to let him or her know that you've noticed and to find out what might make things better.

as there is too much of a chance that this singling out could be experienced as embarrassing.

If the person, for example, is complaining about other people in the group, you could tell her or him that you'd support her or his efforts to voice those complaints in the group. And then, you could help work those issues through. If the person is unhappy with some of the content under discussion, you could ask her or him to provide some alternative suggestions, maybe even lead a discussion in ways that would make her or him feel more included and valued. Negotiate seriously with the person, letting her or him know that you take her or his concerns to heart and that you want to help make this a positive experience for everyone, her or him included. If the person can leave this conversation feeling like she or he has been heard and that she or he has some power to influence how things go, she or he will most likely move from being an obstructer to a facilitator.

HALLMARKS OF THE GROUP THAT IS PERFORMING WELL

It's usually not hard to know whether a group is working well, or not. There will simply be an atmosphere of good will, perhaps some occasional humor, and a sense of bonding that has developed between members. People talk about looking forward to coming to group and about using the group as a silent advisor during their times away from the group. People in the group like one another, and there are possibilities that some of these relationships born in the group will continue after the group ends.

A single determinant of how well a group is doing has to do with its *cohesion.* This is a term borrowed from chemistry, derived from the Latin *cohaerere* (to stick together). The word accurately describes the bond that forms between people in the group when things are working well. While everyone in the group may not like everyone else equally, there is nevertheless considerable camaraderie and a sense of shared purpose (see Figure 9.1)

People in the group will be actively using the skills you have modeled. They will be listening to one another, responding with reflective comments, and will be giving one another feedback. When the group is working well, there simply seems to be a general sense of people caring about one another.

The "working" group will have rounded off some of the rough edges that characterized the "engaging" group. Because people now seem to be involved with one another in more accepting, generous ways, the information that gets shared by way of feedback is typically more positive. This opens the door for more member self-disclosure. When people feel safe, and sense that others genuinely care about them, there is more of an inclination to take risks, to be vulnerable.

Figure 9.1 The Cohesive Group Embraces Individual Differences

One of the shifts I've noticed in groups that have begun to work well has to do with a move away from advice giving toward more active listening and brainstorming about solutions to problems. While in early groups members may try to respond to one another primarily out of their own experiences, now there is a more respectful staying with the person who's sharing. There is less of an inclination to jump into finding solutions to problems people in the group bring up and more of an interest in fully exploring different options for collaborative action with them.

Thus, early in the life of the group, a response to someone whose dog has died may have been "Oh, I'm so sorry about your loss. I know what it feels like to lose a dog, because mine died a year ago. Here's how I dealt with it, and maybe this will work for you." In the later working group, this response might be slightly different: "Oh, I'm so sorry about your dog. This has got to be really hard. Can you tell us about it?" This latter response will be experienced as significantly more supportive and understanding and is indicative of the increased level of sophistication in the group.

This sense of cohesion and shared purpose extend to an acceptance of differences between people. Some of these differences may be attitudinal or relationship-style related (e.g., some people will be more vocal and active), and some may be cultural or ethnic. In the cohesive working group, these differences are embraced, and the people will want to learn more about what's different, while they will at the same time be accepting of those differences. The group that's cohesive creates an environment where differences can be safely explored.

> **HALLMARKS OF THE WORKING GROUP**
>
> - Cohesion
> - A Sense of Shared Purpose
> - Positive Norms Prevail
> - Members Facilitating, Supporting, and Empathizing With One Another
> - Acceptance of Individual Differences
> - Self-Disclosure
> - Giving and Receiving Positive Feedback

ESSENTIAL SKILLS FOR THE WORKING GROUP

It should go without saying that you'll continue to use all the skills we've discussed thus far in your work with a group. You'll want to ask questions, use exercises, and do all the things to lead the working, cohesive group that have helped bring the group to where it is now.

To work with the mature group, you'll also want to add some additional skills to your repertoire. You'll want to help your group dig deeper into personal issues that are brought up and help develop stronger ties between people in the group. The skills that follow should assist in these efforts.

Starting a Session

In addition to starting a new group at the beginning, there is also the need to know how to start each session of the group. You will most likely experiment with trying out some different ways to do this, and there are some typical ways in which experienced group leaders do this that you could try.

Sometimes, the group will have a structured plan or an exercise that you want to use to begin the group. This will then dictate how things get started. If there is no fixed plan, there are two alternative ways by which you could think about starting. One would be to summarize what had happened in the past week or two, and then, say something like "So, given all that we talked about past week, I'm not exactly sure who would like to pick it up from there . . . or maybe introduce something new."

Another common way of starting is to have everyone do a brief "check-in." Each member briefly says something about her or his week and then says whether or not she or he would like some group time to talk about a particular issue. Then, after everyone has checked in, you can come back to give the member time.

Affirming

Affirming is a demonstration of your positive belief in someone in your group. It may be making a statement about his or her ability to do something in the future or it may be a statement of your belief that someone is already doing something well. This might start with something like "I really like it when. . . .," or "I think it's great that you. . . ." Your affirmation of something this person is doing shows your respect for that person's thoughts or actions (Englar-Carlson, 2014).

An affirmation might even demonstrate your affection for this person. Thus, "It's great that you were able to do that. I think you're terrific" is an affirmation of the person and what's been accomplished. Naturally, when you make this kind of affirmation, you need to be aware of how others in the group will take it. Your affirmation of one person should not exclude others; so you'll want to make sure others are affirmed at some point as well. Your affirmations should help set a general group tone that is positive and hopeful (Kiselica & Englar-Carlson, 2010).

Validating

Validating is a lot like affirmation. With this skill, you are telling someone that you believe what's being said and that you have some understanding of the meaning of what's been told (Hall & Horvath, 2015; Howey & Ormrod, 2002). When someone talks about having been bullied as a child, for example, you can validate this by saying—perhaps with some kind of reflection—that you hear what's being said and that you understand, at some level, how difficult it must have been. "Thanks for sharing this really awful bullying experience you had with us. This must have been awful."

You will have people in your groups who have grown up in terribly nonvalidating environments, where they have been given lots of messages, in lots of different ways, about how their experience of what goes on around and inside them is not accurate.

Sometimes, people have been told, even as children, that their feelings— whatever they might be—are unjustified. While your validation of these people's experiences and feelings cannot change those earlier messages, it can help minimize the feelings of craziness one must feel when one is told that one's internal experience (e.g., feeling sad or angry) is inaccurate.

Cheerleading

There are times when you—and the group—can solidly back a member's plan to do something with unabashed encouragement. You can serve as a cheerleader for the things that need to be done (Kral & Kowalski, 1989; Schorr, 1995).

> *Cheerleading Example 1:* "You work hard and deserve more money! We know that you can convince your boss that you need a raise. Go for it!"

> *Cheerleading Example 2:* "You've studied hard and you know the material. We know you can do well on this test—go get 'em!'"

You want to make sure that your cheerleading is for the person, not for how well he or she performs, because there will be times when your cheerleading efforts don't pay off—the person doesn't get the raise or the student doesn't do so well on the test. You want the person to know that your support is for him or her and that it is not contingent on how well he or she does.

Brainstorming

Simply put, this is helping someone outline multiple strategies for dealing with a specific problem or situation (Sarnoff & Sarnoff, 2005). This may involve either you, or one or more group members, offering potential options for looking at someone's problem situation in a variety of different ways. The person in question might also offer some possible options. This way of helping someone strategize about courses of action is preferable to giving advice about one way to go—it's more respectful of an individual's capacity to make intelligent choices for herself or himself.

The following is an example:

Ok, so you say that your boss is intolerant, miserable, and mean. It looks like there could be a number of ways to go with this: You could quit, and find another job; you could get assertive and tell him where to head in; you could just suck it up, and let him do whatever. And I'm sure you've thought about some other options, as well.

Using Deeper Reflections

We've already discussed reflection as a critically helpful skill in letting people know that they've been heard and understood. This skill will continue to serve you well as your group grows and matures, and you can enlarge on its use with your ability to capture the full—sometimes less obvious—meaning and feelings associated with what's being talked about.

By way of an example, consider the woman who has been talking about the difficulties she's been having with her teenage daughter. The woman is a single parent, juggling work and parenting responsibilities, and the daughter has recently been getting into trouble at school. A simple reflection might be "You're having a hard time with your daughter." A deeper, perhaps more meaningful reflection could be "You've got so much on your plate, and being a mom with a kid who's having trouble on top of everything you do . . . this is just really tough."

The deeper reflection captures both the meaning and the feeling of what someone has been talking about. You can use your own experience and feelings associated with those as a guide to how to respond to someone. The more closely you can personally identify with the content of what someone is talking about, the more able you'll be to accurately and empathically respond with a deep reflection.

Summarizing

This is a skill typically used at the end of a group meeting, where you can tie together a lot of what's been said and done in the group that day (Madson, Schumacher, Noble, & Bonnell, 2013; Morran, Stockton, & Whittingham, 2004). You might start by saying something like "This has been quite a group meeting, and we've talked about a bunch of things." and then, you might go on to enumerate what those things are. You might end the summarization with a statement about how you can continue with a discussion of these things the next time you meet.

The best summarizations incorporate some *linking*, meaning that the items that are summarized are talked about in a way that connects the different things—and people in the group who talked about them—together. A good summarization can also serve a cutting off function. If, for example, someone brings up a weighty subject when only a few minutes are left, you can include to your summarization some kind of statement like "Wow, and now, in addition to all the other good stuff we've talked about, we've got this—and it'll be great to get into this next week."

Self-Disclosure

There are times when sharing something about yourself can help move a group in productive ways. In a previous chapter, for example, we talked about using some low-grade self-disclosures early on in the group as a way of modeling how people can talk about themselves.

Remember the "people as onions" analogy? You can model peeling back some of your own layers using some carefully thought-out self-disclosures. Now that your group has moved a bit farther along, you might use self-disclosures of your own experiences as a way of relating to the things people are talking about. You might also share your personal thoughts and feelings about what is being talked about in the group. Thus, there are two ways of self-disclosing: (1) sharing your personal experiences and (2) sharing your ideas and feelings. Using self-disclosure in either of these ways is also a means of modeling what you'd like others in the group to do.

There are some things to think about as you consider whether to make a self-disclosure. The first big consideration has to do with your ideas about the reasons for making a self-disclosure. The only legitimate reason for making a self-disclosure is as a means for helping the group move forward. Using self-disclosure as a way of impressing the group doesn't cut it. The basic question you should always ask yourself is "What purpose will telling the group this about myself—or sharing my ideas—serve?" If you can't come up with anything reasonable, don't share (Goodspeed, McCollum, & Bauman, 2004).

A second proviso about self-disclosure has to do with the kind of information you might share. Be very careful about sharing information that, if someone in the group chooses to, could possibly harm you. Anything you might share can possibly be used against you. Would you really, for example, advise a leader to share the details of her or his past drug use with her or his group of 16-year-old high schoolers?

Finally, do not choose to share anything about yourself that you haven't sufficiently worked through. You may be tempted to share stories of your own losses or other hardships with people who are talking about loss and difficulty; .but don't do it if you think that you won't be able to manage yourself in the telling. As a therapist friend of mine advises, shedding a few tears as you recount some of your personal difficulties is acceptable, even advisable, but sobbing is probably over the top. The group you are running is not the group where you want to do your own therapeutic work.

Hunches/Speculation

We talked about using hunches in the last chapter, and the basics of the use of this skill remain the same when leading the working group. The well-timed hunch, or speculation, can help expand someone's thinking about herself or himself (De Domenico, 1999). The level of hunch, however, like the level of reflections, becomes more sophisticated with the group that's been working together for some time. You and the group have more information about one another with which to form responses, so your hunches about what's going on in one another's world have the possibility of being more accurate.

Sometimes, your hunch can hold an idea of yours about what someone is saying that could be posed as "It's interesting that . . ." or "I wonder what. . . ."

The following is an example of a hunch:

It's interesting that you've been talking about this series of jobs you've had, and how you've never been appreciated for the work you've done. I wonder if perhaps there are some things you've done to undermine the positive contributions you've made.

Immediacy

Whenever you can make the material the group is discussing relate directly to what is happening in the here and now of the group experience, it sets the stage for some great, immediate learning. Bringing the "outside" into the immediate presence of the group is almost always a good idea. You can assume that people typically operate pretty much the same in most group situations, so if there are difficulties someone encounters in his or her world outside the group, those are most likely mirrored in the group. You have direct evidence of someone's positive and negative attributes as they play out before you. Providing the people in the group with information about how these attributes are perceived by the group might help them negotiate their lives outside the group more effectively (Hill, 2014; Sturges, 2012).

For example, given the previous "hunch" about the person's work history, you might make that more immediate by adding, "And maybe what goes on for you at work is just like some of the undermining you do with yourself with us (*and perhaps you could also cite some examples of when this has happened*)."

Silence

Sometimes, the best thing you can say is nothing at all. Unlike at the beginning of a group, where silence on your part can create and help escalate a lot of unwanted anxiety, a group that has grown and matured can likely tolerate some silence on your part. When the group gets quiet, particularly after some of the people have been doing some talking, you might just let things play out without saying anything for a while (Duba, Neufeld, & DeVoss, 2004).

Some silences feel comfortable. It seems that people are simply sitting, ruminating on what's transpired (Wood, 2012). Other silences are different, tinged with tension or pregnant with things that need to be said. Experience will help you distinguish the differences between these and will serve as a guide to when and how to jump in with something to say (Mance, 2011).

Oftentimes, when you're getting uncomfortable with the amount of silence that you're all sitting in, you could simply make a process comment—a *hunch* or *speculation*—about the silence itself. You could say something like "This quiet time is really interesting. Some silences are just quiet times; other silences are just filled with things waiting to be said. I wonder what kind of silence this is."

Another kind of silence can typically unfold in the middle of a group activity. If, for example, you've invited individuals to volunteer to take turns doing something, a number of the people may quickly participate, and others may hang back. You may get to a point where there is silence, as the group waits to find out if there will be another volunteer for the activity. At this point, I might say something like

> You know, this is always one of those tricky times for a group leader. You want to give just enough time so that someone who's a little reluctant to jump in might actually go ahead and do it—but not so much time as to create a lot of undue pressure. Let's give it another couple of minutes, and we'll see what happens.

Then, either another person volunteers or you can decide to proceed.

Reframing

This skill involves helping someone in your group look at a particular aspect of their life situation in a new, more positive way. Your ability to provide a new way of thinking about a difficult life situation can go a long way toward helping someone view his or her own role in the situation more positively (Schneider & Krug, 2014; Singh, Meng, & Hansen, 2014). For the young woman who looks back on her difficult childhood, when she had to take care of her younger siblings because of her parents' drug addiction, you could suggest that while she undoubtedly lost some prized aspects of childhood, she also gained some remarkable life skills. She now has the capacity to understand and care for the needs of others, and she can be reassured in the knowledge that she is a resilient survivor of really difficult situations.

For the new dad, struggling to maintain a job, continuing his education, and supporting his young family, you could encourage him to view his situation as more than just a series of burdens. He can be encouraged to see the heroic aspects of what he's doing—to look at the nobility involved with the struggle to improve himself and provide for his family.

Naturally, you don't want to use reframing in a way that invalidates people's thoughts about their experiences, and you'll want to help them explore and express the thoughts and feelings associated with those experiences. You can, however, also provide them with newer, unique, and alternative ways of looking at their lives. Reframing can help instill hope and inspiration where previously there was little of either (Scheel, Davis, & Henderson, 2013).

Linking

When a number of people have been talking about things in the group, whether these are personal issues, common concerns, or any other matters, it's always helpful if you can draw some common threads out of all this material and make a comment (reflection) about it. "Linking" these different strands of thought together helps people see commonalities between themselves, as well as provides a new way for each person to consider new learning from the ways in which others deal with their particular situations (Davis & Meara, 1982; Morran et al., 2004). This is a skill that helps the people see their own issues in perspective, to appreciate the fact that others may share these concerns. Linking is a skill that, when used effectively, can help connect people to one another in the group and even to people in the wider human community (Wilke, 2003).

For example, let's say that in the group Mary was talking about problems with her young child who doesn't want to go to school, Amy shared some concerns about an elderly parent who might need to go into a nursing home, and Luis talked about his brother's trouble with the law. As a way of linking all this together you might say,

> The three of you have really different situations, but all these are related to family and feelings of responsibility that come up as you consider these difficult situations. This is really hard and hard to figure out what to do.

This linking statement helps Mary, Amy, and Luis see their problems in a more universal light and can serve to bring them into closer alliance. It also serves the function of possibly helping each member learn about how to deal with his or her own difficulty by seeing how the other two deal with theirs.

The best linking comments/reflections capture—just like any reflection—both the common themes/meaning of what's been discussed as well as the feelings attached to the situations.

Drawing Out

You will sometimes have people in your groups who don't say much. They may be shy, they may be intimidated by others in the group, or they may just be naturally quiet. You'll want to develop an ability to get these people involved, to draw them out (Kieffer, 2006; Nosko & Breton, 1997).

As a group leader, you have an ethical responsibility to make sure that everyone has an equal opportunity to participate, so if you think that any of the reasons for nonparticipation have to do with cultural, racial, or other "differences" between this member and others, this quietness takes on some special reasons for concern.

I have found that the best way to draw people out in a group is to use exercises or some kind of structured activity that more or less mandates the entire group's participation. Sometimes, this takes the form of an invitation: "With this next topic we're discussing, it'd be great to hear from everyone. Let's go around the circle, with each of us sharing our take on this." This kind of activity, in other words, is inclusive of everyone in the group.

Less helpful, I've found, are attempts to draw the people out by inviting them, specifically, to participate. When you say to the quiet guy in your group, "It would be great to hear what you think about this, Joe," it can simply serve to make the person feel on the spot, potentially embarrassing him.

If your attempts at drawing someone out via inclusive activities don't work, you can always have a private conversation with him or her outside of the group to check whether there are any inhibiting factors that need to be addressed.

Cutting Off

A very different problem can occur when someone is talking too much or talks about things that are not relevant to the topic at hand. You'll need to be able to stop someone who is talking too much (Harvill, West, Jacobs, & Masson, 1985). Other people in the group will become bored or, even worse, hostile toward someone who overtalks. Taken to extremes, a monopolizer can threaten to drive a group under (Gillam, Coker, & Trippany, 2004).

You'll want to do this cutting off as gently as possible. "Joe, you've talked about this work situation really thoroughly. I think we've all got a pretty good picture of what's going on. . . . Maybe it's time to invite some of other people's perspectives."

You don't want to embarrass someone or cut him or her off in ways that will discourage him or her from sharing anything else in the future. Remember, as the leader, you have a position of power in the group, and you want to use that power

ESSENTIAL SKILLS FOR LEADING THE WORKING GROUP

• Affirming	• Cheerleading	• Validating
• Starting a Session	• Summarizing	• Self-Disclosure
• Silence	• Reframing	• Linking
• Hunches/Speculation	• Immediacy	• Brainstorming
• Deeper Reflections	• Drawing Out	• Cutting Off

judiciously. Some people in the group will be more sensitive about being cut off than others, so you'll have to judge the best way to intervene without causing emotional injury.

THE *NEW DIRECTIONS* GROUP IS WORKING

Gary and Vanessa's group of teens with difficult family situations—the *New Directions* group—moved beyond the period of engaging and then settled into doing some productive work. Some group norms and roles were established, and for the most part, most of those roles that people in the group had adopted were facilitative. Amy was still quieter than most in the group, and Ted was still doing some occasional complaining, but these were not major obstructions. The group had settled into a familiar routine: After a brief check-in with everyone at the beginning of the group (*starting a session*), one or two persons in the group then took some more time to talk about issues at school or home, and then, when time permitted, the group did an exercise together. Things generally went smoothly.

One of these group meetings was characteristic of this productive period. A quieter young woman in the group, Noelle, was visibly upset about something. After everyone had given a brief update about what's been gone on for them during the week, Vanessa came back to Noelle and said, "Noelle, I'm not sure exactly what's going on, but you seem pretty riled up about something" (*drawing out*).

At this point, Ted started to complain, once again, about having to miss some study time to come to group. Vanessa responded with,

> Ted, we can revisit this issue again, for the umpteenth time (*her exasperation is a small self-disclosure*), if it's really important to you, but the first order of business—Noelle—is already on the table (*cutting off*). So, Noelle, what's up?

Noelle looked a little reluctant to talk, but she began to tell the group about the events of the previous evening at her house. Her dad, who was about to move out of the house, had come after work to drink with friends. He was a little drunk and acting kind of mean. She said that he was mostly angry with Noelle's mom, who had told him some weeks earlier that he needed to move out because of his drinking, but he was also needling each of the kids, her brother and her. He started to get on Noelle's older brother's case because of his long hair, and then, he made some nasty comments about Noelle's choice of friends. She said that he went on and on about this, talking about how someone can be judged by the company he or she keeps.

When she took a little pause from telling this story, Vanessa said, "This sounds pretty awful—it's really hard to deal with such unreasonable stuff, especially from a parent (*reflection and validation*)!" Noelle answered, "Yeah. He's great when he's sober, but when he drinks, watch out."

Then, someone else in the group said, "Last night, for you, sounded bad to me, too. And I wonder what your brother thinks about all this." (*This group member is using a reflection and a hunch/speculation—it's always nice to see that the skills leaders have modeled have taken root.*)

Noelle replied, "We don't talk much. I don't have any idea what he thinks about, although I could tell from his reaction that he didn't like the way dad was talking to him." At this, a number of people in the group chimed in. They talked about not talking about family issues with their siblings, and they also talked about how hard that would be to do.

Gary then said,

You know, I remember when I first talked with my sister about some family stuff . . . but years after we'd moved out of the house. We both talked about how we wished we'd been able to talk together more while we were still living under the same roof. I find myself wondering what would happen if you talked with your brother (*self-disclosure and hunch/speculation*).

The group got quiet, and after a bit, Noelle said,

Well, we do get along pretty well. I've always looked up to him, and I think he knows I respect him. Maybe that could work, but I think I'd be pretty nervous about it. I'm not sure that's such a great idea, but I'll think it over.

Gary said, "I'm not advising you to do it, but I'm just wondering how it might roll out." After this little interchange between Noelle and Gary, almost everyone in the group began encouraging her to have a conversation with her brother (*cheerleading*). They talked about how articulate and sincere she was (*affirming*) and about how great it would be to have an ally to talk with in the family. (*Again, how nice it is when the leader can resist the urge to respond and let members use skills they've learned earlier.*)

Then Gary talked a bit about each of the other people in the group who had also mentioned siblings with whom they didn't talk and made a reflective comment about how common it seemed that people in families oftentimes avoid real conversations with one another (*linking*). The people in the group nodded assent, and a couple of them started talking about their own personal family situations and the conversations that needed to happen.

"Sure," Vanessa added,

Talking with a brother or sister can be a great way to go . . . but sometimes that might not be reasonable. Maybe they're not accessible, or for whatever reason you don't think it'll work. Tell me about other options, other people you could recruit as allies (*inviting brainstorming*).

The group responded by quickly listing people they might be able to engage in personal conversations: coaches, school counselors, uncles and aunts, and friends, mostly.

By the time Noelle had discussed her own family situation in a little more depth, adding that she thought that she might consider taking a shot at having a talk about it all with her brother, it was almost time for the group to end. A couple of the other people in the group said that they wanted to talk about their brothers and sisters, too. One person started to launch into talking about his sister and her drug use.

To this, Gary said, "Wow, this is terrific. Great stuff (*affirming*), and I think we should probably wait until next week to get into it so we can give this the attention it deserves (*cutting off*)."

Finally, Gary wrapped things up with a general statement about what the group had done that day, and he also took time to congratulate the group for digging into some important material and for responding in such generous fashion to one another (*summarizing* and *affirming*). He ended by making a specific invitation to the young man who had begun to talk about his sister's issues to lead off with that at the next group. With this, the group ended for the day.

Reflection and Discussion Exercise: The *New Directions* Group

You've just finished reading this *New Directions* group session led by Vanessa and Gary. Following are some questions about this session. Take a few minutes to consider each. Reread the outline of the session, if necessary. Make some brief notes about your responses.

1. Early on in this session, Vanessa cuts Ted off to draw Noelle out. Did you think this was appropriate, and did Vanessa handle this skillfully?

2. Gary self-discloses about talking—and about the times of not talking—with his own sister about their family issues. Was this appropriate?

3. The group has encouraged Noelle to have a conversation with her brother. What do you think about this? Are there any risks?

4. Noelle's situation is, unfortunately, not that uncommon. The group has focused on urging her to talk with her brother and has also encouraged her to consider talking with someone outside the immediate family about this. What other strategies do you think might be helpful for her in dealing with her family situation? Are there any other things that should be happening?

5. What if Noelle's dad had not only been a little verbally mean with Noelle and her brother, but Noelle told you and the group that he had started screaming at them or maybe even hit one of them? What would you have done if you were leading this group?

6. If you had been leading this group, what might you have done differently?

After you've had a few minutes to do some personal reflecting about this session and about these questions, take a few more minutes to discuss this with your colleagues.

WHAT TO DO WHEN IT IS NOT WORKING

There will undoubtedly be the occasion—hopefully rare—when things just don't come together. The group doesn't jell, there's no cohesion, and people in the group generally seem disengaged from one another. Despite your best planning and your close attention to the group's development, it's simply not working. Some people may not trust others in the group. Some in the group may not feel connected to the goals and activities that you've planned. Or maybe, there are one or two big personalities in the group that run rampant over everyone. Any number of things can conspire to threaten the well-being of the group.

Unfortunately, there are no easy solutions for this, particularly in that each situation is unique. There are some things you can almost always do, however. The first—and this is always the suggestion for troubleshooting when things aren't going well—is to talk with your coleader and your supervisor about the situation. Strategize with them about the group and what you might do. You can discuss the personalities who are playing obstructing or facilitating roles and about how to get them to pull together. You can discuss the goals of the group, its activities, and structure, and together you can assess whether adjustments should be made.

Because your coleader has been in the room with you during group sessions, he or she has direct evidence of what's going on and may have some fresh ideas about how to continue that have not occurred to you. This is yet another good reason to colead. Another set of leadership eyes and ears are almost always helpful when problems arise.

This is also why it's so important to have a supervisor who you can trust. You want to be able to talk over your concerns, even your thoughts about your own inadequacies, with someone who you respect. You want a supervisor who will take your concerns and feelings seriously and who will see those concerns in a positive light. Whenever I have been in a position of doing supervision, I have always thought of the vulnerabilities that have been shared as a sign of strength and have been much more concerned when someone was reluctant to talk about any difficulties.

The other significant action you can take—at least with groups of people who are able—is to take a break from whatever is customary and usual and talk over the situation with the group. Simply call a time-out and invite a discussion about the people's perceptions of what is going well and what is going wrong. Just as you did earlier, with the group that was engaging, you can check in with everyone to see what might be changed to make things better, and then, you can think about which of those suggestions you could take seriously and make adjustments around. Oftentimes, the simple fact of being asked and having you responding positively will be enough to turn things in a more positive direction.

If you suspect that part of the reason that things aren't going well has to do with some in the group being intimidated by others, you may assume that having a direct conversation with the group might not be productive. It might be too threatening for people to share their distrust of others out loud. If you think that this is the case, you can always conduct the "discussion" in writing. During the time-out that you call, you could have the people in the group write down their thoughts and give them to you, confidentially.

Working with a group that is having difficulties can be frustrating. If you can keep in mind that the difficulties are not all about you (e.g., personality conflicts, transference, etc.), consult with others and make reasonable adjustments to accommodate the group's wishes, and the chances are that things will get better.

Hang in there through the rough patches, and carry some grit and determination.

TIPS FOR DEALING WITH A GROUP THAT IS NOT WORKING WELL

- Consult with your coleader.
- Consult with your supervisor.
- Call a time-out in the group. Conduct a discussion about what's going on, and ask for constructive suggestions about adjustments that can be made. Take suggestions seriously, and make reasonable accommodations. Don't compromise on those things you believe to be essential.
- Don't allow personal attacks. Remember and utilize rules with the group for giving and receiving feedback during group discussions.
- Conduct written feedback (to you) sessions when you think that it might be too threatening or difficult for some in the group to talk in front of others.
- Think of these tough times as helpful lessons. Some of the things you learn from this experience will help inform your work with future groups.

GROUP FISHBOWL LAB PRACTICE EXERCISE: USING EXERCISES TO PROMOTE GROUP COHESION

This lab practice will need some preparation time. Read the description of the exercise first, and then, determine how much time you'll need to prepare.

For this fishbowl lab, you'll need six people to volunteer to be group members and two people to volunteer to be group leaders. The rest of the people will be silent observers, taking note of how the fishbowl exercise goes, particularly focusing on the leaders' interactions with the group. The observers should be prepared to give feedback to the leaders at the end of the experience.

The group leaders' job is to introduce and conduct a group exercise. There are two exercises provided in the For Further Thought section at the end of the chapter (Item 4). Each of these exercises serves a specific function, but they are each designed to get people working together more cohesively. The leaders should take some time to discuss which exercise they want to use. If neither of the exercises appeal, the leaders may opt to either create or find and utilize another "cohesion-building" exercise.

They should then assemble needed materials (if any) and run this exercise with the group for the amount of time allotted by the exercise's description. Observers should pay attention to how all this goes, and then, should give feedback, primarily to the leaders, about their perceptions of the process. Feedback should be specific, behavioral, and supportive. Observers should focus primarily on the things they think that the leaders did well.

Following their feedback, the leaders and group members should talk about their own participation and observation of the exercise—in particular, what was seen as particularly helpful in moving the group in productive directions and were there things that happened that might have been done differently. If there is time, you could all talk about how this group might proceed if it were to continue as an actual working group.

CONCLUDING THOUGHTS

This is the period in the life of your group when you should be able to lie back a bit and become less active. The group has become more mature and knows, pretty much, what is expected and what it is supposed to do. Naturally, with some groups—children or people with serious and persistent mental illness, for example—you will remain highly active throughout the life of the group. But with most groups, your best strategy will be to let the group assume more responsibility for itself.

However, being less outwardly active doesn't mean to imply not being engaged. While you may be talking less, you'll nevertheless want to remain constantly alert to the dynamics between people, to shifting themes that are discussed, and to any possible problems that are emerging. If you have a coleader, have regular discussions about your respective observations about what's happening in the group.

Pay particular attention to the relative weight given to process and content as the group develops. Is the amount of time spent dealing with process and/or content appropriate to the goals of the group you're leading? Is the amount of time spent talking about the process, the "how" of it that goes with the group, sufficient?

Experiment with silence. When the group gets quiet, try to hang on for a bit, and wait to see if someone will pick up the ball. If no one chimes in and you don't want to chart a new direction in which the group should go, you can always make a process comment, like "We've been dealing with some interesting stuff here, and now it's interesting to see who'll pick things up next."

You'll experience some groups that seem to do better than others. Try to understand what you've done that helped the better ones come together, and capitalize on that for future group work. Remember that there are no bad groups—every group is a source of grist for the experience mill.

FOR FURTHER THOUGHT

1. Interview someone who has led a number of groups. He or she might be a social worker, a psychologist, a clinical mental health or school counselor, or anyone with group experience. Ask about the different experiences he or she has had with levels of cohesion in groups—what does he or she think makes some groups become more cohesive than others? Are there suggestions he or she can give you about leading groups in ways that will promote cohesion? What does he or she remember about groups he or she has run that didn't become cohesive? What did he or she do then?

2. Examine the professional literature about the role cohesion plays in groups.

3. Create one or more structured exercises that are designed to promote group cohesion for a kind of group you might see yourself leading. The exercise(s) should follow the same format as those designed earlier.

4. Following are two student-created exercises, each of which might be used to promote group cohesion. Could you see yourself using either of these? Why, or why not?

ANGER SYMPTOMS BINGO

—Allison Hayes

Goal: To introduce and raise awareness of early physiological warning signs of anger

Target Population: Elementary and middle school–age children with anger management issues

Group Size: Small group size, ideally, no more than six members

Materials: Bingo sheets with symptoms written in grid boxes (each should be in a different order), chips, index cards, or paper with symptoms for "calling," pencils, pens, or markers

Setting: Schools, family centers, or community agencies

Procedures: Begin exercise with a brief discussion, introducing the physiological symptoms associated with anger. A possible introductory statement could be

> Today we are going to talk about how our bodies feel when we get angry. Learning to recognize when we are feeling angry can help us avoid an outburst or explosion. To help us think about ways we can tell when we are getting angry, we are going to play Bingo.

Pass out Bingo cards and chips. It may be useful to have a member be in charge of distributing materials. Check for understanding, and read any words needed. Play game by calling out symptoms and having group members mark corresponding symptoms on their card. The game ends when someone gets a row and calls "Bingo." Process the activity by discussing symptoms and having members identify symptoms they have experienced. They may circle symptoms they identify in themselves on their Bingo card to take home and share with family or caregivers.

Variations:

1. For younger groups (nonreaders), provide Bingo cards with images to depict symptoms rather than words.

2. Older students can brainstorm symptoms to use in the game.

3. Physiological symptoms of anxiety can be used to serve a different population.

EMOTION EXCHANGE

—Michele Longobardi

Goal: The goal of this exercise is to practice mindfulness of emotions. It also serves to show members that they can relate to how one feels about another in the group, promoting acceptance of all different emotions.

Target Population: Ages 12 to 18 (adolescents). The exercise can also be used with a group of young adults who particularly struggle with awareness/acceptance of emotions.

Group Size: Eight members would be best.

Materials: Blank white paper and different colored pens are required.

Setting: Any private room, using chairs/desks, a table, or sitting on the floor will be ideal.

Procedures: Start with a bit of psycho-education on the eight primary emotions: (1) anger, (2) joy, (3) sorrow, (4) shame/guilt, (5) disgust, (6) fear, (7) interest, and (8) surprise. Explain how each of our brains is hardwired with these emotions and that it is okay to feel and accept all of them. Write the name of each emotion on the top of eight different sheets of paper, using different colors (red for anger, blue for sorrow, etc., if you want to make it more creative). Randomly distribute one sheet per person, and tell them that they are to write down different things, experiences, situations, or people (either general or specific) that make them feel that particular emotion. You will give them 2 to 3 minutes to think and jot down what comes to their mind, and then, have them pass their sheet to the right so that they get a new emotion. Have them do this for each emotion, taking 2 to 3 minutes each time. When everybody writes for every emotion, have them volunteer to read the responses of the one they have in their hand. Ask for their reactions at the end and if they were surprised by any similarities or differences among the group.

Variation: If there are less than eight members, you can still do this exercise, giving a random member two emotions to start, and they will get passed around in the same way.

REFERENCES

Davis, K. L., & Meara, N. M. (1982). So you think it is a secret. *Journal for Specialists in Group Work, 7*(3), 149–153.

De Domenico, G. S. (1999). Group sandtray-worldplay: New dimensions in sandplay therapy. In D. S. Sweeney & L. E. Homeyer (Eds.), *The handbook of group play therapy: How to do it, how it works, whom it's best for* (pp. 215–233). San Francisco, CA: Jossey-Bass.

Duba, J. D., Neufeld, P. J., & DeVoss, J. A. (2004). Using silence: "Silence is not always golden." In L. E. Tyson, R. Pérusse, & J. Whitledge (Eds.), *Critical incidents in group counseling* (pp. 265–270). Alexandria, VA: American Counseling Association.

Englar-Carlson, M. (2014). Introduction: A primer on counseling men. In M. Englar-Carlson, M. P. Evans, & T. Duffey (Eds.), *A counselor's guide to working with men* (pp. 1–31). Alexandria, VA: American Counseling Association.

Gillam, S. L., Coker, A. D., & Trippany, R. L. (2004). Cutting off: "It just feels impolite." In L. E. Tyson, R. Pérusse, & J. Whitledge (Eds.), *Critical incidents in group counseling* (pp. 259–264). Alexandria, VA: American Counseling Association.

Goodspeed, P., McCollum, V. C., & Bauman, S. (2004). Leader self-disclosure: "Shouldn't I be a role model?" In L. E. Tyson, R. Pérusse, & J. Whitledge (Eds.), *Critical incidents in group counseling* (pp. 253–257). Alexandria, VA: American Counseling Association.

Hall, M. F., & Horvath, S. F. (2015). Micro-skills: Daily practice for mental health providers. In R. H. Witte & G. S. Mosley-Howard (Eds.), *Mental health practice in today's schools: Issues and interventions* (pp. 125–143). New York, NY: Springer.

Harvill, R., West, J., Jacobs, E., & Masson, R. (1985, March). Systematic group leader training: Evaluating the effectiveness of the approach. *Journal for Specialists in Group Work* [serial online], *10*(1), 2–13.

Hill, C. E. (2014). Skills for immediacy. In *Helping skills: Facilitating exploration, insight, and action* (4th ed., pp. 297–309). Washington, DC: American Psychological Association.

Howey, L., & Ormrod, J. (2002, April). "Personality disorder, primary care counselling and therapeutic effectiveness." *Journal of Mental Health, 11*(2), 131–139.

Kieffer, C. (2006, April). Review of interactive group therapy in addiction: Intervention for dynamic groups. *Journal of Groups in Addiction & Recovery* [serial online], *1*(1), 129–131.

Kiselica, M., & Englar-Carlson, M. (2010, September). Identifying, affirming, and building upon male strengths: The positive psychology/positive masculinity model of psychotherapy with boys and men. *Psychotherapy: Theory, Research, Practice, Training* [serial online], *47*(3), 276–287.

Kral, R., & Kowalski, K. (1989). After the miracle: The second stage in solution-focused brief therapy. *Journal of Strategic and Systemic Therapies, 8*(2–3), 73–76.

Madson, M. B., Schumacher, J. A., Noble, J. J., & Bonnell, M. A. (2013). Teaching motivational interviewing to undergraduates: Evaluation of three approaches. *Teaching of Psychology, 40*(3), 242–245.

Mance, M. (2011, June). Regarding silence: A training group experience. *Group* [serial online], *35*(2), 167–171.

Morran, D. K., Stockton, R., & Whittingham, M. H. (2004). Effective leader interventions for counseling and psychotherapy groups. In J. L. DeLucia-Waack, D. A. Gerrity, C. R. Kalodner, & M. T. Riva (Eds.), *Handbook of group counseling and psychotherapy* (pp. 91–103). Thousand Oaks, CA: Sage.

Nosko, A., & Breton, M. (1997). Applying a strengths, competence and empowerment model. *Groupwork: An Interdisciplinary Journal for Working With Groups, 10*(1), 55–69.

Sarnoff, D. P., & Sarnoff, P. (2005). Assessing interactive creativity in couples. *Family Journal, 13*(1), 83–86.

Scheel, M. J., Davis, C. K., & Henderson, J. D. (2013). Therapist use of client strengths: A qualitative study of positive processes. *The Counseling Psychologist, 41*(3), 392–427.

Schneider, K., & Krug, O. (2014). *Existential–humanistic therapy* (Psychotherapy theories and techniques) [e-book]. Washington, DC: American Psychological Association.

Schorr, M. (1995). Finding solutions in a relaxation group. *Journal of Systemic Therapies, 14*(4), 55–63.

Singh, A. A., Meng, S. E., & Hansen, A. W. (2014). "I am my own gender": Resilience strategies of trans youth. *Journal of Counseling & Development, 92*(2), 208–218.

Sturges, J. W. (2012). Use of therapist self-disclosure and self-involving statements. *The Behavior Therapist, 35*(5), 90–93.

Wilke, G. (2003). Chaos and order in the large group. In S. Schneider & M. Pines (Eds.), *The large group re-visited: The herd, primal horde, crowds and masses* (pp. 86–97). London, England: Jessica Kingsley.

Wood, D. (2012). Opaque silence in groups. In J. Magagna (Ed.), *The silent child: Communication without words* (pp. 269–284). London, England: Karnac Books.

Chapter 10

Ending Your Group

Everything has to come to an end, sometime.

—L. Frank Baum

My colleague and friend, Sally, told me about how she recently wrapped up a 4-day course. This was a course where 17 students, all of whom were preparing for careers in some kind of helping profession, had been learning about some of the skills and tasks necessary for being effective group leaders.

The weekend had been a good mix of activities, and people in the group seemed to be getting a good grasp of the conceptual material. Importantly, they had all interacted well with one another. The days had been long. She said that they were all feeling good about the work they'd done together but that everyone was tired and ready to be finished. She said that the people had begun to talk about what the course had meant to them and how much they'd appreciated the opportunity to get to know one another better.

She then told me about the closing exercise she used to help wind things up with the group. Sally has the luxury of using the retreat center she owns and operates as a space for her group, and there is a large labyrinth painted on canvas and rolled up at the side of the main meeting space. When rolled out, the canvas labyrinth covers the entire floor of this large space.

Sally introduced the labyrinth by explaining that while this particular labyrinth had been modeled after one that is on the floor of the Chartres Cathedral in France, labyrinths are found and have been used in all kinds of spiritual and nonspiritual traditions. She explained some of the historical contexts of the uses of labyrinths and talked about how people in the group could interpret the use of the labyrinth in any way that made personal sense.

She talked about "walking the labyrinth as a group" as a metaphor for how people work with groups and for simply living amid other people—each of us finding our own way, on our own path, while negotiating others. She also talked about the "walk to the middle of the labyrinth" as a metaphor for the journey to find our own center. She used words like *love* and *compassion* to describe this center of the labyrinth—and ourselves—and a message about our journey to find our own internal essence.

She then led the group through some instructions about how to walk the labyrinth—that one person would enter, and after a short time, another would follow.

Then, she said, once everyone had walked to the center of the labyrinth, they needed to walk from the center back out. They needed to return out into the world, in other words, carrying the compassion they'd discovered at the center of the labyrinth, and themselves, to their work with people. Discovering the best within ourselves, she said, carries the responsibility of sharing that with others in the work we do with them.

When she had finished her introduction, the group walked the labyrinth. Sally had put on some soft meditative music, and the group walked the circuit, one at a time, in silence. Sally said that while she'd been a little concerned that maybe some of the people in the group would view this exercise a bit cynically, thinking it too "touchy-feely," she'd occasionally peek up from her own walking to check to see how others were doing. She said that some were visibly moved, some seemed a little unsteady, but that everyone seemed to be taking the walk very seriously.

It took perhaps 45 minutes for the group to walk into the center and then back out. When they had all finished, they gathered together to talk about how the experience had been like for them and about its meaning for their work as a group.

Everyone seemed to have liked the exercise, and some had thought it to be profound.

While you might not ever use a labyrinth as a vehicle for ending a group, you will want to consider how to go about ending. Some kind of exercise or ritual way of ending will be something you'll want to consider. Whatever you do, it should both complement the work the group has done and address what this group ending means to the people in your group.

ABOUT ENDINGS

How people in the group remember the experience will have a lot to do with how it ends, so you'll want to plan carefully for this group ending (Berg, Landreth, & Fall, 2006; Joyce, Piper, Ogrudniczuk, & Klien, 2007).

ENDING A GROUP: CONCEPTS, TASKS, AND SKILLS

- The Meaning of Ending
- Member and Leader Feelings About Ending
- Resistance to Ending
- Unplanned Endings: Dealing With Dropouts
- How to End a Group Session
- How to End a Group: What Needs to Happen
- Skills for Ending
- Measuring Success

In this sense, ending a group is like planning for the ending of any counseling relationship (Novick & Novick, 2006). You should view becoming competent in managing these endings as part of your overall professional competency (Sperry, 2010). This importance of ending well has been shown to be of particular importance if you work with children and adolescents (Delgado & Strawn, 2012; Letendre, 2009).

This chapter will help you plan for ending your group. It will help you look at the scope of concerns associated with ending a group, and it will also help you consider all the specifics associated with what you need to do when you end a group. The chapter will also discuss the skills you'll need to end your group successfully, as well as review the logistics for ending each group session.

As with previous chapters, you will also be provided with an opportunity to do some reflection about endings in groups, as well as a guided format for practicing some of the skills needed for ending a group. Finally, we'll also see how our hypothetical *New Directions* group of high school students wraps up.

THE MEANING OF ENDINGS

This is a time in the life of your group that is laden with meaning. Your group's ending is a reminder that everything ends and that nothing is permanent. Ending and loss are integral parts of life (Donoghue, 1994).

All the people in your group will have had experience with some kind of loss.

There are all kinds of losses that your group members will have endured. They may have experienced the deaths of family members, loved ones, or pets or lost loved ones to suicide or drug overdoses. Some of the people in your groups may have experienced truly terrible things.

In addition to the loss related to death, there are all the other kinds of losses your group members may have endured. They may have had their family lives disrupted by divorce, moving base, or job losses. The children or adults in your groups may have been physically or sexually abused. Some may have been abandoned, either physically or emotionally—as those suffering mental illnesses—by those closest to them. Some others in your groups may have been incarcerated and may have experienced the loss of freedom. Others may have been homeless, moving constantly, never having an opportunity to make attachments with others. For some, loss may be a way of life. The loss of innocence and safety that is the inevitable outcome of such terrible life events can be felt as acutely as the death of a loved one.

The ending of the group is a reminder of all these losses (French, 2012). Every ending is a replication of every loss that's come before. The stronger the bond that's been forged in the group, the more significant will the sensation of the ending be. Endings are proportionally difficult in direct relation to the emotional connections that the people in the group have made. Groups with weak connections will end more easily than those where the connections have been close and strong.

The ending of the group is also, at some level, a subtle reminder that each of us is mortal—that each of us, too, will end. The group's ending is a gentle nudge to our consciousness about our own finiteness (Moraitis, 2009). When added to the reminders of the losses in their lives, the group's ending can make for difficult group leadership challenges.

What will be different about this ending—the ending of your group—is that it will be done with awareness. Planning for the ending of the group is all about providing ample opportunity for all the members in the group to talk about the personal meaning of this ending. This is what makes this ending different from other endings and losses that these people have experienced—it will be done with a discussion of what this means for individuals in the group.

You will need to plan to make time for each of your members to talk about what the group, and the individuals in the group, have meant to them. You will plan to make time for the people in the group to explore the ways in which this ending is a reminder of other endings and losses in their lives. And you will plan to ensure that no one is left with no other place to go if there is significant unfinished personal business that needs attention.

YOUR GROUP'S FEELINGS ABOUT ENDINGS

All these obvious and subtle meanings that are attached to endings translate into feelings and resulting behaviors that the people in the group will be experiencing as the group ends. I'm not sure whether the transference that occurs in a group, where a member views the leader as a representative of some significant figure from the past, is quite as strong as that in individual counseling or therapy. Nevertheless, this transference phenomenon could really add to the sense of loss that some in your group may feel. If some of your members have become emotionally attached to you, the sense of abandonment they may feel because of your impending loss could be acute.

Many of the groups I've run finish with some kind of line like, "I bet this is the best group you've ever had." Groups, and the individuals in them, want to be seen as unique and special. This is an almost universal human need. No one wants to be forgotten.

You, too, will have feelings related to these endings. You may have become quite fond of some of the people in your group, and less so of others. An advantage of having a coleader and/or a supervisor is having someone with whom you can discuss these feelings, as well as to help you decide which of these feelings can be shared with the group.

Both you and your group members will also feel some inevitable relief over the group's ending. However much the people have enjoyed and valued the experience, it has also been one more thing that they've had to do—and there will most likely be some sighs of relief as the group nears its completion.

RESISTANCE TO ENDING

When people have become really attached to a group, there may be some subtle— or less so—ways of undermining the group's ending. People may not be able to talk about their anxiety about a group ending, and they may even behave in ways that suggest that they haven't liked the experience at all.

Back in the days when I worked in residential treatment with adolescents, my colleagues and I observed a fairly typical pattern of behavior that would unfold as a resident came closer to the time of graduation from the program. There would be more incidents of rules infractions and more squabbling with staff and other residents. Some of them who had been doing well, and perhaps had even been models of exemplary behavior, would start to regress, to backslide. They would not be able to talk about their anxiety about leaving, so they would act it out in the only ways they knew. The message was clear: "I'm not ready to leave."

Any parent who has an adolescent "child" getting ready to go to college knows what this so-called regression is about. This is "separation anxiety," and savvy parents know that it's a temporary state of affairs that simply needs to be ridden out. The adolescent is saying with behavior what she or he can't say directly with words: "I'm afraid of this next step—and I'm going to prove to you that I'm not ready by making your life miserable."

> **PREPARING FOR ENDING**
>
> As the group approaches its scheduled ending, make your meetings less frequent. Staggering meetings toward the end is known as *fading*. If you've been meeting weekly, try meeting every other week, or even spacing the last couple of meetings a month apart.
>
> During the life of the group, *periodically refer to the ending time*. Always provide time for talking about ending. If you observe someone's behavior that you think may be linked to feelings about ending, you can always speculate with someone about the meaning of what he or she is doing.
>
> Assess whether you should actually *consider extending the life of the group if the anxiety about ending seems sufficient* to warrant such a move.
>
> Identify and mobilize other resources and sources of support for those who may need them.

Similarly, individuals in groups may say, either directly with words or indirectly with behavior, that they are not ready for the group to end. The group may collectively ask to continue. Some in the group may make a suggestion about having a reunion at some point in the future. You can easily deal with this by saying that you have no objection to a group reunion but that you need to officially end—and then, if someone wants to orchestrate a reunion, to go for it. You can tell the group that you need to end, simply because inevitably someone wouldn't be able to make the reunion.

Sometimes, if a significant number of people in your group are saying it's not time to end, you might want to actually consider extending the time. This, of course, depends on whether you actually can or not. More regularly, however, you'll want to plan to end as scheduled, ensuring that there are plans in place to help individuals who need more get the support that is needed.

Mostly, it's important to remember that there can be people in your group who will try to resist ending and that they may talk about this directly, or they may show it more indirectly by way of how they behave. The more you actively anticipate some resistance to ending and plan for it accordingly, the smoother the transition will be.

UNPLANNED ENDINGS: DEALING WITH DROPOUTS

While some would suggest that people (particularly those who are mandated to attend counseling by parents, courts, or schools) are less likely to drop out of group work than they are when working individually with someone (Csiernik & Arundel, 2013), you will inevitably have those who leave a group before it officially ends. Things happen. Someone might move, take on other commitments, or face unforeseen circumstances that make it impossible for her or him to continue. Or there may simply be insufficient interest in continuing. Whatever the reason, this can be difficult for a group.

Naturally, it's best if someone who is contemplating dropping out can talk about it beforehand ideally with the group as whole, but lacking that, at least with you. This is better than the group having to fantasize about the person's reasons for leaving. Mostly, it will be helpful for the group to know if the person is leaving for personal reasons, as opposed to dissatisfaction with the group.

If the reason does have to do with dissatisfaction, you can always approach this as an opportunity for the person to give you and the group feedback. Maybe there are some reasonable adjustments that can be made to accommodate the complaints and make the experience better for this person. Do what you can, in other words, to reasonably make the group work for someone who is unhappy—but don't feel compelled to make dramatic changes unless there is more widespread discontent.

If someone simply doesn't show up, try to reach out and make contact. Try to find out the reasons for discontinuing, and make a reasonable effort to draw the person back in. You could encourage her or him to come back to the group at least once to say good-bye. Don't overdo it. If she or he does decide to stick with the decision to quit, try not to take it all too personally. Simply take this as an opportunity to think about whether anything could, or should, have been done differently to keep the person engaged. Then move on.

Naturally, if this is someone who is being required to attend the group by a third party—a school or court, for example—you'll need to let the third party know that the person has dropped out. Unless there have been confidentiality waivers signed or there is some danger of physical harm, be wary of sharing anything other than the fact of the person's nonattendance.

HOW TO END YOUR GROUP

There are two kinds of endings that will concern you as you work with your group. The first of these has to do with the ways in which you go about ending each group session, and the second has to do with how you end the entire group experience. Let's consider each of these.

Ending a Group Session

Much of how you go about ending a group session will have to do with the planning you've done for the session as a whole. Managing time well will go a long way toward being able to end well. You'll want to have blocked out time for whatever activities, exercises, or instructional activity—with ample time to introduce the activity and for the group to talk about it afterward—you plan to use during that group time. That time, coupled with whatever time you've allotted for check-ins at the beginning of the group and any other unstructured talking time you want to factor in, will take up the bulk of the group session.

As the session moves along, you can mention how much time is left and when you'll be ending for the day. Then, with just a few minutes left in the session, you can wind things up by asking how the people in the group are doing and if there are any observations about the group's work that day that anyone wants to share. If there was an instructional activity, you might ask each person to quickly say one thing about the lesson that he or she learned—or that he or she is unclear about. If it's a more process-oriented group, you could ask for reflections about how the group is doing. These kinds of questions serve to set the stage for ending and make it clear that it's not time to bring up significant new material.

Despite your best efforts, however, sometimes someone will bring up something important as the group is about to end. This is a variation on the resistance-to-ending theme we discussed earlier. Someone might be reminded of a personal issue by something that's come up in the group. Or someone might be ambivalent about talking about a big issue and waits until there isn't enough time to deal with it. Sometimes, it's just a manipulative way of throwing a verbal wrench into the workings of the group. Whatever the motivation, you'll want to cut this off as gently as possible, saying something like, "Wow, this is a significant thing you've just brought up. I'm wondering if we can start off with this next week, so we'll make sure we have enough time to talk about it?" You could also, if you want, get some internal speculation about the meaning of this by adding something like, "And it's really interesting that you tossed this into the mix, given how little time is left."

If you have a sense that someone has brought up something that is really personally troubling, you can always attend to it yourself, after the group has ended. "You know, we really need to end for today, but I'd love to talk with you for a few minutes after we end." This will allow you time to see if the person will be safe enough to wait until the group meets next week or whether some more intensive intervention needs to be made—for example, individual counseling. Even if you think that someone is being manipulative, using the "significant-issue-brought-up-with-not-enough-time-to-deal-with-it" ploy for more personal attention, I'd suggest affording the extra time to talk.

Ending a Group

The primary thing you'll want to do in ending your group is to make sure that there is ample time for people in the group to talk about what the group experience has meant to them, as well as to reflect on their thoughts and feelings about others in the group and what the future looks like without the group. This is a time for the people to talk about what they have learned about themselves and others and what kinds of things they would like to do similarly or differently in future group situations. If you have had an instructional component in your group, this will also be a time for evaluating the effectiveness of the learning experience.

You'll want, in other words, to provide time for the people to talk about their own behavior in the group, their perceptions of the group experience as a whole, their relationships with others and with you, and what more needs to be done.

This will be, of course, also an opportunity for you to talk about your own perceptions. Try to present your perceptions in a positive light. Again, even if you think that some negative things have happened, present them positively—as ideas about what could be done differently in a next group, for example.

ENDING A GROUP: A TIME FOR PEOPLE IN THE GROUP TO TALK

- What has the experience meant to your group?
- Have the group goals been met?
- How do individuals feel about one another?
- Did you share your own reflections with the group?
- What's left undone?

Figure 10.1   Ending a Group: A Time to Talk About What It All Meant

However, I'd suggest that you wait to share your own ideas until most people in the group have had a chance to talk. You don't want your comments, particularly your positive ones, to short-circuit some of the possible negative things people might have to say (Figure 10.1).

ESSENTIAL SKILLS FOR ENDING A GROUP

Drawing Out and Gently Cutting Off

People in your group who have been relatively quiet will most likely continue to be quiet as the group moves toward its conclusion. Similarly, people in your group who have consistently talked a lot will possibly continue doing this as you wrap things up. You can best deal with drawing the quiet people out by using some kind of activity or exercise that is inclusive, something that calls for everyone to participate.

> *Drawing-Out Example:* "Let's go around the group, and each of us briefly say something about what we've experienced here today."

This same kind of approach can be used for "overtalkers" too, by limiting the amount of time each person can talk. Thus, when you ask people to share something, you can time limit the sharing. In the event that someone continues to share, despite this time limit request, you can use your gentle cutting-off skills.

> *Cutting-Off Example:* "This is great stuff you've learned today. Thanks for all you've told us about this. Let's see how some other folks have reacted to what's happened here."

Reflecting and Summarizing

As you are helping your group move toward its conclusion, you'll want to invite people from the group to share their thoughts and feelings about the experience. It is this sharing and processing of the experience that makes this ending different from many of the other endings in their lives—it is done consciously and with awareness. When people share what they're taking away, you can make reflections about the meanings and feelings about their specific comments, as well as overall reflections (summarizations) about the group's general comments. Oftentimes, these reflections—ones made at the end of the group—are group reflections or summarizations.

> *Reflection to an Individual Example:* "You're saying that the people in this group, and specifically, one or two, have come to mean a lot to you. You're really hoping that these friendships can continue after the group has ended."

Summarization Example: "There seems to be a general sense that while there have been some difficulties that we've had to endure, there's been quite a bit learned about how to deal with this tough family stuff."

Another Summarization Example: "Such a lot of great things have been said about what we've done here—all the friendships that have been made and the hopes for continued contact with one another."

Reframing

You may experience an occasional person in your group who's had a tough time, either with other people in the group or with the experience as a whole. You can always help someone look at what's transpired as a learning experience—to learn how things can be done differently—if he or she wants—in another group experience.

Reframing Example: "Sure, there were some rough spots, sometimes when you had some disagreements with a couple of people in the group, but look at what you've learned about yourself in the process. Knowing how those disagreements unfolded—remember how we talked about those?—allows you to think about how to do it in another way next time."

Affirming

You'll probably want the people in your group to know that you've enjoyed the experience and have faith in them to move forward after this particular experience. You can affirm this faith by telling them about your confidence in their ability to take what's been learned and use it in new situations, as well as of your affection (assuming it's genuine) for them.

Affirming Example: "Look what you've done here. This has been such a great discussion of everything you've learned in this group. I am so appreciative of being a part of this. It's been an honor to get to know you, and I'll look forward to hearing of how things go for you."

Using Exercises

There are many exercises that have been designed specifically for the purpose of ending a group. While I am not someone who uses a lot of exercises in groups that I run, I definitely use them at the beginning and ending of a group, and I would encourage you to consider the use of some kind of exercise in ending. It's a great way to get people in the group talking about ending, as well as a means of including everyone in the discussion. The exercises at the end of the chapter are examples of the kinds of closing exercises that you might use.

ENDING THE *NEW DIRECTIONS* GROUP

Let's revisit the *New Directions* group—the group of high school students we've watched begin, engage, and work together. The end of the high school semester has arrived, and Vanessa and Gary are beginning to talk about ending. This has been a group that has done a lot of good work and has become very cohesive. Vanessa and Gary want to end the group in a way that doesn't undermine the work that's been done or the relationships that have been formed within the group. They want, in other words, to end the group in a way that supports and encourages the ongoing friendships among its members.

Gary and Vanessa are trying to anticipate the issues that these kids will be bringing into the final sessions of the group, and then, they are planning around those to orchestrate the actual things that need to happen in the final session or two.

They have identified two students who do not appear to be well equipped for the upcoming end of the group. Both of these kids have very few resources of support, either external or internal, so Vanessa and Gary have contacted their school counselor for follow-up support.

The group then meets for the last time. They have set the stage for the last meeting of this group by first talking with the group about the importance of ending well and about how sometimes when the ends of things happen it can bring up some feelings related to other, older endings (*using reflections*). They talked about the importance of taking the time to talk about what the group and the people in it have meant to the people (*summarizing*). They circulated a sign-in sheet, asking for names, e-mail addresses, and phone numbers, telling the group that each person would get a copy of this list—and that even though the group is ending, it is hoped that the great friendships formed within it will be continued.

Then, instead of asking the group members to jump into talking about what the group has meant to them—as they thought that this might be too global for the group—they asked each person to say one thing that he or she had learned about themselves and will take away from the experience (*drawing out*). The group responded well to this, and everyone participated, saying something positive about what had been learned. One young woman in the group wanted to talk at length about putting together a reunion. Vanessa suggested that while a reunion was perhaps a good idea, the group really needed to end first—after that a reunion could be planned (*gentle cutting off*). When it came to their turns to talk about the group experience, Vanessa and Gary also shared things that they'd observed and liked about the group (*summarizing and affirming*). Following this, Vanessa and Gary led a more general discussion about what the group had meant to the people in the group, and again, they shared what it had meant to them, as well.

Then, the two leaders introduced a closing exercise (*using exercises*). They had each student take a piece of paper and write his or her first name in large block letters at the top of the page. Then, they asked that each person pass his or her sheet to the person on the left. "Now that you've got a sheet of paper with this person's name on it," said Vanessa, "think about some emotional or physical gift that you could give this person, something you think that he or she could really use—and then, write it down on the paper using just a few words. Certainly, gifts of thanks, or appreciation, can be a kind of gift, too. Then, when you've given that person your "gift," pass the sheet on to the left. Eventually, you'll give a gift to everyone, and everyone will give something to you. When you've got your own paper back, we're done."

Finally, when the exercise was completed, Gary said, "You can read your sheet of gifts now, or you can take it home and read it. Mostly, again, thanks for being such a great, fun, ready-to-take-some-risks kind of group (*affirming*). We're done. Take a few minutes to say good-bye individually to people in the group, and then, let's head out."

REFLECTION EXERCISE: ENDING A GROUP

Here's another situation to consider. Remember the hypothetical group you put together for new parents (the Reflection Exercise section in Chapter 6)? Let's assume that the group came together, engaged, worked productively, and that now it's time to end it.

Begin to think about how you would go about ending this group for these parents. Just as you did in putting this group together, now consider all the potential issues and concerns—the thoughts, feelings, and behaviors—that these people might be bringing in to the ending of this group experience. Once you've considered this thoroughly, think about all the things you'd want to have in place, all the things you'd want to do before and also when the group meets for the last time. Check your plan for ending carefully to make sure that it contains all those things that need to be done to ensure that this group will end well.

What gaps do you see in your plans, and where might difficulties arise because of these? Make some notes about these.

GROUP FISHBOWL LAB PRACTICE EXERCISE: PLANNING FOR ENDING

For this exercise, it will be helpful if you have markers and an easel with a flip pad, or its equivalent, that you can make notes on that everyone can see.

Following the example of group fishbowls described in earlier chapters, assemble a group of your colleagues, all of whom have just completed the previous reflection exercise, with two of you as the designated coleaders. A group of 7 to 10 members, including the coleaders, would be a good number of people for this. This group will sit in a circle, with others watching as observers. The observers will sit silently during the exercise and will take notes on what they see and hear, being prepared to give feedback about the proceedings at the end of the exercise. The observers should, in particular, be watching for those leader behaviors (things that are said or done) that seem to promote productive member interaction. The observers should also keep time, ending the discussion after however much time has been decided should be allocated for this—20 to 30 minutes is probably sufficient.

The leaders' job is to initiate and facilitate a conversation—lasting perhaps 20 to 30 minutes—among the members about their planning ideas for ending the group they were instructed to think about in the preceding reflection exercise. The leaders, or someone designated, could make two lists on the flip chart: one of potential "issues" that the group might encounter and the second of all the things that need to be done before and during the group's last meeting. The leaders will want to do what they can to make sure that everyone is involved in the discussion. They should feel free to add their own ideas about these potential issues and planning concerns.

When this discussion is over, the observers can share their observations and ideas about what has transpired, again focusing on those leader skills that seemed to move the conversation in positive directions. This feedback session should be supportive and positive, while at the same time highlighting things that might have been done differently.

MEASURING SUCCESS

You'll want to establish some way of determining how effective your groups have been, both in terms of the overall satisfaction that people in the group have had with those experiences as well as in terms of the individual growth that people have achieved as a result of their group experiences.

The coursework you'll take in evaluation and measurement can help prepare you to do this kind of research, particularly with regard to individual client growth. You'll find that standardized tests and other kinds of testing tools may help with this (Kenny & Hoyt, 2014; Tingey, Lambert, Burlingame, & Hansen, 1996). Pre- and postgroup questionnaires—about what's been learned, about attitude shifts, and so on—can help you determine the impact a group experience has had on everyone in the group.

You'll also be able to measure individuals' progress in your groups by seeing how well the group members are moving toward goals they've established for themselves. In the addictions treatment programs in which I ran groups, for example, tracking people's drug use pregroup, during, and postgroup was used as an indicator of a group's impact. I also looked at related issues, such as staying out of trouble, maintaining a job, and family stability, as indirect indicators of group success. You may need to become creative in ascertaining ways to measure client growth, and the whole picture becomes even more complicated when you are dealing with people with multiple problems (Hien, Cohen, & Campbell, 2009). You simply do the best you can in trying to measure your members' change in behaviors, knowledge, or attitudes.

You're probably thinking that trying to create some ways of measuring your groups' outcomes is premature, given that you're just starting to lead groups. But it's not. You can begin to think of this kind of integration of research into what you do, at least in part, as a way of measuring your own growth as a group leader. Measuring the effectiveness of your group work will help you identify things that need to be changed in your group work approaches (Jhai & Wu, 2007). Being able to back your qualitative observations of how well your group has worked with quantitative data will also help you in assuring your agency and school supervisors that your group work is worthwhile (Brigman & Webb, 2007).

The more regularly you integrate a research component into the group work you do, and the earlier you start to do it, the easier it will become. Eventually, it will simply seem an automatic part of the planning process. You will not only be able to look at your own progress, but you'll also be able to share your own "best practices" with others (Blinder & Sanathara, 2003; Clement, 1999).

Finally, you should become a savvy consumer of group outcome research and literature. Find out what are best practices in the group work field, particularly for the kinds of groups you want to lead. You'll want to be able to intelligently read research studies relevant to group work. Thus, you'll want to both collect data about the effectiveness of your own groups as well as read about what others are doing with theirs. You'll find that what you learn from the literature will help guide you in decision making about how to shape your own future work (Kelly, 2010; Sexton, 1996; Sexton, Whiston, Bluer, & Walz, 1997).

CONCLUDING THOUGHTS

You might not want to end your group using a labyrinth, but you will want to use some kind of exercise or procedure that helps to end it well, perhaps even with a little drama, or flair. Having members write affirmations to one another, as was done in the *New Directions* group, is certainly a personally meaningful way to end.

A therapist friend of mine who works with kids who've experienced serious trauma and losses often uses an outdoor firepit as an aid in ending her groups.

Kids write regrets, or things that they can't say in person to people in the group, and then, they have a little ritual of burning what they've written. I've heard these children talk about how meaningful a way this can be to end a group. This use of fire certainly has a little drama and flair.

Personally, you can take away from the group the comments and other kinds of feedback people have given you to help you shape how you'll do things differently, or the same, next time around. The feedback from your group that's ending can help inform your work with a future group.

I would encourage you to not take too personally either the flattering or the negative things people in the group have to say about the experience. Use their comments to help you think about how to do your next group, but don't depend on the feedback to shore up—or diminish—how you feel about yourself.

Once again, the importance of self-awareness is highlighted. Your sense of well-being should not depend on what the group tells you about the experience. A supervisor should be able to help you with this.

FOR FURTHER THOUGHT

1. Look for 5 to 10 exercises designed to help groups end. You could start by looking at rituals used by different cultural traditions (e.g., Native American) for group work. Which of these exercises might have applicability for your own work?

2. Create five original exercises for use in ending a group. Each exercise should comprise the following: a title, the goals of the exercise, the target population, size of the group, space and time required, materials needed, and general procedures. Try to create exercises that you might actually use.

3. Examine the research and literature related to group work outcomes. Look at research related to group work outcomes in counseling, psychotherapy, and social work. Then, look at group work outcomes research for specific populations (e.g., addictions, older people, etc.). What implications are there in what you've found for your work?

4. Consider a specific group you might put together, and then, contemplate how you might assess the effectiveness of the group experience, both in terms of the overall experience and in terms of specific outcomes for group members. Write up an assessment plan.

5. Following are 2 graduate student–created exercises, each of which is designed for use with a group that is ending. Read these and consider if you might use

either of these yourself. Are there ways in which you might alter them to make them more suitable for the groups you might lead?

BOWL IT AWAY

—Kathryn Place

Goal: To create a letting-go experience (most likely at the ending of a group)

Target Population: Teenagers and/or adults

Group Size: Small group (4 to 8 people)

Materials: Masking tape, marker, six plastic bowling pins, and a plastic bowling ball

Setting: Enough space to set up a small bowling lane (about 8 to 10 feet). Also, enough room so that members can gather around the lane while each take turns bowling

Procedure: Each member takes three to six pieces of tape. On each piece of tape, the member writes a problem/issue that he or she has been struggling with. These issues can still be a problem for the member or something he or she has worked through in the group already. When it is the member's turn, he or she should put the pieces of tape on the bowling pins and then set the pins up. The counselor should instruct the member to imagine himself or herself as the ball, and the pins represent the problems he or she is struggling with in real life. When the member is ready, he or she can roll the bowling ball and knock down the pins. The member can take as many rolls as needed to knock down all the pins. The other group members will be there to support the member who is rolling. This exercise can be a symbolic representation of working through problems in life.

POSITIVE CLOSURE

—Chris Mitchell

Goal: Increase group members' self-esteem; identify personal strengths

Target Population: age >16 years

Group Size: Small groups, no larger than 15 members

Materials: Pen and paper; each member will need a container (bag or box)

Setting: Classroom

Procedure: Each member will have a number of small pieces of paper (*n* = number of group members). For each member of the group, the other members of the group should write down one positive strength or compliment. At the front of the room, there will be a container for each member (with his or her name on it). Once everyone has written for each member in the group, the members will place the notes in the container that they correspond to. On completing that, each member will go to the front of the room and take his or her container back to his or her seat.

This exercise is for closure of the group and is designed so that everyone in the group will have something to take home with them. Leaders will want to use this cautiously because they will not be able to screen the content that each member is giving the other. This is designed for a mature group.

REFERENCES

Berg, R. C., Landreth, G. L., & Fall, K. A. (2006). *Group counseling: Concepts and procedures*. New York, NY: Routledge/Taylor & Francis.

Blinder, B., & Sanathara, V. (2003). Review of "Outcomes and incomes: How to evaluate, improve, and market your psychotherapy practice by measuring outcomes." *Bulletin of the Menninger Clinic, 67*(4), 367–368.

Brigman, G., & Webb, L. (2007). Student success skills: Impacting achievement through large and small group work. *Group Dynamics: Theory, Research, and Practice, 11*(4), 283–292.

Clement, P. (1999). *Outcomes and incomes: How to evaluate, improve, and market your psychotherapy practice by measuring outcomes*. New York, NY: Guilford Press.

Csiernik, R., & Arundel, M. K. (2013). Does counseling format play a role in client retention? *Journal of Groups in Addiction & Recovery, 8*(4), 262–269.

Delgado, S. V., & Strawn, J. R. (2012). Termination of psychodynamic psychotherapy with adolescents: A review and contemporary perspective. *Bulletin of the Menninger Clinic, 76*(1), 21–52.

Donoghue, K. (1994). The impact of the termination of brief psychotherapy, and its implications for counselling practice. *Counselling Psychology Review, 9*(3), 9–12.

French, L. (2012). The ending process. In L. French & R. Klein (Eds.), *Therapeutic practice in schools: Working with the child within: A clinical workbook for counsellors, psychotherapists and arts therapists* (pp. 187–197). New York, NY: Routledge/Taylor & Francis.

Hien, D., Cohen, L., & Campbell, A. (2009). Methodological innovation to increase the utility and efficiency of psychotherapy research for patients with co-occurring mental health and substance abuse disorders. *Professional Psychology: Research and Practice, 40*(5), 502–509.

Jhai, Z., & Wu, P. (2007). Exploring the intimate world of adolescents in group counseling. *Chinese Annual Report of Guidance and Counseling, 22,* 119–155.

Joyce, A., Piper, W., Ogrudniczuk, J., & Klien, R. (2007). *Termination in psychotherapy: A psychodynamic model of processes and outcomes.* Washington, DC: American Psychological Association.

Kelly, T. (2010). Editorial. *Groupwork: An Interdisciplinary Journal for Working With Groups* [serial online], *20*(2), 3–5.

Kenny, D. A., & Hoyt, W. T. (2014). Multiple levels of analysis in psychotherapy research. In W. Lutz & S. Knox (Eds.), *Quantitative and qualitative methods in psychotherapy research* (pp. 157–167). New York, NY: Routledge/Taylor & Francis.

Letendre, J. (2009). Working with groups in schools: Planning for and working with group process. In C. R. Massat, R. Constable, S. McDonald, & J. P. Flynn (Eds.), *School social work: Practice, policy, and research* (7th ed., pp. 595–609). Chicago, IL: Lyceum Books.

Moraitis, G. (2009). Till death do us part. *Psychoanalytic Inquiry, 29*(2), 157–166.

Novick, J., & Novick, K. (2006). *Good goodbyes: Knowing how to end in psychotherapy and psychoanalysis.* Lanham, MD: Jason Aronson.

Sexton, T. (1996). The relevance of counseling outcome research: Current trends and practical implications. *Journal of Counseling and Development, 74*(6), 590–600.

Sexton, T., Whiston, S., Bluer, J., & Walz, G. (1997). *Integrating outcome research into counseling practice and training.* Alexandria, VA: American Counseling Association.

Sperry, L. (2010). *Core competencies in counseling and psychotherapy: Becoming a competent and highly effective therapist.* New York, NY: Routledge/Taylor & Francis.

Tingey, R., Lambert, M., Burlingame, G., & Hansen, N. (1996). Clinically significant change: Practical indicators for evaluating psychotherapy outcome. *Psychotherapy Research, 6*(2), 144–153.

Chapter 11

Groups Across the Life Span

The old believe everything, the middle-aged suspect everything, and the young know everything.

—Oscar Wilde

Most of what you've read about groups, thus far, has to do with working with groups of adults. The developmental issues, the skills you'll need, and all the theories related to groups apply to that population of people.

Most likely, however, you will not exclusively lead mixed-gender groups of adults. You may be called on to work with other kinds of groups—of different ages, with different developmental issues, and with different problems. The chapter following this one deals with a few of the specific problems, or themes, that a group you construct might share.

This chapter deals specifically with some of the challenges posed by different age groups and single-gender groups of adults.

GROUPS FOR DIFFERENT AGES

- Groups for Children and Adolescents
- Groups for Women
- Groups for Men
- Groups for Older People

GROUPS FOR CHILDREN AND ADOLESCENTS

Children have never been very good at listening to their elders, but they have never failed to imitate them.

—James Baldwin

I spent the last semester of my senior undergraduate year as a college student (more than a few years ago) doing some student teaching in a middle school in a rural Vermont community. My classes were filled with poor farm kids, most of whom received free or reduced price meals at school before the day officially began. Many of these kids had done chores before arriving at school in the early morning, and a few of them still wore their farm boots, rich with the smells of the chores they'd done, when they came in for class.

These were classes in social studies, a curriculum of mixed instruction about history, politics, and a smattering of rudimentary sociology and psychology. Frankly, I don't remember a lot about what the content of these classes was, but I do vividly recall many of the stories the children told me about their lives. While I did what I could to make the time in class stick to the instructional material, around the edges I learned about the hard times their parents had, about their dreams for the future, about their sorrows, and a lot about their own personal struggles.

I don't know how much of the formal material about politics and history they retained, but I do know that my own view of the world was profoundly affected. Those children began to open my eyes to the realities of childhood that are too often not acknowledged. I began to wake up to the fact that childhood is not always the safe harbor from life's challenges that I had wished it to be.

Special Features

Over the years, in a variety of work settings with children and, more usually, adolescents, I have found that many children face extraordinary challenges. Poverty, family turmoil, and living environments that are crime infested are an unfortunate fact of life for too many children. And even for those children born into privileged circumstances, the pressures associated with performance and achieving success can be formidable. Providing opportunities for kids to talk with one another can be a real asset in helping them deal with these pressures and in helping them feel better about themselves (Egbochuku & Aihie, 2009).

Learning to work effectively with children and adolescents starts with dropping the idea that childhood is an easy time. To communicate well with children, you'll need to be open to hearing about the tough things they see and experience. It'll mean letting go of the denial of the pain that so many endure. This, too, like any work with people, means being open to the diversity issues they bring to you.

Children and adolescents don't receive much attention in the counseling theory literature. Counseling theories, by and large, focus on adults. Most counselors in training receive little training specific to working with children (Hollis, 1997). With the exception of some analytic theory (attachment and object relations theory, in particular), most counseling theories about working with people focus on adults. When they do talk about children, they typically try to adapt the theory that was designed for adults to work with children.

Conversely, the people who work with children the most—teachers—receive little, if any, training in how to work with groups. They do get training around classroom management and methods, some of which has information related to groups, but it has always seemed to me that straightforward coursework in group work could be a great asset for the beginning teacher.

Working with children and adolescents in groups calls for a special skill set.

There is a distinct need to talk with children and adolescents in a way that is different from talking with adults. While you'll be able to use many of the general relationship-building skills you use with adults, like engagement questions and reflections of content and feeling, you'll also want to be even more spontaneous, warm, and transparent than in your work with adults. Unless there's been significant abuse or trauma, children will most likely be less guarded with you, and it will be helpful if you can reciprocate.

If you're going to work with children and adolescents, it certainly helps if you actually like them. There are, unfortunately, people who do work with children who really don't seem to like them much. You'll need to be aware that many children and adolescents will be able to pick up what you're really thinking about them, even though you may not be saying it explicitly. I like to think of adolescents, in particular, as having built-in radar that allows them to intuitively read your real intentions behind the things you say.

Thus, I'd suggest that in working with kids, particularly adolescents, you can allow yourself to be even more authentic and genuine than in working with adults. While you'll want to be careful about what personal information you share with the children and adolescents in your groups (anything you say about yourself can and possibly will be later used against you), you can, at least occasionally, wear your heart on your sleeve.

Very broadly speaking, children and adolescents fall into two groups: (1) those who have some facility and interest in talking about themselves and the world around them and (2) those who don't. There are the "thinkers and feelers," and then, there are the "action lovers." Why not create group experiences that address and play into their relative strengths and interaction style?

I once worked in a residential treatment facility for adolescents with drug problems. The community was sited on a 300-acre working farm, with a large vegetable garden and a barn full of animals. This was not a fancy place—it was located, in fact, on the grounds of the area's old poor farm (in pre-Medicaid days, these were places in rural areas that housed the indigent), but it did afford some unique possibilities for building groups that suited the different interaction styles of our population of kids.

For our adolescents who liked to talk about things—their feelings, themselves, and their families—we created talking groups led by talking-oriented leaders. While we still encouraged the leaders to use a considerable amount of structured activities, like exercises and games, in these groups, the groups were designed primarily for talking.

With the kids for whom talking was a challenge, either because of reluctance or ability, we designed groups that were action oriented. Gardening, working with animals, helping out in the kitchen, and running and walking together became our vehicles for group work. We found that once the kids were fully engaged in these activities, they would often open up and begin to talk about themselves. You probably won't have access to a farm for your work with children and adolescents, but you can nevertheless create different kinds of groups that are designed to capitalize on the strengths of the children in them (see Figure 11.1).

Leader Considerations

Bear in mind that when we talk about children and adolescents as a group, we're talking about a population of people within whom there is a tremendous

Figure 11.1   Games Can Be Used With Children as Effective Teaching Tools—Like This One
Promoting Cooperation

developmental range of age and ability. There may be large differences in cognitive and emotional development, even within the same age group, and attention spans may be highly varied. You'll want to create groups, particularly through member selection and planning for activities, which take these developmental differences into consideration. You'll want to choose activities and exercises that are age and ability appropriate. This is particularly true when you are designing programs and groups that will be used multiple times in school or in agency settings (Fazio-Griffith, 2013).

You can create groups that address specific concerns. You might have specific theme groups that deal with, for example, bullying issues, social skills (Lopez & Burt, 2013), anger management (Splett, Maras, & Brooks, 2014), or changing families. Many such group themes have excellent curricular packages that have been developed to address these specific concerns. This means that you can look for and adopt an already-developed package and adapt it for the specific group you're putting together.

In general, the younger your group, the smaller the number of participants you'll want. A good rule of thumb in constructing groups for children is to have the group size number about the same as the age of the children, or maybe one or two more. With adolescents, a range of 6 to 12 participants is probably appropriate.

You'll want to make similar adjustments for the time of each group session, as well. With young children, 20 to 30 minutes is the maximum time. With adolescents, 50 to 90 minutes should work well. Reality factors, like a school schedule, may mandate time boundaries. Work within these as best you can.

You may work with children who have experienced real difficulties. Poverty, abuse, neglect, and violence are a part of many children's lives. You may be working with groups of children, some of whom have incarcerated parents (Lopez & Burt, 2013), or parents who have deployed with the military overseas (Curry, 2013) or who are homeless (Dugan, 2013). In some cases, your job will be not only to create groups where they can talk about and deal with these issues in a safe and supportive environment but also to serve as an advocate to intervene in some dangerous situations (Cox et al., 2012). A good supervisor—and possibly legal advice—can be helpful in negotiating appropriate intervention strategies, as in knowing when to report suspected abuse.

Unlike working in some groups with adults, you'll want to assume that you're going to maintain a high profile, active status during the life of the group. With adults, you want the group to assume more responsibility for itself as it matures, sometimes to the point where you can really back off and act more like a member than as a visible leader. This is the leadership transition from autocratic to democratic to laissez-faire that we talked about in an earlier chapter. With adolescents, and particularly with younger children, you'll remain active throughout the group's life span. While you do want members to assume more responsibility for what happens, you'll most likely never want to move into full laissez-faire mode.

Pay attention to gender issues in your groups of children and adolescents. Meeting in groups can be a great way for children to begin talking about some of the social forces at play in defining sex roles and stereotypical assumptions about girls, boys, men, and women. In coed groups of boys and girls, you can make your discussions more immediate by looking at, and pointing out, the ways in which some of those assumptions may be at play in the group (as with relative talking time by boys and girls, who steps up to lead in activities, etc.). You might want to occasionally experiment with creating single-sex groups, particularly when you think that this might make your kids more comfortable in talking about some of these gender-related issues. Depending on the relative safety of the setting, this may also be a time when they can discuss issues related to their emerging sexuality.

Finally, build therapeutic games and activities into your groups. Expressive arts and the use of art materials (paints, clay, etc.) can be useful vehicles for expression in your groups (Ceballos & Williams, 2013; Goicoechea, Wagner, Yahalom, & Medina, 2014; Rosselet & Stauffer, 2013). Working with groups of kids in adventure- or action-based ways is also a great way to engage them and to get them to work together (Lee, 2009).

Always remember that the goal of the game should be to suit some therapeutic goal—the group isn't just playing a game. Manage your time boundaries, so that the activity can be easily handled within the time frame you've got, and make sure that the ground rules are well-defined and maintained, so that safety is ensured. Finally, there should be adequate time built in to talk about the activity after its completion. The meaning that the members make out of the game is what's really important.

Reflection Exercise: Remembering Your Adolescence

Your ability to remember and present the thoughts of your own adolescence will be a huge asset in your ability to work effectively with this population of people. This exercise is designed to help you do a quick review of a snapshot of a period of time in your own teen years.

You'll want to read through this entire exercise, even a couple of times, before actually doing it. Alternatively, you could have someone read it to you; ask her or him to put on her or his best guided imagery voice and then slowly lead you through the instructions.

Start by sitting in a comfortable chair, with your feet uncrossed and planted solidly on the floor. Your hands should be in your lap or on the arms of your chair. Let your eyes close, and begin to focus your attention inward. Note how quickly

TIPS FOR WORKING WITH ADOLESCENTS

- Think of yourself as a mentor, and set appropriate expectations for the adolescents with whom you work. Find other mentors for young people who need appropriate adult role models. Children move through adolescence into adulthood most productively via healthy connections with adults and compelling interests. Help make these connections happen.
- Be real. Remember children's ability to intuitively know the "you" behind your words. Be honest—as in, real—with them.
- Remember that taking risks is a natural part of being an adolescent. Pushing the boundaries of what is safe is a teenager's job. Our job is to tolerate the teenager's need to take risks while trying to minimize what is truly dangerous.
- Try not to be put off by a child's obnoxious behavior. Every child yearns to be known and accepted, but he may have had lots of experiences that tell him people are not trustworthy. Accept the fact that the obnoxious behavior is part of a defense system that has been built as a survival strategy, and look for the beauty of the child behind the behavior. Work with kindness, patience, and grit.
- When you plan activities for the youth with whom you work, plan activities that you think will be fun for you as well as for the kids. If the activities are fun for you, they'll most likely be fun for them, too.

your breathing begins to slow and how comfortably heavy you become in just sitting there.

On a screen you can pull down behind your mind's eye, cast a picture of yourself as you might have looked at age 15. See yourself standing there, with your hair as it might have looked then, your facial features then, and the clothes you wore then. Are you smiling or frowning—what kind of expression do you have on your face? Note the feelings you have—and had then—as you see yourself standing there.

Then take this image of yourself and place it in a classroom you might have been in at that age. Maybe this is a traditional classroom or maybe it's another kind of room, like a lab. See the details of the room, the black or whiteboard, the chairs or desks, the walls and windows, and the other kids and the teacher.

Listen to what the other kids and teacher are saying. Maybe they're joking around; maybe they're serious. Note the smells of this classroom—some rooms have distinctive smells, like of chalk, dry erasers, or chemicals. Let all your senses take in this experience—take it all in. Note your feelings in this place. Do you feel like you belong there? Are you connected to these people?

Finally, consider where you might have left for that morning, before you went to school. Were you at home, or were you somewhere else? Did you have breakfast or just dash out the door? Did you see and talk to anyone? Who? Again, note the feelings you have as you see all this. Did you feel connected with people, like you belonged there? Did you feel loved?

When you've allowed yourself to experience all this, let your attention shift back to the present. Come back to the place where you started this little journey. Give yourself some time to make this reentry, and finally, allow your eyes to open.

Take a few moments to jot down some of your immediate thoughts and impressions of this experience.

Group Fishbowl Lab Practice Exercise: Remembering Adolescence

This fishbowl exercise will afford you some time to share your thoughts about the reflection exercise you just completed with others. Whether you wish to share and what you choose to share is, of course, voluntary.

As with earlier group fishbowl exercises, this practice session will have two group leaders, six to eight group members, with the rest of your group as group observers. Set an amount of time you'd like to take for the group to talk about this reflection exercise, perhaps 30 to 45 minutes, and then, simply have a discussion about it. Members can talk personally about what they saw in this guided imagery experience, or they can talk more objectively about how the exercise suggests implications for working with adolescents.

The members and leaders who participate in this group fishbowl exercise should remember that this is not a group therapy session, so there shouldn't be intent to analyze or go into too much depth about any personal observations that are shared. This is simply an opportunity, if the members choose to share what their personal memories of being 15 years old are, to provide a snapshot glimpse of what was remembered.

The leaders might want to talk about how they'll approach this before the group fishbowl discussion actually starts. Their primary job is to get the discussion going and to draw individuals out. They should try to eventually include everyone in the discussion, using all the skills we've discussed to move the conversation along.

The observers should actively watch and listen to the interaction between members and leaders. If you're an observer, pay attention to the stories members share. What kind of differences between stories did you hear? Were there some reflections that seemed "happier," or "sadder," than others? Could you relate to any of these? What kinds of role did culture and the range of diversity issues (e.g., race/ethnicity, religion, or gender) play in how recollections of adolescence are portrayed? Talk about your impressions with the group.

The observers should also actively watch and listen to how the group leaders manage the discussion. How did they get things started? Did they go around the circle, asking each member in turn to share his or her observations or simply open it up for whoever wanted to go first? Did they draw members out, and did they manage to get everyone involved? What other observations can you share with the leaders?

Finally, the entire group should discuss what's transpired. Talk with the group about how this experience has affected you and what implications there are in it for your work with adolescents.

GROUPS FOR WOMEN

If you want something said, ask a man.
If you want something done, ask a woman.

—Margaret Thatcher

Some years ago, I attended a workshop for professionals titled "Psychotherapy and Women." The focus, as the title suggests, was on the special issues that women might bring into counseling or therapeutic relationships. It had been a great day, and a good deal of helpful information had been shared.

As we were about to wrap up and end, a woman in the back of the room raised her hand and asked to add some last thoughts. She then took out a notepad and said,

> You know, in this workshop, which is ostensibly about women's issues in psychotherapy, we had 43 women and 8 men in attendance. All of us in this room, women and men alike, are professionals who work with women. I took the liberty of tracking talking time, and simply want to let you know that—in this workshop about women—where women clearly make up more than 2/3 of the attendees, during the period we had for discussion, the men talked over 85% of the time.

With this very brief intervention, this woman made the whole issue of "women in psychotherapy" more immediate and real for us. She brought the theoretical down to the real and made us confront some of our own personal "issues" in working with women. For those of us who were involved in doing a significant amount of group work, it was a "heads-up" about the potential impact of gender issues in our groups. It was a quick and clear look at how men's voices can potentially overpower those of women and a persuasive argument for "women-only" groups.

Special Features

Making any sweeping generalizations about the nature and goals of women's groups would be dangerous. There is a wide array of support- and theme-based groups (e.g., groups having suffered sexual abuse, having eating disorders, with health concerns, and dealing with relationship issues) for women that embrace all kinds of political and values orientations. There may be no such thing as a typical women's group, just as there may not be any typical women's issues (Leech & Kees, 2005).

While it is probably risky for me, a man, to make recommendations about what makes for good leadership in a group for women, let me nevertheless highlight some observations from the literature and personal observation that you might find helpful. Many women's groups are about helping women find and use their own voices. They are about helping women identify and acknowledge their strengths and learn to utilize those strengths in the world more effectively.

Most feminist approaches to working with women emphasize helping women recognize how their ways of operating in the world have been shaped by a social–political paradigm that has been designed and supported by men. Much of the work in helping women, then, has to do with raising their political awareness and teaching them about those forces that shaped, and continue to control, their lives. This can be tricky, because while, on the one hand, women's groups want to help women become more personally powerful and "individuated," they typically also want women to retain the best of the relational qualities that they've learned by virtue of growing up in a society that teaches women the importance of connections with others.

Power and love are two of the significant themes that are often heard in discussions in these groups. Women's groups generally serve both to empower women and also to help them look at how their searches for love can become more productive. Regarding the theme of power, women can be helped to recognize and mobilize their own internal resources on their own behalf; regarding the theme of love, women are helped to recognize that loving well begins with loving oneself.

I once heard Gloria Steinem, the well-known feminist and founder of "Ms. Magazine," talk about how women with eating disorders, addiction issues, and terrible self-esteem problems would come to work at the magazine she edited, "Ms. Magazine," and slowly get better. She maintained that simply having contact with, learning from, and being supported by powerful, self-aware women served a healing function. This is the healing function that groups can serve, as well.

Closely related to this issue of power in women's groups are the ways in which these groups can help women recognize the ways in which their searches for love and affection may have gotten them into trouble in the past. Many women have looked for love in all the wrong places. Groups can be a wonderful way for women to connect with one another to talk about the search for love. Groups may serve this purpose even more effectively than working one-on-one with someone (Csiernik & Arundel, 2013).

For many women, learning how to care for others is intricately tied into notions of their own self-worth (Kasl, 1990). Caring for others can be a way of indirectly caring for one's self, in other words. One of the best things that groups can do for

Figure 11.2 Groups Afford Women Unique Opportunities for Sharing and Learning

women is to help them learn how to more directly attend to their own needs, not via caregiving. Thus, work with women in groups can serve to help women acknowledge their own power as well as their ability to love themselves and others more effectively (see Figure 11.2).

Leader Considerations

While there may be some central themes of concern that a lot of women share, there are also very real differences that you'll want to take into consideration. You'll want to make sure that you create a good fit between a particular woman and the group she's joining. This means that the goals and style of the group should, to the best of your ability, match those of the individuals signing on for the experience (Paquin, Kivlighan, & Drogosz, 2013).

One of the things a group for women can do is to raise the general level of awareness of how social forces have shaped their lives. Books, films, or even bringing guests into the group to talk about their personal experiences with some of the politics of gender can be powerful tools in helping raise this awareness. Strong women in the group can provide support and role modeling for others.

Given that many women feel that they haven't been listened to or adequately heard when they talk about life and relationship difficulties—and this may be particularly acute when sexual violence and abuse are involved—your group can

TIPS FOR WORKING WITH GROUPS OF WOMEN

- Use the group as a vehicle for teaching women about how larger social–political forces affect their lives.
- Books, films, and guest speakers can help your efforts to inform and raise awareness.
- Encourage stronger women in the group to act as mentors and role models.
- Teach skills, such as assertiveness, mindfulness, relaxation, anger management, and so on.
- Hear the stories of the women in your groups, and validate their perceptions of those experiences.
- Use expressive arts (e.g., clay, paint) to help the women in your group explore and articulate strong emotions.
- Help women in the group reframe their experiences in a way that helps them recognize their hidden strengths.

provide a great opportunity to validate the reality of their stories. Affording women the opportunity to talk, for the group to actively listen to what they have to say, and then to affirm and validate the truth of what's been spoken can be a powerful force for personal empowerment.

Relatedly, you can sometimes help women look at the events of their lives, their personal stories, in a new light. The woman who thinks of herself as a failure, for example, because she continues to stay with an abusive partner, could be helped to reframe her staying as a heroic effort to provide a good life for her children. Economic realities keep many women locked in unhappy relationships, and while your group can help raise awareness of—and maybe even change—some of these realities, it can also help women not blame themselves for their circumstances.

In addition to providing an opportunity for support and raising awareness, women's groups can also teach skills. While women will indirectly learn from others in the group, you can also consider utilizing specific training packages that you think might be helpful to teach things like assertiveness, mindfulness, or relaxation.

GROUPS FOR MEN

Every man is a volume, if you know how to read him.

—William Ellery Channing

During the past couple of years of my graduate work in Buffalo, I joined a men's support group. The group was composed mostly of fellow graduate students. While the program I was in expected us to do group work, this men's group was an "add-on" for me, not part of a program requirement.

Generally, each of us in the group was looking for some support and validation in dealing with the challenges of the graduate program, our concerns about our careers and futures after leaving the program, and, mostly, about the changing nature of the relationships we had with our partners. We all had spouses or partners, some of whom were also doing graduate work. All of us were meeting new people and changing in some unpredicted ways. The changes were exciting and sometimes scary. These changing relationship issues were the primary reason for each of us in joining this men's group.

School can create a lot of new and unexpected pressure in a couple's relationship. One person can feel that he or she is outpacing the other, particularly in terms of personal growth. This can be particularly acute when one person is involved with a school experience and the other is not. In our cases, each of us felt that our relationships were undergoing seismic change, and joining the group was an attempt to find some stability and understanding of what was going on in our love lives. One of us was also experiencing some new feelings and recognitions about his sexual identity, and that added further fuel to his own relationship questions.

We stumbled a lot in the beginning. We knew that we didn't want to take to the woods with drums (that was a big trend in men's groups in those days), so we turned, instead, to the kitchen. In the early days of our meeting together, our group time was essentially a series of meals. Our tastes in food and wine weren't particularly sophisticated, but we experimented with new dishes and collectively assembled some pretty good meals together. Around the edges of our cooking and eating, we talked. And in this, too, we experimented. We found that our level of sophistication in our conversation with one another was roughly equivalent to our unsophisticated tastes in food. We found that it was really hard to talk about personal things with other men.

To our credit, we hung in with one another and tried to become more personal and vulnerable. We tentatively shared some of our fears and failures with one another and tried to support one another in our efforts to push the limits of what was comfortable.

Over time, we left the kitchen and did more things together outside. We went on hiking trips and a couple of overnight backpacking trips. We found that our best conversations still usually happened around the edges of doing things together, rather than while sitting in a room looking at one another. We found that whatever activity we shared, whether it was centered in the kitchen or in the outdoors, was better for our talking than when there was no activity at all.

The group ended when we graduated, and each of us left the Buffalo area. All of us moved on to other things, some of us with intact relationships, others embarking on change and new relationship directions. I've fallen out of touch with most of those guys but have maintained contact with a couple, and one remains a best friend.

I remember this men's group now, nearly 40 years later, with fondness. I don't know if the group helped me actually survive my graduate school experience, but it certainly made it a lot richer.

Special Features

Most men are in some kind of group, but they don't call what they do "being in a group." More typically, the groups they are in are called sports teams, hunting camps, rotary clubs, book clubs, or poker nights. These are groups that are defined by the activity that ties them together.

While the times may be changing and more men will seek out group experiences on their own, some men may only join a "talking" group when they're mandated to. Typically, the reason for being there has to do with being leveraged by the court— or some other—system because of legal offenses. In these instances, someone in the court system has suggested that treatment (for substance abuse violations, domestic assault, sexual offenses, etc.) might be a preferred option to incarceration. The hope is that these men can be taught some skills and ways of behaving that will not continue to cause harm to themselves or to others (Wexler, 2013).

Rarer are the groups that men participate in where talking and personal sharing are the defined reason for being there. Men simply don't usually gravitate to that kind of group without some serious prompting. There are, of course, exceptions, and some might argue that more men are now seeking out those kinds of groups.

All this is an introductory way of saying that if you want to work with men in groups, you're going to have to think carefully about men, about men in groups, and, mostly, about your own attitudes about men in groups. Men labor under some heavy cultural stereotypes that can make involvement in anything that looks "touchy-feely" really tough.

We see, in considering groups for women, that there is a need to respect and validate how a woman may struggle for autonomy and individuation, while also supporting her ability to thrive in relationships with others. Similarly, most men generally want to retain what is culturally thought of as masculine while push-ing the boundaries of personal expression. For those of us who work with men in groups, the struggle is to maintain the best of what is thought of as masculine while challenging some unproductive assumptions that continue to burden men.

When an atmosphere of trust is established in a men's group, some wonderful things can happen. When they feel safe enough to take the risk and sense that they won't be judged, men will talk about past incidents of abuse, of their vulnerabili-ties, and of their difficulties being a "man," with all the ambiguities that it entails (Rabinowitz, 2014).

When I worked in the addictions treatment field, it was common knowledge that women seeking addictions treatment faced an even greater challenge with stigma than did men. While both men and women had to deal with stigma and shame in seeking—or being leveraged into—treatment, it was a much tougher road for women to traverse.

The same could be said for men who seek treatment for depression or other mental health concerns. Where there is potentially stigma for both men and women seeking this kind of help, it seems clear that for men seeking help for emotional or mental health the stigma they perceive is even greater. The good news about group work with men is that once engaged, men will be more inclined to stay involved with a group than they will in some other kind of therapeutic intervention, like individual counseling (Csiernik & Arundel, 2013).

To appreciate the challenge that confronts you in working with men in groups, you only need to look at how men are represented in the helping professions. In my own professional organization, the American Counseling Association, less than a third of its members are male. Counseling and related helping professions are more stereotypically female congruent, which means that women are the primary service deliverers and service recipients.

If you want to work with men, particularly in groups, you'll need to think of yourself as a countercultural subversive. You'll be challenging some traditional norms and assumptions, and how you do this will have to do with your own personal attitudes about masculinity and what it means to be a male in this culture.

Leader Considerations

The first thing you'll need to consider in working with men in groups is how you're going to find men with whom to work. It might require you to go where men are and to figure out how you can infiltrate those groups that they're already in. This will mean that you'll need to get out of the comfortable confines of your office and search out the places where men congregate.

I've had students who have been coaches of teams who built personal growth activities into their team-building activities. I've known counselors and psychologists who do presentations with rotary clubs about some of the hazards of being a male in this culture. And there are certainly counselors and social workers who provide services to men who are in residential treatment for war-related issues or who are required to receive services for addiction problems.

If, on the other hand, you are creating new groups for men, you'll need to consider the best ways to intelligently market new group experiences to men. Think about how you can make a group sound appealing to the men you're identifying as your target population. I've found that men are oftentimes drawn to experiences where they'll be helping other men, as in vet-to-vet support groups, than they'll be

TIPS FOR WORKING WITH GROUPS OF MEN

- Teach men active listening skills. Men have a tendency to automatically jump to "fix-it" solutions when asked to listen to the difficulties that someone else is having. Teach them how to listen and respond—particularly how to use good reflection skills—without trying to give advice or fix anything.
- Challenge traditional notions of what success means. Once the primary needs have been met and the ability to make a living has been established, all evidence suggests that simple accumulation of more wealth and status are not as satisfying as doing things that are intrinsically rewarding. Help the men in your groups identify those individually specific, intrinsic "satisfiers" (e.g., coaching, playing with kids, cooking, being in nature, etc.).
- If the group is interested, use this as an opportunity to examine traditional notions of masculinity. Use books, film, and other materials to fuel your discussions. Ask about definitions of *courage*. What do men think about the courage involved in physical risk taking versus the courage involved in taking emotional risks (i.e., becoming emotionally vulnerable)?
- Use the group as an opportunity to talk about diversity issues within the group. What kinds of racial/cultural and other issues of diversity exist, and what implications do these have for being a man? If one of these "diversity" issues is sexual orientation, this will be a great opportunity to expand on the discussion of what it means to be a man.
- There is a saying that goes, "Men talk best shoulder-to-shoulder, women face-to-face." This suggests that your groups of men will best relate when engaged in some activity together.
- Friendship and fatherhood are two topics that should receive ample talking time in your men's groups. The importance of having enduring friendships with other men can be discussed, as can the experience of having been fathered—and, perhaps, of being a father.

to experiences that are designed more directly for themselves (Buitenbos, 2012). They may also be more easily drawn to groups that are activity oriented than to groups that are geared toward discussion of personal issues and feelings. Consider all this as you are planning for a new group, and get very strategic as you think about how to sell your new group to men.

Then, whether you are working with a group that is already up and running or working with a group that you've formed, you'll want to think about the kinds of things that will be the most productive sources of learning for the men in your groups.

Following are some of the things that I have personally emphasized in my own work with men. You may find some of this helpful, and you will undoubtedly want to change or expand on this to make the list your own.

GROUPS FOR OLDER PEOPLE

Treasure the wisdom of old age. Learn from elder people and be wise.

—Lailah Gifty Akita

Working with older people in groups provides a group leader with some unique joys and challenges. Many older people hunger for contact with other people and yearn for opportunities to talk. If you work in groups with older people, you may certainly encounter some difficulties with individual behaviors—as with people who talk too much or too little—but rarely will you have to deal with the kinds of disruptive behavior that a group of challenging adolescents might display. Some suggest that working with groups of older people is superior to working with them individually (Drown, 2008).

There are some unique pleasures in leading groups of older people. When older people are primed to talk, it is a real privilege to be a witness to the stories of lives lived a long time ago. Most of the stories you hear will be rich, filled with the adventures of living. Some will talk of lives lived well; some may talk of regrets. Rarely will the stories be boring—though you may hear some of those stories more than once. Working with older people in groups can be truly rewarding, both for you and for the people in these groups (Alle-Corliss & Alle-Corliss, 2009).

Special Features

There is a danger in thinking that this is a uniform population of people. There are vast differences among this population. In addition to the usual cultural, ethnic/racial, and other kinds of diversity that you might encounter in any group, there are also great differences in physical health, cognitive functioning, personal attitudes about aging, and individual interactional styles. Some people may be visible, living in some kind of assisted-living facility; others may be isolated and difficult to locate.

You may encounter some wariness regarding your attempts to engage older people in groups. There used to be an expression that went, "Never trust anyone over the age of 30," which characterized a generation of youths' distrust of older people. When working with older adults, you may encounter a similar distrust of younger people, which could perhaps be expressed as, "Never trust anyone under the age of 60." Some older people, on the other hand, may naturally embrace someone younger who wants to hear about their lives.

I recall one conversation I had with a colleague who talked about one generational issue that could potentially affect interactions in your groups with older adults. He talked about how his father had said,

> You know, when I was a young guy like you and I tripped over a lamp cord in the living room and broke the lamp, I'd say, "Dang, broke the lamp. Time for a new one." But your generation of psychology-types will do the same thing and you automatically start worrying about what motivated you to break it. Maybe, you think, you're angry with your mother who bought the lamp, or your boss, or some such nonsense. You should just get over it and get on with things.

Figure 11.3 Groups Are a Great Way to Connect Older People

You will have older people in your groups who approach life's circumstances in very different ways. Some will want to talk about their lives "psychologically," and others will not. Additionally, some older people will have stigmatized notions of what it means to be in a group. They may think that involvement implies weakness or an inability to manage their own lives without help. Thus, you may face their reluctance to join a group and then different interactional styles once people have engaged in the group.

Older people may have multiple medical issues, including cognitive impairments, which make involvement in a group challenging. Some of these difficulties may be so distracting that effective participation may be seriously compromised. Some of the people may be really depressed about their life circumstances and their diminished ability to do things. Naturally, if they are able to engage (Figure 11.3), this can be a wonderful opportunity to give and receive support (Johnson, 1996). Involvement in groups might even help ameliorate some people's symptoms (Kessel, Merrick, Kedem, Borovsky, & Carmeli, 2002; Rishty, 2000; Spector, Gardner, & Orrell, 2011).

Leader Considerations

If you're going to work with older people, you'll need to come to grips with your own attitudes about aging, about older people, and about all the issues that accompany this population. Your attitudes about dealing with physical infirmity, mental incapacity, and your own mortality will all come into play here, so it is best to do some close examination of these attitudes before being called on to actually lead a group. How are you around older people? How do you feel about yourself getting older?

You might want to include some older people in your group who are reluctant to become involved. How can you reach out to them and make your group experiences attractive enough to them so that they'd want to join? Are there older people in your community who are isolated or avoid contact because of cultural differences? Are there people in the group who will need transportation if they're going to become involved? You'll need to think very strategically about finding people and creating effective recruiting strategies for your groups of older people.

Once you do get a group together, you'll want to assess the strengths of the people in the group and capitalize on those. Activities and games might help to get the people talking together. You could ask them to show their photos as a way of prompting talk about families, work, and their lives.

Be careful, however, to match the activities to your members' abilities, which might mean having groups of different activity levels.

I remember going with one of my relatives to an afternoon of games in her nursing home. She had some physical mobility problems, but she still had all her mental faculties, and she was a true intellectual. The activities leader had the group playing animal bingo, and my relative just rolled her eyes at me. She was a good sport and played, and there were certainly some of the residents who truly enjoyed

---

TIPS FOR WORKING WITH GROUPS OF OLDER PEOPLE

- Get creative about marketing your group to older adults. Think carefully about the incentives you can use to bring these people into your groups. Transportation and food are usually helpful.
- It can be helpful to consider making physical activity part of your group work with older adults. This kind of activity has been demonstrated to be helpful in keeping the people in the group physically mobile (Salmon, 2011).
- Treat the people in your groups with respect. Do not infantilize them or talk down.
- You don't need to be serious all the time. Appropriate use of humor can be an effective therapeutic tool (Scott, Hyer, & McKenzie, 2015).
- Encourage people in the group to share their life stories. Asking the people to talk about their families or their work or to share photos of their friends and family can be a great way to honor their history and helps create bonds between people.
- Form groups where people congregate: community and senior centers and nursing homes. These places are oftentimes eager for fresh faces and new activities to supplement what they do (Weiss, 1995).
- Some of the group work you do might be with the staff. Instead of working directly with groups of older people yourself, you could train interested on-site staff about the use of active listening skills, and maybe some of them would want to lead discussion groups themselves.

the game, but I did think that it might have been better to have had two levels of group activities, with one that could have better suited people like her. You will certainly want to do what you can to match activities to people's ability levels—both mental and physical.

Working with older people may push you out of your comfort zone. They may want to talk about spiritual concerns, or they may want to pray together. They might want to talk about sexuality issues and concerns, or they might want to be touched or massaged. How will you be able to respond and talk with them about these matters? When they want to talk about death, dying, and loss, will you be able to go there with them?

A common theme that runs through many groups with older people is that of a desire to reminisce. Some of the people may want to talk about their lives, their families, and their work. They may want to talk about their joys, their successes, and their regrets and sorrows. It can be a wonderful honor to sit in the midst of people who share freely their life's journeys.

CONCLUDING THOUGHTS

There are two final thoughts about this chapter that I want to share with you. The first has to do with the age of the population you consider might be best suited for you. You might have a real affection for young people and envision running groups for them as the best way for you to go. Perhaps you've already worked with children, or adolescents, and know that you have a knack for working with them.

I would encourage you to remain open to thinking about group work with other ages. I've encountered many student interns who, when exposed to groups in age groups they hadn't been familiar with, find themselves drawn to a very different population than they thought they'd have interest in—"I always thought I wanted to work with kids, but I really like this bunch of older women. This is the work I want to do."

This happened to me, as well. My original idea was that I'd do my best work with older adults but then happened to find myself in a job where I worked with incarcerated young people. I loved my group work with that population. In particular, I found myself drawn to work with the most resistant—or reluctant—young men. I think that I thrived on the challenge.

So stay open. Try to experience as much as you can of different age groups and of groups run for them. Choose your field or volunteer experiences carefully, and try not to always go with the familiar. If you can, work with different groups for different ages.

The other thought I want to leave you with has to do with the values you bring to your work with these different groups. Your ideas and values regarding what it means to be a woman or a man, for example, will be at play in your groups for women and men. If you come into leading a women's group thinking, again by way of example, that a woman's primary roles in social life should be as a homemaker and a mother, that will be a very different influence than that of another leader who sees such roles for women as suffocating and too narrow.

It's important that you get clear about what you believe and that you think about the ways in which your beliefs can influence your work. It's also important that the people who join your groups know, as much as you are able to tell them, about the value bias that a group you lead might have. This should be seen as an integral part of the informed consent process that you do with anyone joining your new group.

FOR FURTHER THOUGHT

1. Make arrangements to visit a local nursing home. Call them ahead to talk about the best way and time to visit. Engage one or two residents in a conversation, and find out as much as you can about them. Do the same with one or two staff. Ask the staff about the joys and frustrations of their work.

2. Do an Internet search of adventure-based programs for adolescents. Find out as much as you can about these programs: staff (and their qualifications), programming, costs, and so on. Do any of these programs, or this way of working with youth, appeal to you?

3. Visit a local elementary school and meet with a school counselor or school-based clinician. Ask about what kinds of groups, if any, are run in the school for children. If you're able to, sit in on one or two of those group sessions.

4. Consider forming a same-sex support group with five to six people you don't know well. Perhaps there will be a common theme you're all interested in talking about (e.g., parenting, school, or relationships). Be clear with fellow participants that this is a support group, not a counseling or therapy session.

5. Pick one kind of group discussed in this chapter, and do a literature search on that kind of group. Explore what the literature says are the best ways of working with that population and what approaches seem to be the most effective.

REFERENCES

Alle-Corliss, L., & Alle-Corliss, R. (2009). *Group work: A practical guide to developing groups in agency settings*. Hoboken, NJ: Wiley.

Buitenbos, P. (2012). "Good grief! It's a men's group, Charlie Brown." *Canadian Journal of Counselling and Psychotherapy, 46*(4), 335–343.

Ceballos, P. L., & Williams, J. M. (2013). Using play techniques to address student grief and loss. In J. R. Curry & L. J. Fazio-Griffith (Eds.), *Integrating play techniques in comprehensive school counseling programs* (pp. 19–42). Charlotte, NC: IAP Information Age.

Cox, G. R., Robinson, J., Williamson, M., Lockley, A., Cheung, Y. D., & Pirkis, J. (2012). Suicide clusters in young people: Evidence for the effectiveness of postvention strategies. *Crisis: The Journal of Crisis Intervention and Suicide Prevention, 33*(4), 208–214.

Csiernik, R., & Arundel, M. K. (2013). Does counseling format play a role in client retention? *Journal of Groups in Addiction & Recovery, 8*(4), 262–269.

Curry, J. R. (2013). Using play therapy techniques in counseling children with deployed parents. In J. R. Curry & L. J. Fazio-Griffith (Eds.), *Integrating play techniques in comprehensive school counseling programs* (pp. 105–123). Charlotte, NC: IAP Information Age.

Drown, E. C. (2008). Group work with older adults. In L. VandeCreek & J. B. Allen (Eds.), *Innovations in clinical practice: Focus on group, couples, and family therapy* (pp. 61–70). Sarasota, FL: Professional Resource Press.

Dugan, E. M. (2013). Helping homeless children in schools: Play therapy interventions. In J. R. Curry & L. J. Fazio-Griffith (Eds.), *Integrating play techniques in comprehensive school counseling programs* (pp. 367–380). Charlotte, NC: IAP Information Age.

Egbochuku, E. O., & Aihie, N. O. (2009). Peer group counselling and school influence on adolescents' self-concept. *Journal of Instructional Psychology, 36*(1), 3–12.

Fazio-Griffith, L. J. (2013). Social skills development and school based play techniques: Engaging and empowering students. In J. R. Curry & L. J. Fazio-Griffith (Eds.), *Integrating play techniques in comprehensive school counseling programs* (pp. 343–365). Charlotte, NC: IAP Information Age.

Goicoechea, J., Wagner, K., Yahalom, J., & Medina, T. (2014). Group counseling for at-risk African American youth: A collaboration between therapists and artists. *Journal of Creativity in Mental Health, 9*(1), 69–82.

Hollis, J. W. (1997). *Counselor preparation, 1996–98: Programs, faculty, trends* (9th ed.). Philadelphia, PA: Accelerated Development.

Johnson, W. Y. (1996). Group counseling for depressed older adults. In *The Hatherleigh guide to managing depression* (pp. 65–92). New York, NY: Hatherleigh Press.

Kasl, C. (1990). *Women, sex, and addiction: A search for love and power.* New York, NY: HarperCollins.

Kessel, S., Merrick, J., Kedem, A., Borovsky, L., & Carmeli, E. (2002). Use of group counseling to support aging-related losses in older adults with intellectual disabilities. *Journal of Gerontological Social Work, 38*(1–2), 241–251.

Lee, F. W. (2009). Adventure-based counselling (ABC) approach: Working with young people in a world of conflicts. *International Journal of Child Health and Human Development, 2*(4), 403–408.

Leech, N. L., & Kees, N. L. (2005). Researching women's groups: Findings, limitations, and recommendations. *Journal of Counseling & Development, 83*(3), 367–373.

Lopez, A., & Burt, I. (2013). Counseling groups: A creative strategy increasing children of incarcerated parents' sociorelational interactions. *Journal of Creativity in Mental Health, 8*(4), 395–415.

Paquin, J., Kivlighan, D., & Drogosz, L. (2013, June). Person–group fit, group climate, and outcomes in a sample of incarcerated women participating in trauma recovery groups. *Group Dynamics: Theory, Research, and Practice* [serial online], *17*(2), 95–109.

Rabinowitz, F. E. (2014). Counseling men in groups. In M. Englar-Carlson, M. P. Evans, & T. Duffey (Eds.), *A counselor's guide to working with men* (pp. 55–70). Alexandria, VA: American Counseling Association.

Rishty, A. C. (2000). The strengths perspective in reminiscence groupwork with depressed older adults. *Groupwork: An Interdisciplinary Journal for Working With Groups, 12*(3), 37–55.

Rosselet, J., & Stauffer, S. (2013, October). Using group role-playing games with gifted children and adolescents: A psychosocial intervention model. *International Journal of Play Therapy* [serial online], *22*(4), 173–192.

Salmon, J. (2011). Physical activity and sedentary behavior across the lifespan. *International Journal of Behavioral Medicine, 18*(3), 173–175.

Scott, C. V., Hyer, L. A., & McKenzie, L. C. (2015). The healing power of laughter: The applicability of humor as a psychotherapy technique with depressed and anxious older adults. *Social Work in Mental Health, 13*(1), 48–60.

Spector, A., Gardner, C., & Orrell, M. (2011). The impact of cognitive stimulation therapy groups on people with dementia: Views from participants, their caregivers, and group facilitators. *Aging & Mental Health, 15*(8), 945–949.

Splett, J. D., Maras, M. A., & Brooks, C. M. (2014). GIRLSS: A randomized, pilot study of a multisystemic, school-based intervention to reduce relational aggression. *Journal of Child and Family Studies, 24*, 2250–2261.

Weiss, J. C. (1995). Universities for the second phase of life: Counseling, wellness, and senior citizen center programs. *Journal of Gerontological Social Work, 23*(3–4), 3–24.

Wexler, D. B. (2013). *The STOP program: Innovative skills, techniques, options, and plans for better relationships: Handouts and homework* (3rd ed., rev. and updated). New York, NY: W. W. Norton.

Chapter 12

Specialized Groups

It is never too late to be what you might have been.

—George Eliot

You will most likely find that you have a special talent for working with some specific population of people. You might really like working with children and find that you're less interested in working with older people. Or you might prefer working with groups of adults. Many of these adults will be people who have made some difficult, even harmful, life choices and are now trying to get back on track—to become what they might have been.

Beyond that, you may find further that you have some real interest in working with some specific theme or interest area group: for example, women with serious health problems, adolescents with eating disorders, or older people who are grieving the losses of their partners. All the usual guidelines for running groups will apply to the specialized theme and age-group-specific groups you run. There will be, however, special considerations that you'll want to factor in as you plan for these groups.

This chapter discusses four such specialized groups, groups that you might commonly encounter and be asked to run in your community. Each of these theme-specific groups has special features that will shape your considerations for developing and leading them.

> ### SPECIALIZED GROUPS
>
> Special Features, Leader Considerations, and Tips for Group Work
>
> - Addiction Issues
> - Serious and Persistent Mental Illness
> - Criminality and Violence
> - Grieving

GROUPS FOR PEOPLE WITH ADDICTION ISSUES

Special Features

I don't need to tell you that the problems related to addiction are of epidemic proportion. You most likely have a close friend, colleague, family member, or even yourself who you could identify as having been seriously affected by an addiction problem.

The problems associated with addiction run rampant through all our social, health, and mental health institutions. Our correctional facilities are filled with people who have problems associated with addiction. Our problems of domestic violence, child abuse, homicides, and suicides are all directly correlated with addiction problems, and our schools have too many children who live in homes where drug and alcohol abuse are prevalent. The costs associated with dealing with these problems are staggering, as is the cost to our economy in terms of lost productivity (Doweiko, 2011). The problem is huge.

Working with people who have problems associated with drug/alcohol addiction can be incredibly rewarding. While the work can be challenging, and there are certainly people with whom you will work who will make positive life changes only to relapse, there are nevertheless significant joys in working with addiction groups. You'll often see people make visible, positive changes in their lives. Treatment works (van Wormer & Davis, 2003). People get well, and you'll recognize that in ways that are more difficult to see in other kinds of therapeutic work.

I look back with great fondness on the time I spent working with people who had developed addiction problems. Some of those were among the most creative people on the planet—really bright and interesting people. I came to think of many of these people as searchers—people who had simply gotten stuck in some patterns of searching that were no longer working. The therapeutic struggle I think, with both individual and group work, is to help someone uncouple from drugs in order to find more productive ways to continue the search.

Groups have been proven to be one of the best ways to work with a population of people dealing with addiction problems (Line & Cooper, 2002). Working in groups has been demonstrated to be a particularly effective treatment modality for adolescents with drug and alcohol problems (Tanner-Smith, Jo Wilson, & Lipsey, 2013), as well as for working in addiction prevention programming with adolescents (Malekoff, 2005).

However, there are some issues related to drug and alcohol abuse and addiction that make for some particular challenges in running groups for this population. The first of these is the stigma associated with drug addiction. Despite the fact that virtually all of us know someone, perhaps even in our own family, who has some kind of addiction problem, there are still significant negative connotations that we associate with addictions. The stigma associated with addiction is probably most acute for women (Taylor, 2010).

This problem of stigma is a primary reason why people may be reluctant to seek help. In addition to the public's stereotypical ideas regarding people with addiction, many have internalized these negative ideas, so there can be significant shame attached to seeking help.

Another barrier to people getting the help they need is related to denial. The person with an addiction problem may be the last to know it. While denial is a natural defense mechanism we all use to manage the realities of our lives, it takes on magnificent proportions when an addiction is involved (Golden, 2009). You can frequently hear someone with such a problem say, "It's not such a big deal. I can quit anytime I want to."

Thus, harsh social judgment and a personal minimizing of the extent of the problem often work together to keep people from seeking the help they need. This means that oftentimes the people you'll see in some of your groups have been leveraged, or coerced, into being there by someone else. An impaired driving offense may have forced a man into the psycho-educational group on the hazards of drinking and driving that you're leading. Being caught using drugs may have forced an adolescent into your "teens-at-risk" group. A spouse may have told his wife that he was leaving her unless she sought help via one of your groups. There are all kinds of reasons why or ways by which someone might be "convinced" into joining your group. Coercion can come in many different forms, but it can typically result in people being in your group who are there under duress and may be quite reluctant to be there.

Complicating the picture even further is the fact that many people in your group with problems related to addiction may also have other significant mental health and living problems. There may be multiple, co-occurring issues, which means that caring for the addiction issues have to be handled in the context of dealing with all those other issues too.

Recent years have seen the increased use of medications to assist people with addiction problems. Historically, when people entered the treatment system, the expectation was that they'd be working toward becoming drug free—abstinent. More options are available to people now. They may opt for abstinence or they may opt for any variety of medications that satisfy cravings, but that are prescribed and monitored, and help people avoid the dangers (e.g., disease transmitted via dirty needles) of illicit drug use. People involved in these harm reduction programs may have goals that are different from the goals of those pursuing abstinence, and there may be implications for you in these different goals, as you select people for your groups.

Leader Considerations

Confrontation used to be the name of the game in treating people with addiction problems. If you were in a group 30 years ago because of a drug or alcohol problem, most likely you'd have people, encouraged by the leader, hammering away verbally at your "denial." The hope was that this challenging would put a serious dent on your denial and that then you'd be ready to seriously work on your issues.

Fortunately, the treatment field has gotten a lot less confrontational. Clinicians are more respectful. There has been a significant amount of research about what is effective in helping people with addictions in groups that suggest utilizing ways of working that are much more collaborative—less confrontational techniques will most likely be more effective.

Some of the basic things you'd do with any group apply to these groups as well. You are looking to create a safe, respectful atmosphere so that people in the group can explore their concerns and ideas about how their lives might be better—in this case, without the use of drugs or alcohol. Safety is a big deal. Some of the people in your groups may have been in physically and emotionally very unsafe situations, and some members may have helped create unsafe situations. Practical considerations, like where and when your group is held, and constantly reinforcing confidentiality (and its limits) guidelines will help ensure safety. It will also be most helpful in building trust and relationships between members, if your group has a closed membership.

This safety issue begins with screening potential members to ensure that the people coming into your group are appropriate for it. You'll want to see if there are any outstanding things—serious problems with mental illness, for example—that might suggest another way of working, like individual counseling, with someone who might be more appropriate. You'll also want to make sure that the people in a given group have more or less the same goals for being there. If the group is composed of people who are trying to maintain abstinence, not use drugs at all, it will most likely not be helpful to have people in it who are not.

I recently visited an addictions treatment program that had a waiting room filled with people waiting to be seen by their therapists. Some of the people there were in a harm reduction program and were waiting for medications; others were trying to maintain abstinence. It was not a comfortable mix. Why not avoid undue difficulty and create different groups for people with different goals?

In addition to safety, respect is also a big deal. You want to create an environment that promotes group cohesion, like an extension of the therapeutic alliance we strive so hard to help create in individual therapeutic work. Cohesive groups create an atmosphere where it is safe for members to really support one another, and you certainly want the people in the group to offer support and to learn from one another about what has worked in helping them deal with their addiction problems.

You will have people in the group who will seriously test your desire to be respectful. They will be reluctant to be there and may be quite vocal about their resistance. The best way of dealing with this will be to employ your best reflective listening skills and remind them of the voluntary nature of their participation. It will help if you can keep in mind that their resistance is most likely rooted in fear (Rasmussen, 2002). Trying to remain cool and maintaining a nondefensive posture when faced with a lot of resistance will be your best strategy. Take a look again at Chapter 9, where we talked about dealing with challenging behavior. Keep cool and rely on your grit to get through the tough times.

On occasion, you may have someone who is intoxicated or high show up for your group session. I would suggest that you do what you can to head an intoxicated person off before he or she gets into the group, or tactfully (maybe by taking a break) remove someone if the group has started. Allowing an intoxicated person to remain in a group will not be productive for the person or for the group. Then, of course, you also need to do what you can to ensure that the person gets home safely.

Perhaps your largest task will be to plan for the activities and the kind of structure you'll use in your group. Research suggests that there are two theoretical approaches that are most effective in group work. One of these is cognitive behavioral therapy (CBT), where people are taught a variety of coping strategies and skills; the other is motivational interviewing (MI), which headlines respect for the individual as a foundation for beginning a process of helping people examine the role of drugs—and their ambivalence about stopping its use—in their lives (Rollnick & Miller, 1995). MI's effectiveness in addictions treatment—and in a variety of other settings—has been clearly demonstrated (Easton, Swan, & Sinha, 2000; Young, Gutierrez, & Hagedorn, 2013).

Using a combination of these theoretical approaches can be a potent combination in building effective addictions treatment groups. Using MI to help build alliances with people in the group and CBT to help them develop a variety of skills (learning how to say "no" effectively, relapse prevention, mindfulness, etc.) can go a long way in helping people maintain sobriety and improve their quality of life.

You can begin to learn more about MI by visiting the Web site www.motivationalinterview.org. A good beginning to look at the use of CBT in groups would be

TIPS FOR WORKING WITH GROUPS OF PEOPLE WITH ADDICTION ISSUES

- Screen for appropriateness—someone with unreasonable levels of resistance can destroy a group, as can someone needing unreasonable amounts of attention.

- Keep it safe. Think about safety when you plan for the meeting space and time.

- Be careful about self-disclosure. People in the group will ask you about your own drug history. Sharing that information is far less important than showing that you have the capacity to understand and relate. Only share if you really believe that it will serve some therapeutic purpose.

- Meet resistance with nondefensiveness. Think of this as a martial art—roll with the resistance. The resistance is usually about fear and bad past experiences—assume that behind that wall of defense is probably a person yearning to be known.

- Teach coping and life skills. Help your group members teach one another.

- In addition to the groups you run, encourage your members to become involved with the self-help community: Alcoholics Anonymous, Narcotics Anonymous, and so on.

- Discourage (maybe even establish ground rules against) romantic entanglements between group members. They're not good for the group, and they're not good for members' personal recovery.

- Avoid further stigmatizing the people in your groups. You never need to use the words *alcoholic* or *addict*.

- If you work with groups of adolescents with addiction issues, you'll probably want your groups to run for a longer period of time. The job with them is more "habilitation" than rehabilitation. Many of them will never have learned some of the basic skills for living.

Bieling, McCabe, and Antony's (2009) *Cognitive-Behavioral Therapy in Groups*. Naturally, coursework, trainings, and supervision in these approaches will best prepare you to actually use them in your group work.

Above are a few thoughts about working with groups of people with addiction issues that you may find helpful.

GROUPS FOR PEOPLE WITH SERIOUS AND PERSISTENT MENTAL ILLNESS

Special Features

We must stop criminalizing mental illness. It's a national tragedy and scandal that the L.A. County Jail is the biggest psychiatric facility in the United States.

—Elyn Saks

Have you ever seen *One Flew Over the Cuckoo's Nest*? This is a film from 1975, which quite graphically portrays how we used to house and treat people with serious and persistent mental illness. While fictional, the film accurately shows institutional life, the use of electroconvulsive therapy, and the use of groups in such institutional settings. The film's iconic Nurse Ratched, who leads the daily men's group in the institution, is a model of how a group leader can misuse power to control and intimidate. If you do watch the film—and I recommend that you do—view Nurse Ratched's role as typifying how you don't want to be with your groups.

Times have changed. The big institutions are mostly gone, now used only for those who are truly at risk for harming themselves or others. We've replaced them with community-based housing and services and with medications that are designed to help people control the symptoms of their mental illnesses. If, for whatever reason, a mentally ill person isn't housed in a community care home, he or she often winds up homeless on the streets or in a correctional facility. Refining and adequately funding a system of care that is truly humane for those with serious and persistent mental illness is one of our largest social challenges.

For someone with serious and persistent mental illness who is involved with receiving mental health services in a community setting, group work will most likely be part of the treatment regimen. The economy of groups and the ability to teach a number of things to a group of people at the same time are appealing to agency administrators.

If you work in community mental health, you will very likely be asked to lead a group; so it will be helpful for you to know about some of the special features and concerns for group work that are specific to this population.

First, understand that when we talk about serious and persistent mental illness, we are talking about a complex range of behaviors, thought patterns, and symptoms. There are often multiple problems in addition to mental illness. There may be housing issues, including some people who refuse offers of housing, so homelessness may be a significant problem. For people with mental illness living on the streets, abuse is an everyday fact of life. Too many people with mental illness wind up in jails, usually incarcerated for victimless, senseless crimes. This is a vulnerable population of people, too often exploited and harmed.

Some people in the group may be using illicit drugs, in addition to the medications they are prescribed. Work, or the lack of it, can be a significant problem, in part because there may be difficulties with interpersonal relationships. People with serious and persistent mental illness oftentimes have serious deficits in social skills, and this may make it really difficult to hold a job. All these issues, these co-occurring problems, conspire together to create a complicated mix of things that can be difficult to manage (Drake & Noordsy, 1994).

Because of the negative connotations many people associate with mental illness, there is also significant stigma associated with these issues. Thus, in addition to all the struggles that a person with serious and persistent mental illness must endure because of the dynamics of her or his illness, she or he may also have to suffer the negative social indignities inflicted by uneducated people.

Leader Considerations

Creating groups for people with serious and persistent mental illness is a great way to help people learn socialization skills. What better way to learn the inter-personal skills necessary for work or educational settings than by practicing them in real-life situations? Furthermore, you could create a group that could teach interpersonal skills, and it could also have a curriculum of material (e.g., skills for daily living) that could be taught simultaneously. Groups, in other words, are an extremely efficient and practical way to work with people with serious and persistent mental illness.

The people in these groups will most likely receive the most help from an experience that is highly structured and where you are very active. You'll want to plan group sessions that have every minute of time taken into account, and then, do your best to try to stick to the plan. Additionally, the kind of structure that will be most helpful is that which instructs: Skills of daily living and socialization should most typically be the focus. These groups could include field trips to local stores and supermarkets—managing a budget and shopping for food in a public place can be a great way to combine learning a set of daily living skills and socialization skills.

People in your groups may want to address other concerns in your groups as well (e.g., the biological nature of their illness, spirituality concerns, the pharmacology of their medications, etc.), so you might want to explore relevant curricular packages in those areas too.

You can begin to check out some curriculum suggestions online. The federal Substance Abuse and Mental Health Services Administration and the National Alliance on Mental Illness Web sites have curricular packages for people struggling with mental illness—and for their families (www.nami.org).

I would suggest that you keep the discussions in your group very concrete—nonabstract. The psycho-educational focus of your group will allow you to be quite directive, taking a teaching stance, and you'll want to avoid letting people in the group give lengthy voice to the delusional world they may live in.

Finally, I would encourage you to think expansively of your role as a group leader when working with people with serious and persistent mental illness. Think beyond the actual time that these people are actually in the group, and consider what other needs they may have. Particularly, when you are working with people

> **TIPS FOR WORKING WITH GROUPS OF PEOPLE WITH SERIOUS AND PERSISTENT MENTAL ILLNESS**
>
> - Screen for appropriateness. Someone who is too severely disturbed may need more care than a group can provide.
> - Use lots of structure and utilize an active leadership style.
> - Keep it concrete. Teach skills.
> - Be respectful. Avoid using diagnostic labels loosely. There's enough stigma attached to some of the terminology of mental illness without using labels in dehumanizing ways.
> - Beyond the group work you provide people, think of how else you might assist them find services and assistance they can't find for themselves.
> - Become an active advocate for the people in your groups. Get political. Help lend a voice to those who have trouble speaking up for themselves.

with multiple problems—homelessness, addiction issues, and so on—consider what role you might play in helping them find other services to assist them. Collaborate with others in the community who provide services for these people (Baier, 1987; McClellan, 1998; Pratt, Gill, Barrett, & Roberts, 1999). If someone in your group has difficulty finding the help she or he needs, and has no one else helping her find these services, consider providing these case management services as an extension of the work you're doing in the group.

More than this, even, you should become an advocate on behalf of your mentally ill clientele in the community. Fight discrimination where you see it, actively support funding for increasing treatment services, and generally become a voice for fair treatment of this disenfranchised, vulnerable population of people (Kiselica & Robinson, 2001; Ratts, 2011).

Here are some specific suggestions you might find helpful in working with people with serious and persistent mental illness.

GROUPS FOR PEOPLE WITH ISSUES RELATED TO CRIMINALITY AND VIOLENCE

Special Features

What is a good man but a bad man's teacher?
What is a bad man but a good man's job?

—Lao Tzu

Working with perpetrators of violence presents some unique challenges, and you'll want to consider some features of this population of people—and strategies for working with them—that may make your groups go more smoothly.

First, your group will most likely be composed of people who are involved with some kind of criminal justice program. They may be incarcerated inmates or they might be in some kind of probation/parole outpatient program. Many of the people in these kinds of programs are male and a disproportionate number of those African American (Brinkley-Rubinstein, Craven, & McCormack, 2014). The fact that a young African American man may more likely be incarcerated than be studying in college is a stunning, unfortunate fact.

For some of the people with whom you work, some act of violence may have been a part of the reason for incarceration. For some, this would have been part of a larger lifestyle that is involved with criminal activity, like drug dealing (Figure 12.1). For others, the violence may have been domestic or related to sexual violence. Many of these people will themselves have been the victims of sexual and/or other kinds of physical abuse, not to mention of poverty and inadequate family support.

There are any number of ways by which people might be involved with the criminal justice system, from being in minimum or maximum security correctional facilities to house arrest and probation and parole oversight. You might be running groups in any of these settings. The kinds of groups you construct should reflect the relative safety needs of each setting.

Figure 12.1   Criminality and Violence May Be a Way of Life for Some in Your Groups

Many of the people with whom you'll work will have a distrust of authority and may see you as an extension of the system that has taken away or limited their freedom. Fairly typically, these are people who will also minimize their own responsibility for what they've done, and they may blame others, including their victims, for their plight. Additionally, some may have become very adept at conning people to get what they want.

I've certainly had my own experiences with being conned. I was once scammed by a group of youthful offenders whom I'd taken on a canoeing trip. While some of the "kids" had entertained the staff with games and singing by the campfire, others—who we thought were being supervised—were looking for beer by breaking into some unoccupied local camps. Needless to say, we spent a long time repairing some of the damage caused by that night's activities, not to mention cleaning up our own supervision protocols.

People who are involved with the criminal justice system face considerable public stigma. They may have internalized some of society's negative perceptions and see themselves as "bad." Negative public perceptions and negative personal self-image may have conspired together to form a very difficult constellation of thoughts and feelings about oneself and one's place in the world.

Additionally, for many people who find themselves involved with the criminal justice system, there may be addiction, mental health, and a collection of other co-occurring concerns. You'll have to consider this complicated mix of problems as you plan your groups.

Leader Considerations

Your primary concern should be with safety: yours, the people with whom you're working directly, and others who might be affected by the people with whom you work. Think carefully, for example, about where and when you hold your groups. There should be people around to help in the event something bad begins to unfold, and you want to avoid putting yourself in situations where you will feel physically unsafe (e.g., home visits with potentially violent people).

You'll also want to be aware of the fact that some kinds of activity that you might promote in other groups may not be appropriate with people who are involved with the criminal justice system. Encouraging people to be vulnerable might be a wonderful thing to do in most groups but perhaps not where someone is going back into a living situation where that vulnerability will put them at risk.

Much of what you will most likely be doing in your groups will be trying to help people deal with the denial of responsibility related to what they've done

TIPS FOR WORKING WITH GROUPS OF PEOPLE WITH ISSUES RELATED TO CRIMINALITY AND VIOLENCE

- Use your group as a place where people can develop new skills (e.g., anger management) and reorganize harmful thought patterns.
- Work toward helping people in the group take responsibility for themselves, what they do, and what they have done.
- When working with resistant members, you can always remind them of the voluntary nature of the group experience. Though the alternatives (like a cell) might not be attractive, they can always leave.
- Think about safety issues, including helping members stay safe when they leave the group.
- Work nonjudgmentally. Remember to look for the person behind the offenses that have been committed. Avoid further stigmatizing the people with whom you work.
- Keep an eye out for conning behavior—but try not to become overly suspicious or cynical.
- Beyond the work you do in your groups, become an advocate for the ongoing reform of our criminal justice system.

and helping them explore ways to manage a life that doesn't involve violence or involvement with the criminal justice system. You can investigate specific anger and violence reduction programs that can help you design constructive group experiences to teach these skills (Gerhart, Holman, Seymour, Dinges, & Ronan, 2015). You can also encourage people in your groups to share their stories of how they have avoided repeating the use of violence in confrontational situations (Chovanec, 2014).

You'll also want to help the people in these groups take a look at some of the self-defeating thoughts they have about themselves, thoughts that contribute to them continuing to be in trouble. This will inevitably include looking at the ways in which their thinking and behaving patterns lead to trouble and helping them find ways to short-circuit and change the trouble-making thinking. Much of your group work with this population, thus, will be psycho-educational, and the recommended way of working will be with cognitive-behavioral treatment approaches.

You'll want to do the best you can to avoid buying into the stigmatization that may destructively affect the people with whom you work. While you may have some strong negative feelings about some of the things that people have done, it is a behavior. I have frequently heard from students who intern and then work in correctional facilities about how much their personal perceptions of this population shift once they have actual contact with these people—"I never thought I could even stand to be around people who've done these kinds of things . . . and now I find that I actually even like a lot of them."

GROUPS FOR VICTIMS OF VIOLENCE

Special Features

A significant hurdle you'll have to clear in working with victims of violence, particularly when the violence has been domestic, will be the fact that many of these people, usually women, tend to blame themselves for the violence—"I talked back to him. I just asked for it." Victims of violence may thus see themselves as responsible for what has happened to them. They may be caught in a web of self-defeating thoughts and perceptions of themselves as weak and unworthy of love that isn't infused with violence.

Some women live in a subculture that supports violence as a way of dealing with assertive women. There may have been generations of domestic abuse within some of the families with whom you work, and violence may simply be seen as an acceptable way of settling arguments.

A victim of domestic violence, nearly always a woman, may have to remain in close contact with the person who has been violent, oftentimes because of economics. She may have to financially rely on someone who has been physically abusive, particularly when children are involved, which means that she will have a continued relationship with someone who may have done terrible things to her.

In some cases, victims of violence have not been believed when they told people about what has happened to them. Even worse, some people may have reinforced the notion that the victim bears responsibility for the violence that transpired—"What did she think was going to happen, wearing that dress?"

Leader Considerations

As the brief description above implies, you'll have your hands full in trying to work effectively in groups with victims of violence. You'll have the difficult realities of some situations with which to deal. You may be working with someone who continues to live with a person who commits acts of violence on her, and that may be within a culture that supports that violence; and, on top of all that, she may have a personal belief system that thinks that the violence is deserved.

Your work as a group leader—work that all of us who are concerned about reducing violence share—is to bolster a victim's sense of self while dealing with some of the practical and political realities that reinforce the use of violence. This means that you'll need to continually validate the truth of the realities of the violence the victims with whom you work tell you about. You can do this in an atmosphere of respect and with an identification and affirmation of the strengths these people have. They are not only victims but also have great strengths in some areas of their lives. Help identify and build on those.

> **TIPS FOR WORKING WITH GROUPS OF VICTIMS OF VIOLENCE**
>
> - Validate the reality of the things victims tell about themselves and what's happened to them.
> - Help make your groups places where people feel supported with affection and respect.
> - Do what you can to help people stay safe, particularly when they are still in close contact with the perpetrators of violence.
> - Use your groups to highlight people's strengths. Feminist and strengths-based approaches may serve you best in this effort. These groups can also be a place where people can learn new skills.
> - Advocate for reform of laws and legal procedures that further victimize victims.

You'll most likely need to think politically, as well. How can the system in which a victim lives be positively affected to be more believing of her stories and concerns, be more respectful? How can a culture of belief that supports violence as a way of dealing with conflict be at once respected and challenged? While you can focus your attention on honing your group work skills to work with victims of violence in groups, you'll also need to think of your work as an advocate for change in the ways in which we deal with violence in the larger social context.

Your groups that work with victims of violence can be both personally supportive and politically active. Your strong group members can serve as role models for some of the other, less sure, people in the group. You can teach people about the right to be assertive and then use your groups to teach assertiveness skills.

GROUPS FOR GRIEVING PEOPLE

Special Features

Everyone has dealt with some kind of loss.

There are losses associated with separation or divorce, losses associated with moving from one place to another, and losses associated with death. Some losses, like the death of a loved one, may seem more serious than others, like the losses associated with moving from one place to another, but the feelings related to any kind of loss can be intense regardless of the kind of loss suffered. The loss of a pet can throw someone into a state of real turmoil.

How someone responds to loss is a little like how she or he responds to any kind of crisis situation: It's not about the specifics of the crisis; it's about the individual's ability to tolerate and respond to it. Similarly with loss—it's not about what kind of loss it was; it's about how someone is able to grapple with it and move on in life. This does not mean "getting over" the loss. Some kinds of losses are never gotten over, and all losses become a part of the fabric of our lives.

Some people seem to be immobilized by their grief. The pain is so acute that you may be concerned for their safety. In some settings, like schools, a student suicide can create an explosion of feelings among other students, and particularly for those students who have a lot of personal difficulties, the risk of other suicides is a real possibility.

One high school near where I live endured three suicides in 1 year—counselors in the school surmised that the first triggered the other two. The director of school counseling services there told me, "This was really awful. The aftermath of suicide is the last thing we want to get good at handling, but we do think that some of the groups we created may have prevented even more loss."

People have written about the so-called stages of grief, either about the feelings associated with the impending loss or about the grieving that follows the loss. Many know of Elizabeth Kübler-Ross's (1969) work in this regard. You'll recall that she suggested that people move through a sequence of reactions to a terminal diagnosis: denial, anger, bargaining, depression, and acceptance.

While her work did much to draw attention to how we deal with death and dying in this culture, most who work with people around grief issues (Kübler-Ross included) suggest that there is no clearly delineated, linear movement through grief. The feelings and personal reactions are mixed and flow together. People may deny the severity of their illness one moment, then bargain (e.g., trying to make a deal with God to become a "better" person), and then move back to denial as a remission of the disease occurs

The grief associated with the impending loss is probably a very complicated mix of emotions (Rando, 1993). My friends who are intimately involved with hospice work and regularly care for dying patients suggest that in addition to talking about anger and denial, we also need to acknowledge the complicating role of other variables. The hope for a cure—or barring that, for a lengthy remission—and the role that physical pain can play are simply two of those.

Similarly, the ways in which people respond after a death or other significant loss are complex and individually specific. Rando (1988) suggests that there is an initial attempt to simply understand the loss and that this is followed by a period of disorganization and real difficulty. Finally, with help and luck, there can be some accommodation and transformation of the loss—again, words like *getting over* do not apply.

Mothers Against Drunk Drivers is a political action group that models a collective transformation of grief. This is a way that parents who have lost a child in an impaired driving accident can channel their grief in political directions. Compassionate Friends, for families of children who have died, is another vehicle for grief transformation. Helping other families who have had children who have died is a way of helping oneself.

I know one woman who turned her career path on its head, quitting her job and going to medical school to learn how to do research on the kind of cancer that had stricken her child. After a significant loss, each of us needs to mobilize some personal meaning and mission in response to the loss (Frankl, 1962). The alternative is despair.

It's best to think of a reaction to grief as idiosyncratic. Each of us has our own unique way of responding and coping, our own style of grieving. Some people seem to respond to loss with equanimity and no visible difficulty, while others seem to be immobilized.

When I was a senior in high school, my younger brother died in a drowning accident. This was a terrible event. It was truly awful for me and for my family. In the aftermath of the tragedy, my parents put up pictures of my brother all over the house—and I took them down. We had our individual styles of grieving. They wanted to immerse themselves in the feelings of loss, and I couldn't tolerate it.

Some people's grief will not subside. The feelings become frozen and complicated—all kinds of things will start to fray around the edges of the grief (Rando, 1993). There may be drinking or drug problems, serious relationship problems, or other destructive behaviors that appear.

In my case, the years following my brother's death were a time of complicated mourning. I didn't make the best of my undergraduate college experience—it's all something of a haze. I may have looked like I was coping decently, but under the surface, all was not well.

Fortunately, I eventually stumbled into a profession that made me help myself as a prerequisite for helping others. My own work, both in groups and in individual therapy, has made it possible to work with others around their losses without becoming immersed in my own. This has helped cement my belief in the importance of help for helpers, the importance of a therapist's self-awareness.

Looking back, I think that my parents' style of grieving, immersing themselves in the loss, was probably a better way to go. I often wonder whether involvement in a group of my peers, led by a competent adult while I was still in high school, would have helped me deal more immediately and effectively with the loss.

Thus, there are two broad kinds of groups that can be helpful for people dealing with some kind of grief: (1) those that are geared for people dealing with the impending loss and (2) those for whom a loss has already occurred. In working with loss related to death, helping people in groups who have been given a terrible, terminal diagnosis is an example of a group dealing with the impending loss; the other kind of group helps people grieve after the death (Figure 12.2).

Culture plays a huge role in shaping how people deal with grief. In some cultures, death and loss are seen as a natural outgrowth of life; in others, it is feared and denied. I remember the funeral I attended while working as a Peace Corps volunteer

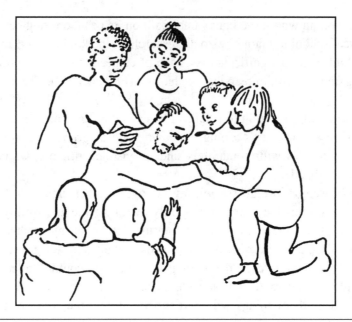

Figure 12.2   For Some People in Grief, Groups Can Be the Best Way to Provide Comfort and Support

in Jamaica. The men spent the night before digging the grave, and the women cooked. There was a fair amount of white rum involved in both the digging and the cooking. The funeral itself was a mix of tears and festivity. As one woman put it, "He had a hard, hard life. . . . Now it's not hard at all." This was a very different kind of funeral than most of those I've attended in this country.

All kinds of cultural differences will affect how people grieve—their family, their community, and their religion—and all of these have implications for the groups you'll create to assist them. The best thing you can do is to become a student of all these wonderful differences.

Leader Considerations

Providing opportunities for someone in grief to talk with others can be a wonderful way to offer support and comfort. For someone dealing with a difficult illness, sharing with others the fears and problems associated with being sick—particularly those people who have similar concerns—can be a great help. For someone who has lost a loved one to death, sharing the loss with others can provide a great sense of relief. It can also be a way of taking a step toward transforming the loss in a way that is healing.

Working with people in groups who have some kind of terminal diagnosis can be remarkably rewarding. Hospice therapists and volunteers talk about the incredible

TIPS FOR WORKING WITH GROUPS OF GRIEVING PEOPLE

- Create theme-specific groups (e.g., for people with a similar diagnosis or for people with a similar kind of loss).

- Be very active at the beginning of the group; try to back off and let the group do most of the talking as it matures.

- Screen members for appropriateness for a given group. Some people in the group may need individual help. Trust when someone says that he or she is not ready to be in a group. Keep a close eye out for those people who are having real difficulty—assessment is an ongoing process.

- Using different art forms in your group can be very helpful. Clay and paints can be useful vehicles for helping people express themselves. Books and film can provide a good way to stimulate group discussions.

- If you are uncomfortable with conversations about death or being around really sick people, try to find time to put yourself in situations where you are exposed to those—before the time comes when you are leading a group and are responsible for responding.

- Try to encourage—and not be unduly afraid of—the expression of deeply felt emotions.

- Avoid "the Kleenex effect." Handing someone a tissue is a comforting gesture, but it also suggests that the person should clean up his or her act and get it together.

- Don't be afraid to be human. Showing, emotionally, that you are moved by something that is being said in your group is a wonderful kind of self-disclosure.

- Crying with your group can be a great asset—sobbing, however, will not be so helpful.

- Always bear in mind that you are leading this group to help the people deal with their grief. While it is appropriate and helpful to be moved by the things they say, this is not the primary place for you to deal with your own grief issues.

- Allow for time and space after a group meeting for the people to get their "game faces" back on. People going back into the everyday world will most likely not want to still be visibly awash in emotion.

- Try to help people in the group see glimpses of possible movement in positive directions.

- Have a life outside of the work you do with grieving people. This is the best way to ensure that you're fully present when you need to be.

feeling of privilege in working with people who are confronting their own death. All the unimportant issues are discarded, and people can get down to talking about what is closest to the heart. Therapeutically, there is nothing to fix, and it is simply about being with and caring for someone.

Working in groups with people who have endured loss is also remarkably rewarding. Being privy to stories of people who have died is a real honor, as is the opportunity to help people see the gifts that have been bestowed on them by the death, the loved one's legacy.

It can also be a really difficult and challenging work. If you're going to work with people who are grieving, it's important that you have a handle on your own emotional life. This doesn't mean that you need to have all your personal issues resolved. You don't need to be perfect, but you do need to be prepared to manage your group's strong emotions. You don't want to become swamped by your own strong reactions to what you hear.

There are some special considerations you'll want to factor into your work with groups of people who are grieving. Following are some of these.

REFLECTION AND GROUP FISHBOWL LAB PRACTICE EXERCISE

Take a few minutes to consider and think about these specialized groups you've just reviewed. Is there any one of these groups—or perhaps one that is not discussed here—that has an appeal for you and that you could see yourself running? What is it about a kind of group that particularly interests you or, conversely, that you would not like to run?

For this fishbowl lab, you'll again need six people to volunteer to be group members and two to volunteer to be group leaders. The rest of the people will be silent observers, taking note of how this fishbowl exercise goes, particularly focusing on the leaders' interactions with the group. The observers should be prepared to give feedback to the leaders at the end of the experience.

The leaders' job is simply to initiate and stimulate conversation related to the reflection exercise: What kinds of groups are people most interested in leading? They should encourage members to talk about their rationale for wanting to lead one kind of group over another. What values or personal experiences, for example, influence a desire to work with one kind of group of people over others? I would encourage the leaders to talk about their own preferences as well.

Take approximately 30 minutes for discussion, and then, allow time for the group to talk about the experience and for observers to provide feedback.

CONCLUDING THOUGHTS

If you make group work a part of your work life, you will most likely gravitate to working with some kind of specialized group and maybe with an age group that you find attractive. Thus, you might work with young adults with problems of addiction and criminality or with older people with grief issues, for example. If you do specialize in this way, you may very likely become known in your community as the go-to person for referrals of people with those kinds of characteristics.

As you gain proficiency in working with groups, and as you gain special skills in working with the specific issues people have, you'll most likely also become aware of some of the larger political realities that shape these people's lives. Many of the people with whom we work are marginalized by society, and they have to deal with considerable stigma. You will become aware of the problems they encounter.

Your increasing awareness of the stigma and negative political realities that affect the people in your groups should drive you to become an advocate for the people with whom you work. Your groups can become a vehicle for heightening your members' awareness of these political issues (e.g., the paucity of treatment resources for those with addiction problems, overmedication and neglect in some nursing homes or facilities for those with serious and persistent mental illness, etc.). Some of the people in these groups will want to become politically active around these issues themselves.

Beyond what you can do within your groups, however, I would strongly encourage you to think expansively about your professional role. Involvements with your group members' communities, as well as with statewide political action groups that influence social policy, are legitimate extensions of your group work. Your best professional work will include both the work you do directly with people in your groups as well as the indirect work you do on their behalf as an advocate.

FOR FURTHER THOUGHT

1. Contact professionals in local correctional centers, hospice programs, addictions treatment centers—any place where you might see yourself leading groups. Set up a time to talk with these people about their work and about the groups they lead. What are the particular joys and frustrations of their group work in these settings?

2. Pick one or more of these specialized groups and review some of the literature about the theory and research related to these groups. Explore what seems to be the "best practice" in working with these kinds of groups.

3. Examine the literature related to evaluating the success of each of these kinds of groups. What implications can this have for your work with groups? How, in other words, would you be able to measure whether your specialized group had any impact?

4. Consider what kinds of structured exercises might be helpful in working with any of these specialized groups. Try to find exercises that have already been designed for these groups. Alternatively, design (following guidelines that have already been established for these in previous chapters) some exercises of your own.

REFERENCES

Baier, M. (1987). Case management with the seriously mentally ill. *Journal of Psychosocial Nursing and Mental Health Services, 25*(6), 17–20.

Bieling, P., McCabe, R., & Antony, M. (2009). *Cognitive-behavioral therapy in groups.* New York, NY: Guilford Press.

Brinkley-Rubinstein, L., Craven, K. L., & McCormack, M. M. (2014). Shifting perceptions of race and incarceration as adolescents age: Addressing disproportionate minority contact by understanding how social environment informs racial attitudes. *Child & Adolescent Social Work Journal, 31*(1), 25–38.

Chovanec, M. G. (2014). The power of learning and men's stories in engaging abusive men in the change process: Qualitative study across programs. *Social Work With Groups: A Journal of Community and Clinical Practice, 37*(4), 331–347.

Doweiko, H. (2011). *Concepts of chemical dependency.* Pacific Grove, CA: Brooks/Cole.

Drake, R., & Noordsy, D. (1994). Case management for people with coexisting severe mental disorder and substance abuse disorder. *Psychiatric Annals, 24*(8), 427–431.

Easton, C., Swan, S., & Sinha, R. (2000). Motivation to change substance use among offenders of domestic violence. *Journal of Substance Abuse Treatment, 19,* 1–5.

Frankl, V. (1962). *Man's search for meaning: An introduction to logotherapy.* New York, NY: Washington Square Press.

Gerhart, J., Holman, K., Seymour, B., Dinges, B., & Ronan, G. F. (2015). Group process as a mechanism of change in the group treatment of anger and aggression. *International Journal of Group Psychotherapy, 65*(2), 181–208.

Golden, G. (2009). *In the grip of desire: A therapist at work with sexual secrets.* New York, NY: Routledge/Taylor & Francis.

Kiselica, M., & Robinson, M. (2001). Bringing advocacy counseling to life: The history, issues, and human dramas of social justice working in counseling. *Journal of Counseling & Development, 79,* 387–397.

Kübler-Ross, E. (1969). *On death and dying.* New York, NY: Macmillan.

Line, B. Y., & Cooper, A. (2002). Group therapy: Essential component for success with sexually acting out problems among men. *Sexual Addiction & Compulsivity, 9*(1), 15–32.

Malekoff, A. (2005). Group work in the prevention of adolescent alcohol and other drug abuse. In G. L. Greif & P. H. Ephross (Eds.), *Group work with populations at risk* (2nd ed., pp. 76–93). New York, NY: Oxford University Press.

McClellan, K. (1998). Managing care for the seriously and persistently mentally ill. *Employee Assistance Quarterly, 13*(4), 23–32.

Pratt, C., Gill, K., Barrett, N., & Roberts, M. (1999). *Psychiatric rehabilitation.* San Diego, CA: Academic Press.

Rando, T. (1988). *Grieving: How to go on living when someone you love dies.* Lexington, MA: Lexington Books.

Rando, T. (1993). *Treatment of complicated mourning.* Champaign, IL: Research Press.

Rasmussen, P. (2002). Resistance: The fear behind it and tactics for reducing it. *Journal of Individual Psychology, 58*(2), 148–159.

Ratts, M. (2011). Multiculturalism and social justice: Two sides of the same coin. *Journal of Multicultural Counseling and Development, 39*(1), 24–37.

Rollnick, S., & Miller, W. (1995). Motivational interviewing: Resources for clinicians, researchers, and trainers. *Behavioral and Cognitive Psychotherapy, 23,* 325–334.

Tanner-Smith, E. E., Jo Wilson, S., & Lipsey, M. W. (2013). The comparative effectiveness of outpatient treatment for adolescent substance abuse: A meta-analysis. *Journal of Substance Abuse Treatment, 44*(2), 145–158.

Taylor, O. (2010). Barriers to treatment for women with substance abuse disorders. *Journal of Human Behavior in the Social Environment, 20*(3), 393–409.

Wormer, K. van, & Davis, D. (2003). *Addiction treatment: A strengths perspective.* Pacific Grove, CA: Brooks/Cole.

Young, T. L., Gutierrez, D., & Hagedorn, W. (2013). Does motivational interviewing (MI) work with nonaddicted clients? A controlled study measuring the effects of a brief training in MI on client outcomes. *Journal of Counseling & Development, 91*(3), 313–320.

Chapter 13

Final Thoughts

Taking Care—the Personal and the Political

Your visions will become clear only when you can look into your own heart.
Who looks outside, dreams; who looks inside, awakes.

—C. G. Jung

I want to leave you with some thoughts about what I believe are two critical areas of concern for group workers: (1) maintaining a focus on your own well-being and (2) also becoming a force to help promote the well-being of the people you serve in your groups—a force for advocacy and action. The first of these, maintaining a focus on your own health, will help ensure that you don't get burned out and disillusioned in your group work.

The second, establishing yourself as an advocate and activist on behalf of your clients, will not only help the people in your groups but also help you maintain some perspective on the importance of your own personal problems.

STAYING HEALTHY

It should be obvious that your ability to be an effective group leader will largely depend on your personal well-being (Mutchler & Anderson, 2010). Nurturing your own health, in other words, is a professional obligation. We talked in the chapter on leadership about the importance of self-awareness and about how different aspects of yourself, taken together, constitute your "whole person" (Evans, Duffey, Erford, & Gladding, 2013).

You can think about self-awareness as an ongoing assessment of these various "selves" (Wegscheider, 1986).

It should be clear that self-awareness is singularly important as a determinant of effective group leadership. This self-awareness is something that should translate to all aspects of who you are—your total "whole person." You will want to bring awareness to each aspect of yourself and realistically assess which of these areas might need some of your attention and, perhaps, work.

This can be tricky, a bit dialectic, actually. On the one hand, you want to be able to accept these different "selves," while, on the other hand, working to change some things. This process can be sometimes assisted with the help of others—a nutritionist or a personal trainer to help with your physical self, a therapist to help with your social-familial and emotional selves, or a career counselor to help with your concerns about working, as only a few examples of these.

You don't need to be perfect. You don't need to resolve all your personal emotional issues, repair all your relationship concerns, or have an ideal body. Forget striving for perfection. Rather, strive for some balance. Maintain an ongoing awareness of these different aspects of yourself, ask for help from others when you see some changes that you'd like to make, and accept the rest. To paraphrase a line from the well-known prayer, "Grant me the serenity to accept what I cannot change."

All that being said, take a look at some questions, some suggested ways as to how you might survey seven different aspects of yourself, your own seven "selves," and then consider what additional questions you'd like to add to these.

Your Physical Health

You live in your body. Your physical self is the first part of you that your new groups will encounter, and many people will jump to some immediate conclusions about who you are based on what they see (Vargas & Borkowski, 1983). This might not seem fair, but it's what happens. Even more important than others' perceptions, however, are your own perceptions of yourself and your physical being.

How much attention do you pay to your physical well-being? Do you exercise and pay attention to what you eat—not obsessively but with awareness? Do you get regular checkups? Are there some health concerns you have that need attention? Do you drink—or use legal or illegal medications—in a way that is harmful? You don't need to be a physical fitness fanatic to make some commonsense decisions about eating, exercising, and paying attention to your physical self.

We in North America live in a culture that sends a lot of confused messages our way about how we should treat our physical selves. Our magazines are filled with tips about how to diet—along with recipes for calorie-rich deserts. We talk about the health benefits of walking, but many of us live in suburban or urban neighborhoods that have no sidewalks or other safe places to walk. We live in a culture that produces vast quantities of food, yet healthy, affordable foods are out of the reach of many people, and many others are harmfully affected by eating disorders. We work in organizations that tout the benefits of physical fitness, yet many of those job sites provide no time or incentives for employees to get healthier.

It can be difficult to make sense of these contradictions, but it's important that you try to negotiate a path amid all these contradictions that makes sense to you. This doesn't mean having a "perfect" body, whatever that is. It means making sensible decisions about what's good for your body and maintaining a healthy awareness and acceptance of your physical self. This can be as much of an attitudinal adjustment as it is an adjustment in what you're doing physically.

The people in your groups will definitely be affected by how comfortable you are in your body. Some theories of psychotherapy—like bioenergetics and the use of yoga—actually maintain a primary focus on the body as a way of promoting emotional health. Some medical schools are now helping new physicians deal more effectively with nutritional issues, both for themselves and for their patients. Your awareness of your body and the attention you pay to it will be one of the most important modeling messages that you convey to your groups.

Your Emotional Health

It's pretty obvious that your emotional state will affect how you are with your groups. Whatever is happening inside will somehow manifest itself outside. This means that maintaining an awareness of your feeling states and paying attention when things seem to be going awry is important. This doesn't mean being "happy" all the time, rather simply paying attention to the movement of your emotional life. You can think of your "happiness" not as a fixed state but as a fluid series of "happenings."

Part of the reason this is so important is that it will have a lot to do with how you let the people in your groups express their feelings. If you are out of touch with, or even afraid of, some of your own emotions—anger, for example—it will make it very difficult for you to allow the people in your group to express theirs.

Just as you want to be able to monitor your own emotional state, part of what we called your "intrapersonal" world, while you're leading a group to gauge your responses to what's unfolding there, so you'll also want to be able to do this in your day-to-day life. Check in with yourself periodically; see what's going on. You can do this informally, or you can establish some kind of regular emotional monitoring practice, as with prayer, meditation, or mindfulness.

Ask yourself whether you're generally positive about your life. If not, why not? Try to be honest with yourself. If you think that you're feeling depressed and negative about most things, try to unravel what that is all about. I often think of some kinds of depression as a result of feeling stuck between a rock and a hard place—between two untenable sets of choices. Oftentimes, this is between what one thinks one should do versus what one wants to do. Sometimes, this may involve your work, directly. If, for example, you stick with a job or a line of work primarily because of the extrinsic satisfactions it holds (the money and security) at the expense of what you find intrinsically rewarding (e.g., time to pursue what you really love), you will most likely be unhappy and depressed. Could you make some difficult choices to help make yourself feel better?

In addition to asking yourself about what's happening in your emotional life, you could also seek out some help for your exploration. A good therapist—or a supervisor—can help you articulate, give language to, and help sort out your complicated mix of emotions. She or he can help you think through what kinds of changes you might have to look at making in order to make yourself more emotionally satisfied and what the consequences of those changes might be. This search, even the fact of simply giving voice to your emotions with someone who you really trust, can be a real adventure.

Your Social–Familial Health

The family you grew up in has had a great influence on how you work with people (Softas-Nall, Baldo, & Williams, 2001). Whatever your family looked like, whatever the circumstances, it has played a really important role in your life.

Life in this world is not played on a level playing field. While some of us grow up in families that are nurturing and supportive, others have had to face abuse and neglect. Some of us are born into wealth, some into poverty. There are injustices of race, of socioeconomic class, and of gender in our society that are played out daily in our families.

"At some point, we all need to give up hope for a better past" (Yalom, 2011). No matter what kind of family upbringing and circumstances we were born into, this saying suggests that, at some point, we each need to assume responsibility for our lives. As adults, we need to give up blaming others for our circumstances and act as the architects of our own lives. Not blaming, however, does not imply not being angry about those injustices and taking action to correct whichever of those you can.

You will be much better equipped to be that architect of your life if you have an understanding of the forces that have helped shape who you are. This includes the intimate family surroundings you grew up and lived in as well as the larger social context of your life. A sophisticated understanding and appreciation of those will be invaluable as you make choices as to how to proceed with your life. That understanding will also help you better appreciate the forces that shaped and continue to influence the lives of the people in your groups.

Some would suggest that you are perhaps better equipped to understand the difficulties others have experienced in their lives if you've had those difficulties yourself (Wilcoxen, Walker, & Hovestadt, 1989). While there may be some truth to that, there is the risk of your own history unduly influencing your relationships with people in your groups. This is the phenomenon sometimes referred to as "the wounded healer," which suggests that while our own difficult family backgrounds may provide us with some heightened intuitive skills in working with people, we might also look toward our clients/people in our groups to help mend some of our own history (Hayes, 2002). This is yet again a good reason to have a therapist and/ or a supervisor who can help us recognize when this may be happening.

It is also important that you have a social life apart from your work life. You will want social relationships with people other than those in your groups, with people with whom you are on an equal footing (Minor, Pimpleton, Stinchfield, Stevens, & Othman, 2013). Having good friends and family, perhaps children, is a great counterbalance to an active work life.

Your Spiritual Self

Until recently, with the advent of psychotherapy approaches that deal specifically with spirituality, scant attention was paid to the spiritual questions that the people in our groups (or we) might have. This lack of attention paid by the therapeutic community to spiritual issues led one famous psychoanalyst, Otto Rank (1952), years ago to suggest that our "mechanistic, reductionistic" ways of looking at people has meant that modern psychotherapy is emotionally impoverished and that it works incompletely with people. Most of modern psychotherapy, he argued, ignores a primary human need: to have our lives mean something (Rank, 1952).

The existentialists who followed him—Rollo May, Victor Frankl, and Irvin Yalom—would certainly echo that concern. They began to infuse the psychotherapy world with these questions that people have about the meaning of their lives.

If you are involved in some kind of professional training program in social work, counseling, or psychology, it is unlikely that much of your required coursework includes much about spiritual concerns. Unless your program is decidedly religious in nature, your program will most likely take a secular approach to working with people. Coursework in theories of psychotherapy have begun to include approaches that focus on spiritual concerns, but by and large, you will be left to your own devices to consider how these concerns will be woven into your own work. I would suggest that it is legitimate for you to pay as much attention to addressing spiritual questions as a part of your professional life as it is to any other aspect of your professional training.

As you consider how you'll address spiritual concerns that people in your groups may bring up, you'll need to think about your own relationship to these issues. What gives your life meaning? In what do you believe? Is there any kind of organizing force in the universe, or are we all left to our own devices? These questions, and many more, are ones you'll need to address—or else you'll inadvertently address them by not addressing them. Not believing in anything is, in fact, a belief system too.

You may or may not be interested in following the path of an established religious doctrine. You may have grown up in a family with a belief system that you have adopted as your own or you may as an adult have been on a search for a spiritual path that feels personally meaningful. This may include an adherence to beliefs in an established religion. Alternatively, you may decide to make your own way in this and negotiate a path that is strictly your own. Walking in the woods, for example, or meditating by a river, might be exactly what you need to maintain a sense of perspective and balance in your life (Milton, 2009).

The more grounded you are in your own spiritual beliefs (meaning, the more aware of them that you are), the better prepared you'll be to hear the spiritual concerns of the people in your groups (van Asselt & Senstock, 2009), and the better you'll be prepared to serve as an advocate for them when they run into trouble because of their beliefs (Wiggins, 2010).

While people won't bring up spiritual concerns in every group you run, you can assume that they'll be in the mix of things somewhere. And in some groups, particularly in those dealing with life and death issues, spiritual concerns will be at the forefront. How ready will you be to hear these? Will you be able to hear, appreciate, and accept those belief systems that run counter to your own, or do you need to work in a setting that reflects a clear belief system that fits who you are?

Your Intellectual Self

Are you a curious person? Do you approach the world with an inquisitive mind? I'm not asking whether you're brilliant, but rather whether you have interest. Do you want to know how things work, about what makes people do the things they do, and about how people come to feel better about themselves, for example. Your quest for answers, your inquisitiveness, is an indication that you are feeding that part of you that craves intellectual stimulation.

When you embark on a professional training program, like the one that helps prepare you to run groups, you pay a great deal of attention to this intellectual side

of yourself. You learn about theories of human behavior, about systems of intervention that can help people resolve personal difficulties, and about research and
evaluation. The courses you take and the intellectual interactions you have with
other people in your program help give you the knowledge base you need to begin
to work effectively with people.

But there's more that's intellectually required of you. You'll need to extend your
intellectual self beyond what you are expected to do in coursework. The coursework is just a foundation, a beginning.

Think of yourself as a lifelong student, with much of your necessary learning
needing to take place in the world at large. You can read widely, and not just about
your own professional field. You can immerse yourself in discussion with mentors
and people who will force you to challenge some of your closely held assumptions
about the world. You can travel, experience other cultures, and seriously expand
your appreciation of the diverse world we live in. Consider all this as an integral
part of your professional preparation.

Your Aesthetic Self

A number of therapists I know have incorporated the arts into their work with
people. One of these therapists loves to use clay. She believes that the act of shaping something with your hands, the emotional release such a tactile action can
facilitate, is a great asset to the talking work she does with people. I have frequently
brought artists into my groups to help people learn how to give voice visually—or
sometimes musically—to things they're feeling inside. These guests take care to
call what they're doing "making things," as opposed to doing "art," mostly to minimize the performance anxiety people may feel when trying to think of themselves
as creating a work of art.

It will be easier for you to work this kind of activity into your groups if you
are creatively engaged with your environment artistically as well. This nurturing
of your aesthetic self can take many forms. It might be in painting or drawing, in
writing poetry, or in making music. This nurturing might be less in creating new
works yourself and more in appreciating what others have done. Or it might be
even more elemental, like digging in the dirt and planting things. You don't need,
in other words, to be an artist to have some artistic, or aesthetic, appreciation for
the world around you. Creating beauty can take many forms. Even how you deco-
rate your home, or your office, reflects your sense of the aesthetic, and you can
approach that thoughtfully.

My family and I used to have a little running commentary about the buildings
we'd drive by on road trips. When we'd pass a large brick building, one of us would

invariably say, "Well, there's another school . . . or is it a prison?" The people who designed many of those buildings were clearly more invested in the buildings' functions than they were in the buildings' beauty. I would suggest that you not carry this same attitude into the space you create for your groups.

Think about aesthetics when you create your groups. Do the best you can with the space you have to make it reflect your own aesthetic appreciation. The space you select and the ways in which you use it reflect your respect for your group and for the things that can happen there. I am convinced that better things happen in groups that are run in aesthetically pleasing places, so factor these concerns for aesthetics into your group planning.

Your Working Self

You most likely already spend a lot of time contemplating your working life.

A lot of your waking hours are spent working, and you probably give this part of your life a lot of thought. You think about your interactions with people, about advancement, and maybe about whether what you're doing is right for you.

Much of this contemplation of your work life has to do with the degree to which it satisfies you extrinsically and intrinsically. The extrinsic rewards, like money and recognition, are most likely less satisfying to you—and this is a guess—in the long run than are those that are intrinsic, like feeling good about helping people connect with one another. Naturally, you need a certain amount of money to live decently, but beyond that, there may not be a great deal of additional satisfaction. Again, this is a personal decision. How much money do you need from your work to afford a decent living?

You may be someone whose real vocation is not what pays the bills. Your real love may be music, the fine arts, or theater, but you work in the "helping" field to pay the bills. You have a job, and then you have your work. Is there some way to make these two worlds into one? Could you create something that could help you help others, while making a living from doing what you love?

Or maybe you need to make a change. I've known many people who have made midlife career changes to make their working lives more satisfying. Invariably, this has been a shift away from work that satisfied extrinsically to work that is more intrinsically rewarding. One of my friends recently said, "Banking was very good to me. I made a ton of money, but now I want to shift my focus to working with people. I want to be able to make a positive difference in people's lives, not just fatten my savings account."

What is the balance between extrinsic and intrinsic rewards that feels right to you?

REFLECTION AND GROUP FISHBOWL LAB PRACTICE EXERCISE: FOCUSED AWARENESS OF YOUR VARIOUS "SELVES"

Start by finding a time and place where you can sit quietly for a few minutes, and then, begin to focus your attention internally. Close your eyes and take stock of the thoughts and feelings that are in the foreground.

Then, survey the seven different areas of your life we've just discussed: (1) the physical, (2) the emotional, (3) the social–familial, (4) the spiritual, (5) the working, (6) the intellectual, and (7) the aesthetic. Pass through each area briefly, and note your level of satisfaction with each. Do you see areas that deserve more of your attention? Take note of those. Try not to be judgmental. Simply take note.

After you've spent a few minutes in this focused attention, open your eyes.

Then, assuming that you have a group of people with whom you are sharing this material, create a group fishbowl lab exercise: two leaders, members, and observers. As with previous group fishbowls, the leaders should lead a discussion, this time about members' perceptions and levels of satisfaction of the seven different aspects of themselves. And, again, the leaders should function as participant-leaders, and they should feel free to add their own perceptions. To the best of their ability, the leaders should foster a discussion where members are interacting with one another, using skills discussed in earlier chapters. Members should be encouraged, in other words, to reflect on one another's disclosures and to help one another increase the meaning of their understandings of their perceptions of themselves.

At the end of the allotted time (perhaps 30 to 40 minutes), the observers should provide feedback, and the group, as a whole, should process the exercise. Again, take care to ensure that the feedback is specific, constructive, and supportive. Finally, reiterate the confidential nature of the exercise.

STAYING FRESH AND ALIVE AND AVOIDING BURNOUT

As you periodically engage in the review of your various "selves," you can look particularly at those areas that seem to be receiving too little of your attention. You might be spending considerable time on your working and intellectual selves, for example, and very little on your social–familial and spiritual selves. Look for those areas of yourself that need more attention, and strategize about the ways in which you can commit more time and energy to nurturing those parts of yourself.

Your goal here is to achieve some balance. Your ability to take care of these different aspects of yourself translates directly into how effective you'll be in your work life (Bakker, Van Der Zee, Lewig, & Dollard, 2006). You don't want your life

WARNING SIGNS OF BURNOUT

- Exhaustion and Fatigue
- Insomnia
- Negative Attitude About Work
- Increased Use of Tobacco, Alcohol, or Drugs
- Negative Self-Concept
- Psychosomatic Illness
- Negative Attitude About Clients
- Poor Performance, Absenteeism
- Eating Difficulties
- Guilt
- Passivity

—Maher (1983)

to be so skewed that only one or two aspects of yourself are receiving all your time and attention. While there may be some times in your life when that is inevitably going to happen (e.g., when you're finishing school), in general you want to be able to have the time and energy to commit to all those various aspects of who you are.

Make an examination of your work a constant in this process. How satisfying does the work you're doing with groups continue to be? Does the place where you're doing this group work value and support what you're doing? Some workplaces, of course, are more supportive than others, and some are simply filled with stress and an unrelenting crisis mentality (Senter, Morgan, Serna-McDonald, & Bewley, 2010).

Monitor your satisfaction and enthusiasm for your work. Your level of enthusiasm has a huge impact on your effectiveness (Lanham, Rye, Rimsky, & Weill, 2012). You may know people who seem dispirited and unhappy in their work. They don't seem to have much energy and exude negativity and cynicism (Kesler, 1990). You may have a colleague who makes derogatory remarks about people in his or her groups or even calls them by their diagnostic labels (my "borderlines" group). Someone like this seems to me to be simply marking time, struggling to make it to the retirement finish line. Even worse, it may be someone who is far from retirement, someone who's just hanging on for the paycheck.

You don't want to be one of those people. You want to look forward to the next group you'll be doing and think about your work with excitement and a sense of challenge.

TIPS FOR AVOIDING BURNOUT

- Continue to remember the importance of your work—assisting people to connect more effectively with others in their groups and in the world and in their learning new skills.
- Connect with people who are vibrant, committed to their work, and generally upbeat.
- Be engaged with your community. Your contributions as an advocate and activist serve as a different way to assist your clients and provide another way of involvement that can help keep you excited about what you do. It can bring you in contact with some very different kinds of people.
- Have a life outside of work. Have friends and a family with whom you can have fun and who can serve as a counterbalance to the things you do at work.
- Spend an adequate amount of time with just yourself.
- Watch your tendencies to "overdo": You're not the only one who can serve on the committees, work with specific people, or do certain tasks. You don't always have to say "yes."
- Be enthusiastic, and keep yourself upbeat. Be the kind of person you want to be around. On some days, you might have to pretend to be upbeat until the real thing kicks in—fake it until you make it.

If you find yourself dealing with any of these warning signs, it might be time to take a break—a vacation or a leave of absence—to do something different. Maybe that could be time spent in a review of what you need to do differently in your work situation, maybe doing a different kind of work for a while, or maybe consulting with colleagues about trying some other strategies.

BECOMING AN EFFECTIVE ADVOCATE AND ACTIVIST

One of the great things about working with groups is that it provides a vehicle for people to get outside of themselves and connect with others. The people in your groups can begin to think of themselves as part of a larger whole and expand their appreciation of how their own particular issues or concerns about life are shared by others. This is the concept of "universality" that we talk about as one of the primary therapeutic outcomes of an experience in a group.

A sense of connection with others and to the larger world—and to the ways in which the world affects people's lives—is a significant departure from what we, who work in the psychotherapy world, think about, when we're trying to help people. We have had a tendency to reduce all of a person's problems to the psychological, and we help people adjust to situations or help make personal changes in order to become happier. With the exception of social workers, who have historically been very savvy about considering the social systems in which people live, most of us in the helping professions have more or less ignored the larger social forces that seriously affect people's well-being (Hillman & Ventura, 1993).

The people we serve might not be particularly aware of those larger "forces" either. Certainly, some racial and ethnic groups might have a great deal of awareness about the political world in which they live (racial profiling, inequitable drug laws, etc.), but many of those who live in the racial and cultural majority may be oblivious. People have a tendency to blame themselves for their circumstances, a blaming that is reinforced by a prevalent "pull yourself up by your bootstraps" message from society. Our credo of personal responsibility may run counter to some very powerful forces that inhibit the possibilities for self-improvement. Our professions need to fully acknowledge the fact that the political and the psychological are inextricably entwined.

Our professions are changing, however. Increasingly, counselors and psychologists—in addition to social workers—are being challenged to see advocacy and activism as being part of their professional identity (Goodman & Anderson, 2015; Ratts & Wayman, 2015).

This implies that you and we together have a responsibility to ramp up our own awareness of those social forces that affect our clients' lives and to improve— outside of our group and therapy rooms—those social forces in ways that are better suited for the people with whom we work (Glosoff, Durham, & Whittaker, 2012; Lewis, Toporek, & Ratts, 2010). We can raise our own awareness of those issues and do some consciousness raising in our groups as well.

Most directly, as has been suggested in earlier chapters, we can advocate for the people in our groups. We talked, particularly in the chapter about working with specialized groups, about the stigma that many people in our groups face. People with addiction problems, people coming out of jail, and people with serious and persistent mental illness, all have to deal with social notions about themselves, which are steeped in negativity. While you can help the people in your groups unravel some of the shame they personally feel about this, you can also become a voice in your community to combat the stigma associated with these conditions (Snook & Marvarene, 2015).

We can also work with the agencies and service providers our clients are involved with to help them get the assistance they need. This might be in the form of housing, adequate mental health or addiction treatment services, or financial assistance. What this means is that you will need to become familiar with, and develop relationships with, those service providers who can help. You can become astute about the ways in which services are provided and paid for and help the people you serve get what they deserve.

The people you work with in your groups may be unaware of how to go about accessing the services they are entitled to. I distinctly remember trying to sort through and understand my parents' financial and insurance documents when they were elderly and ill and thinking then how incredibly hard it must be for people who don't have a lot of education or experience with the public and private insurance industry to negotiate the bureaucracies that affect their lives. We can help the people we serve identify and access the services that can improve their lives.

Unfortunately, the sad fact is that, typically, the services for people who need them are underfunded. There are never enough treatment dollars, public assistance, or residential beds available for those who need them. This means that you'll be competing with other people who are also advocating for their particular population of people in need. It's always frustrating to watch nonprofit agencies that provide essential community services vying with one another for a shrinking pool of dollars.

This means that you will eventually find yourself looking at things that are going on in your groups, in your community, in our world, that simply don't seem fair to you. You may have children in your groups who come to school hungry. You may have young men in your groups who seem to have done jail time for what seem like insignificant crimes. You may have women in your groups, victims of domestic violence, who live in neighborhoods that are riddled with crime and violence.

At some point, you can decide to become more of an activist on the side of social justice. While you'll want to continue your service to people in your groups, and to act as their advocate in the service delivery system, you can also commit to trying to change those things that contribute to the poverty, violence, and injustice that directly and indirectly affect people's lives. You can align with those groups in your community that are promoting change, and you can become involved with groups in your profession who are similarly inclined (e.g., Counselors for Social Justice).

If you do decide to become more politically active, to become a force for social justice, you should be aware that you will be looking at an uphill struggle. If you are concerned about income disparities in your community, state, or nation, for example, don't naively think that everyone thinks similarly or that the people who have power will want to share it.

People in our professions oftentimes have a hard time dealing with the political world, where very different rules of engagement apply. The world of power politics can be extremely challenging, particularly for people who haven't been steeped in the tradition (Smith, Reynolds, & Rovnak, 2009). It's always hard for people who fight fairly to deal with people who don't, and this can be really rough work. You'll need to care for yourself when working in this arena as well as when you work with groups (Edwards & Rodriguez, 2013).

A caution—in your activism, beware of appearing to be self-serving. You want to be a force for change on behalf of your clients, and that's the message you want people to hear. If people think you're simply trying to promote your own self-interest, your message will fall on deaf ears. As an example, in my own state a number of years ago, a group of us who provided mental health and addiction services

TIPS FOR EFFECTIVE ADVOCACY AND ACTIVISM

- Advocacy—working within the services delivery system to assist people in getting the services they need.
- Develop an effective network of relationships with people who provide services.
- Use all your relationship skills to nurture these relationships. Make sure that people are aware of your appreciation for their help.
- Identify and collaborate with other advocacy (e.g., political action, faith-based) groups.
- Activism—work to correct the injustices perpetrated by that system.
- Learn how the political process for change works—both the official and the unofficial rules.
- Identify some key players in the system you want to influence; recruit some as allies.
- Identify other community activists, and join forces.
- Focus your energy—on one or two important issues. Best to make your initial choices local ones, for things you might be able to affect. Save tackling income inequality for another time.
- Assume that if you start to threaten the status quo, you will be marginalized and discredited. Develop a thick skin. This is tough work.
- Join your professional organization's division that fights for social justice (e.g., the American Counseling Association's Counselors for Social Justice).
- Study the works of well-known community activists (e.g., Saul Alinsky).
- Make effective use of the press and social media.

became very politically active in trying to initiate insurance reimbursement for our services to people. We had to effectively demonstrate that it was our clients—not us—who would be the primary beneficiaries of this reimbursement. We did, in fact, successfully make the case, but only after a number of our courageous clients willingly gave up their anonymity to testify about the effectiveness of treatment—and, not insignificantly—that dollars would be saved by treating problems earlier rather than letting them get worse.

Reflection and Group Fishbowl Lab Practice Exercise: Activism

This will be the final personal reflection and group fishbowl lab exercise you'll do with this book. For the personal reflection, take some time by yourself to consider two or three particular things that affect the people in your groups—or your community—that could be improved. The stigma associated with problems of addiction or mental illness; the lack of affordable housing, health care, or nutritious food; the lack of access to safe walking and biking paths; or the prevalence of crime—any of these, or any others—could be issues you identify.

What is it about these issues that have captured your attention? How strongly do you feel about them? How did these issues come to be, and what would be the barriers to resolving them? Who else in your community might feel similarly?

Have you already committed energy to working on these things, or do you see yourself as having the time, energy, and inclination to become more involved?

When you've had a chance to consider these questions, write down some notes to yourself about your thoughts.

Once again, assuming that you have a group of people with whom you are sharing this material, create a group fishbowl lab exercise: two leaders, a number of members, and some observers. As with previous group fishbowls, the leaders should lead a discussion, this time about members' perceptions about social issues they'd like to improve for their group members and communities. Members can be encouraged to talk about the reasons for selecting the particular issues that concern them and about ways in which they might get involved to make these situations better. If there is time, there could also be some brainstorming about strategies to utilize in approaching others about these concerns.

And, again, the leaders should function as participant-leaders, and they should feel free to add their own particular concerns. To the best of their ability, the leaders should foster a discussion where members are interacting with one another, using skills to engage and better understand one another. Members should be encouraged, in other words, to reflect on one another's disclosures and to help one another increase the meaning of their understandings of the social issues that concern them.

At the end of the allotted time (perhaps 30 to 40 minutes), the observers should provide feedback, and the group, as a whole, should process the exercise. Again, take care to ensure that the feedback is specific, constructive, and supportive. Finally, reiterate the confidential nature of the exercise.

CONCLUDING THOUGHTS

On the surface, it may seem that taking care of your personal self, or selves, and social advocacy and activism are very different kinds of activity, but I think that they feed one another. They are parallel paths. Caring for others by way of promoting causes that address issues of social justice is a way of caring for oneself. When you act on behalf of others, you inevitably feel better about yourself. "What goes round," as they say in Jamaica, "comes round."

I've often suggested to the people with whom I've worked in groups that they consider getting involved in some kind of community service. They can put the interpersonal skills they've learned in a group into action in the community. This makes what they've learned even more immediately relevant. This kind of involvement in the community is a great adjunct to the group experience (Hacifazlioğlu, Özdemir, & Uzunboylu, 2010). People who can use some help can also learn how to help. At some point in our lives, each of us needs to be helped—and at other points, each of us needs to help others.

Similarly, your involvement in your community as an activist is a great adjunct experience to the direct service work you do with people. Your involvement in the community as an advocate and activist serves the people with whom you work and, indirectly, yourself. It's obvious how your social activism and commitment to promoting social justice can benefit others, but just as important are the ways in which this activity ties you to your community and promotes your sense of belonging there (Blando, 2011).

We talk a lot about the importance of empathy, about being able to see the world as the people in our groups see it. Becoming engaged in your community as an activist for social justice is simply an extension of that empathic ability. If we truly see the world as those people see it, we will also awaken to the injustices and challenges they face every day. A commitment to promoting causes that aim to make the world a better place for all people is one of the best ways by which we can put our empathy into action.

FOR FURTHER THOUGHT

1. Pick one of the seven areas of the "whole person" written about in this chapter, and read what some people have written about this. Some of these readings might be of the self-help variety, and some might provide more depth.

2. Examine the literature about burnout in the specific field in which you work or contemplate working. Think about the implications this has for your own work.

3. Identify and begin to read some of the writings of well-known political activists (e.g., Howard Zinn, Saul Alinsky). Consider how the work of these activists might help inform and shape your own activism.

4. Begin to explore the branches of your professional organization that devote themselves to social justice. Consider affiliating with one of these.

5. Identify one or more political activists in your own community. See if one of these would agree to an interview. Ask them about their motivations for the work they do and about their joys and frustrations associated with their work.

6. If you are on a college campus, find out about organizations that are involved in service learning, community service, and activism—what are the origins of these organizations, and who is involved with them? Consider joining one of these.

REFERENCES

Asselt, K. van, & Senstock, T. (2009). Influence of counselor spirituality and training on treatment focus and self-perceived competence. *Journal of Counseling & Development, 87*(4), 412–418.

Bakker, A., Van Der Zee, K., Lewig, K., & Dollard, M. (2006). The relationship between the big five personality factors and burnout: A study among volunteer counselors. *Journal of Social Psychology, 146*(1), 31–50.

Blando, J. (2011). *Counseling older adults.* New York, NY: Routledge/Taylor & Francis.

Edwards, K., & Rodriguez, R. (2013). Counseling internationally: Caring for the caregiver. In J. A. Kottler, M. Englar-Carlson, & J. Carlson (Eds.), *Helping beyond the 50-minute hour: Therapists involved in meaningful social action* (pp. 210–221). New York, NY: Routledge.

Evans, M., Duffey, T., Erford, B., & Gladding, S. (2013). Counseling in the United States. *Counseling around the world: An international handbook* [e-book] (pp. 323–331). Alexandria, VA: American Counseling Association.

Glosoff, H. L., Durham, J. C., & Whittaker, J. E. (2012). Supervision: Promoting advocacy and leadership. In C. Y. Chang, C. B. Minton, A. L. Dixon, J. E. Myers, & T. J. Sweeney (Eds.), *Professional counseling excellence through leadership and advocacy* (pp. 185–205). New York, NY: Routledge/Taylor & Francis.

Goodman, J., & Anderson, M. L. (2015). Professional development: Who we are and what we do. In P. J. Hartung, M. L. Savickas, & W. B. Walsh (Eds.), *APA handbook of career intervention: Vol. 1. Foundations* (pp. 419–432). Washington, DC: American Psychological Association.

Hacifazlioğlu, Ö., Özdemir, N., & Uzunboylu, H. (2010). Student teachers' reflections of a community service learning experience. *Journal of Psychology in Africa, 20*(3), 453–454.

Hayes, P. (2002). Playing with fire: Countertransference and clinical epistemology. *Journal of Contemporary Psychotherapy, 32*(1), 93–100.

Hillman, J., & Ventura, M. (1993). *We've had a hundred years of psychotherapy and the world's getting worse.* New York, NY: HarperOne.

Kesler, K. (1990). Burnout: A multimodal approach to assessment and resolution. *Elementary School Guidance and Counseling, 24*(4), 303–312.

Lanham, M. E., Rye, M. S., Rimsky, L. S., & Weill, S. R. (2012). How gratitude relates to burnout and job satisfaction in mental health professionals. *Journal of Mental Health Counseling, 34*(4), 341–354.

Lewis, J. A., Toporek, R. L., & Ratts, M. J. (2010). Advocacy and social justice: Entering the mainstream of the counseling profession. In M. J. Ratts, R. L. Toporek, & J. A. Lewis (Eds.), *ACA advocacy competencies: A social justice framework for counselors* (pp. 239–244). Alexandria, VA: American Counseling Association.

Maher, E. (1983). Burnout and commitment: A theoretical alternative. *Personnel and Guidance Journal, 61*(7), 390–393.

Milton, M. (2009). Waking up to nature: Exploring a new direction for psychological practice. *Ecopsychology, 1*(1), 1–13.

Minor, A. J., Pimpleton, A., Stinchfield, T., Stevens, H., & Othman, N. A. (2013). Peer support in negotiating multiple relationships within supervision among counselor education doctoral students. *International Journal for the Advancement of Counselling, 35*(1), 33–45.

Mutchler, M., & Anderson, S. (2010). Therapist personal agency: A model for examining the training context. *Journal of Marital and Family Therapy, 36*(4), 511–525.

Rank, O. (1952). *The trauma of birth.* New York, NY: Robert Brunner.

Ratts, M. J., & Wayman, A. (2015). Multiculturalism and social justice in professional counseling. In *Introduction to professional counseling* (pp. 139–160). Thousand Oaks, CA: Sage.

Senter, A., Morgan, R., Serna-McDonald, C., & Bewley, M. (2010). Correctional psychologist burnout, job satisfaction, and life satisfaction. *Psychological Services, 7*(3), 190–201.

Smith, S. D., Reynolds, C. A., & Rovnak, A. (2009). A critical analysis of the social advocacy movement in counseling. *Journal of Counseling & Development, 87*(4), 483–491.

Snook, J.-D., & Marvarene, O. (2015). Perceptions of wellness from adults with mobility impairments. *Journal of Counseling & Development, 93*(3), 289–298.

Softas-Nall, B., Baldo, T., & Williams, S. (2001). Family of origin, personality characteristics, and counselor trainees' effectiveness. *Psychological Reports, 88*(3), 854–856.

Vargas, A., & Borkowski, J. (1983). Physical attractiveness: Interactive effects of counselor and client on counseling processes. *Journal of Counseling Psychology, 30*(2), 146–157.

Wegscheider, S. (1986). *Another chance.* Palo Alto, CA: Science & Behavior Books.

Wiggins, M. I. (2010). Religion and spirituality and the ACA advocacy competencies. In M. J. Ratts, R. L. Toporek, & J. A. Lewis (Eds.), *ACA advocacy competencies: A social justice framework for counselors* (pp. 75–83). Alexandria, VA: American Counseling Association.

Wilcoxen, S., Walker, M., & Hovestadt, A. (1989). Counselor effectiveness and family of origin experiences: A significant relationship? *Counseling and Values, 33,* 225–229.

Yalom, I. (2011). *When Nietzsche wept: A novel of obsession.* New York, NY: Harper.

Index